Media and January 6ᵗʰ

JOURNALISM AND POLITICAL COMMUNICATION UNBOUND

Series editors: Daniel Kreiss, University of North Carolina at Chapel Hill,
and Nikki Usher, University of San Diego

Journalism and Political Communication Unbound seeks to be a high-profile book series that reaches far beyond the academy to an interested public of policymakers, journalists, public intellectuals, and citizens eager to make sense of contemporary politics and media. "Unbound" in the series title has multiple meanings: It refers to the unbinding of borders between the fields of communication, political communication, and journalism, as well as related disciplines such as political science, sociology, and science and technology studies; it highlights the ways traditional frameworks for scholarship have disintegrated in the wake of changing digital technologies and new social, political, economic, and cultural dynamics; and it reflects the unbinding of media in a hybrid world of flows across mediums.

Other books in the series:

Journalism Research That Matters
Valérie Bélair-Gagnon and Nikki Usher

*Voices for Transgender Equality: Making Change in the
Networked Public Sphere*
Thomas J. Billard

Reckoning: Journalism's Limits and Possibilities
Candis Callison and Mary Lynn Young

*News after Trump: Journalism's Crisis of Relevance in a
Changed Media Culture*
Matt Carlson, Sue Robinson, and Seth C. Lewis

*Press Freedom and the (Crooked) Path towards Democracy:
Lessons from Journalists in East Africa*
Meghan Sobel Cohen and Karen McIntyre Hopkinson

*Data-Driven Campaigning and Political Parties:
Five Advanced Democracies Compared*
Katharine Dommett, Glenn Kefford, and Simon Kruschinski

Borderland: Decolonizing the Words of War
Chrisanthi Giotis

The Politics of Force: Media and the Construction of Police Brutality
Regina G. Lawrence

Authoritarian Journalism: Controlling the News in Post-Conflict Rwanda
Ruth Moon

Imagined Audiences: How Journalists Perceive and Pursue the Public
Jacob L. Nelson

*Pop Culture, Politics, and the News: Entertainment Journalism
in the Polarized Media Landscape*
Joel Penney

The Invented State
Emily Thorson

*Democracy Lives in Darkness: How and Why People Keep Their
Politics a Secret*
Emily Van Duyn

*Building Theory in Political Communication:
The Politics-Media-Politics Approach*
Gadi Wolfsfeld, Tamir Sheafer, and Scott Althaus

Media and January 6th

Edited by

KHADIJAH COSTLEY WHITE, DANIEL KREISS,
SHANNON C. MCGREGOR, AND
REBEKAH TROMBLE

OXFORD
UNIVERSITY PRESS

Oxford University Press is a department of the University of Oxford. It furthers the University's objective of excellence in research, scholarship, and education by publishing worldwide. Oxford is a registered trade mark of Oxford University Press in the UK and certain other countries.

Published in the United States of America by Oxford University Press
198 Madison Avenue, New York, NY 10016, United States of America.

© Oxford University Press 2024

All rights reserved. No part of this publication may be reproduced, stored in a retrieval system, or transmitted, in any form or by any means, without the prior permission in writing of Oxford University Press, or as expressly permitted by law, by license, or under terms agreed with the appropriate reproduction rights organization. Inquiries concerning reproduction outside the scope of the above should be sent to the Rights Department, Oxford University Press, at the address above.

You must not circulate this work in any other form
and you must impose this same condition on any acquirer.

Library of Congress Cataloging-in-Publication Data
Names: Costley White, Khadijah, editor. | Kreiss, Daniel, editor. | McGregor, Shannon C., editor. | Tromble, Rebekah, editor.
Title: Media and January 6th / [edited by] Khadijah Costley White, Daniel Kreiss, Shannon C. McGregor, and Rebekah Tromble.
Description: New York : Oxford University Press, 2024. | Series: Journalism and political communication unbound | Includes bibliographical references and index. |
Identifiers: LCCN 2023043766 (print) | LCCN 2023043767 (ebook) | ISBN 9780197758533 (paperback) | ISBN 9780197758526 (hardback) | ISBN 9780197758557 (epub) | ISBN 9780197758564
Subjects: LCSH: Capitol Riot, Washington, D.C., 2021—Press coverage. | Mass media—Political aspects—United States. | Political violence—Washington (D.C.)—History—21st century. | Riots—Washington (D.C.)—History—21st century. | Trump, Donald, 1946-
Classification: LCC E915 .M43 2024 (print) | LCC E915 (ebook) | DDC 973.933—dc23/eng/20231214
LC record available at https://lccn.loc.gov/2023043766
LC ebook record available at https://lccn.loc.gov/2023043767

DOI: 10.1093/oso/9780197758526.001.0001

Paperback printed by Marquis Book Printing, Canada
Hardback printed by Bridgeport National Bindery, Inc., United States of America

Contents

Acknowledgments	xi
List of Contributors	xiii

1. Understanding Media's Role in January 6, 2021   1
   Khadijah Costley White, Daniel Kreiss, Shannon C. McGregor,
   and Rebekah Tromble

PART I HOW SHOULD WE UNDERSTAND JANUARY 6, 2021?

2. It Was an Attempted Coup: The Cline Center's Coup d'État
   Project Categorizes the January 6, 2021, Assault on the U.S.
   Capitol   17
   Scott L. Althaus, Joseph Bajjalieh, Jay Jennings, Michael Martin,
   Buddy Peyton, and Dan Shalmon

3. What January 6th Was Not   23
   Danielle K. Brown

4. Remembering January 6th: An Insurrection, the Media,
   and the Shadow of the Tea Party   30
   Khadijah Costley White

5. "Stop the Steal" and the Racial Legacy of Election
   Disinformation   44
   Francesca Tripodi

6. "Fake and Fraudulent" vs. "An American Right": Competing
   Imaginaries of the Vote in the 2020 U.S. Presidential Campaign   54
   Jennifer Stromer-Galley, Brian McKernan, Christy Khoury, and
   Pyeonghwa Kim

7. The Changing American Racial Landscape and January 6th   61
   Andrew Ifedapo Thompson

8. Asymmetrical Identity-Driven Wrongness in American Politics   70
   Dannagal G. Young

viii CONTENTS

9. January 6th as Logical Extension of Conservative Populism 79
   Paul Elliott Johnson

10. Antidemocratic Publics: The January 6th Mob and Digital
    Organizing 86
    Silvio Waisbord

11. The Ordinary Insurrection: January 6 and the Mainstreaming
    of Political Violence 95
    Alice E. Marwick

12. The Antidemocratic Feedback Loop: Right-Wing Media
    Responses to January 6 104
    Becca Lewis

PART II WHAT SHOULD RESEARCH LOOK LIKE AFTER JANUARY 6, 2021? HOW CAN WE PREVENT ANOTHER JANUARY 6, 2021?

13. Online Data and the Insurrection 121
    Megan A. Brown

14. What Can "We" Do? Reflections on Politics after January 6 128
    Cynthia Burack

15. Political Communication Research at a Time of Democratic
    Crises 136
    Daniel Kreiss

16. It's Not Just the Fruit, It's the Factory Farm: Assessing the
    Past, Present, and Future of January 6th 146
    Whitney Phillips and Regina Lawrence

17. Not Just Higher Truths: Critical Inquiry into Conservative
    Media after January 6th 153
    Anthony Nadler

18. Rethinking Right-Wing Media in the Wake of an Attempted
    Coup 163
    Yunkang Yang

19. The Local Roots of January 6th: A Mixed-Methods,
    Multilevel Approach to Political Communication 173
    Sadie Dempsey and Jianing Li

CONTENTS ix

20. Afflicting the Comfortable 183
    Dave Karpf

21. Taking It to the States 192
    Lewis Friedland

22. Reparation through Reporting 199
    Meredith D. Clark

23. Epilogue 207
    Daniel Kreiss, Shannon C. McGregor, Rebekah Tromble, and Khadijah Costley White

Index 215

Acknowledgments

Daniel and Shannon would especially like to thank Katy Peters, former executive director of the Center for Information, Technology, and Public Life (CITAP), for her help in coordinating the January 6th event on its one-year anniversary that gave rise to this volume.

They would also like to thank all those at CITAP and many others in our extended network who have informed this event and helped craft our Center's intellectual agenda over the years. This agenda animates much of this volume. We are indebted to Parker Bach, Bridget Barrett, Tressie McMillan Cottom, Yvonne Eadon, Kirsten Eddy, Deen Freelon, Rachel Kuo, Alice Marwick, Nanditha Narayanamoorthy, Meredith Pruden, Madhavi Reddi, Carolyn Schmitt, Francesca Tripodi, and Yiping Xia.

Shannon also especially thanks her family for their unwavering support while she completed this work—especially the long baseball games and practices Dave and Finnegan attended (with Daniel) during which she worked on and completed this volume. Thank you also to her mother, Dorothee, who spent a life demonstrating a commitment to equality and justice, and to her sister, Sara, whose tireless work for this country should inspire us all to engage in the hard work to reach its full potential.

Khadijah sends thanks and love to her family: Anthony, Akin, Ella, and baby Ominira, who was carried in her belly when work on this volume first began and carried in her arms when it was completed.

Rebekah would like to thank Margo Cunniffe and Alyse Mier of the Institute for Data, Democracy & Politics (IDDP) for their help in organizing the George Washington University side of the January 6th workshop that led to this volume. She would also like to thank her colleagues at IDDP, as well as her colleagues and students in the School of Media & Public Affairs, for intellectual engagement and inspiration. The events of January 6, 2021, loom particularly large for those who live, work, and study in Washington, D.C., and Rebekah is especially grateful to those who have helped to process, make meaning of, and chart a path forward from that dark day for American democracy.

Contributors

Scott L. Althaus is director of the Cline Center for Advanced Social Research, University of Illinois, Urbana-Champaign.

Joseph Bajjalieh is a research manager at the Cline Center for Advanced Social Research, University of Illinois, Urbana-Champaign.

Danielle K. Brown is the 1855 Professor of Community and Urban Journalism and an associate professor at Michigan State University. She is an award-winning political communication researcher investigating the intersection of digital media, underserved and historically excluded communities, and social justice efforts. Her research focuses primarily on injustices in media and their effect on society in three core areas: race and racism, protest and social movements, and health inequalities. Brown has authored dozens of peer-reviewed articles that appear in communication, journalism, and political science journals, and her work also appears in popular media outlets like *Salon, Yahoo News,* and *The Conversation.* Brown serves as associate editor for the *International Journal of Press/Politics.* Prior to joining the academy, she was a photojournalist, writer, and later a nonprofit public relations professional. Brown received her doctoral degree in journalism from the University of Texas at Austin in 2017. She received a bachelor's and master's degree in journalism and public Relations from Baylor University.

Megan A. Brown is a PhD student in the School of Information at the University of Michigan and is a research affiliate with the Media and Democracy Data Cooperative at University of Texas at Austin and the Center for Social Media and Politics at New York University. Her research is centered on the online information ecosystem. Brown studies research infrastructure to support computational social science and the effect of platform governance, affordances, and moderation policies on the spread of political content online. Formerly, Brown was a Sr. Research Engineer at NYU's Center for Social Media and Politics where she collected and maintained large-scale collections of social media data and digital trace data for social science research.

Cynthia Burack is a political theorist and professor of women's, gender, and sexuality studies at The Ohio State University. She is the author or editor of eight books, including *Sin, Sex, and Democracy: Antigay Rhetoric and the Christian Right.* Her most recent books are *Because We Are Human: Contesting U.S. Support for Gender and Sexuality Human Rights Abroad* (2018) and *How Trump and the Christian Right Saved LGBTI Human Rights: A Religious Freedom Mystery* (2022). All three were published by SUNY Press in the Queer Politics and Cultures book series Burack co-edits with Jyl J. Josephson.

xiv CONTRIBUTORS

Meredith D. Clark is an associate professor in the School of Journalism and the Department of Communication Studies at Northeastern University, where she also serves as an affiliate faculty member in Africana studies. She is the director of Northeastern's Center for Communication, Media Innovation & Social Change. Her first book, *We Tried to Tell Y'all: Black Twitter and Digital Counternarratives*, is forthcoming from Oxford University Press. Her current project is an explication of reparative journalism, a concept she introduced in a 2020 prediction for Nieman Lab.

Khadijah Costley White is an associate professor in the Department of Journalism and Media Studies at Rutgers University–New Brunswick. She researches politics, social change, and identity in media. Her book, *The Branding of Right-Wing Activism: The News Media and the Tea Party* (2018) examines the rise of the Tea Party in online, print, broadcast, and cable news. She has been a White House intern on the Obama broadcast media team, a National Association of Black Journalists and United Nations fellow, and an assistant producer for an Emmy-nominated team on the show *Now* on PBS (formerly *Now with Bill Moyers*). She has also served the MacArthur Foundation as an external advisor in journalism and media. In 2020, she received a Whiting Public Engagement Fellowship to complete a community media project on lockdown culture in schools. Costley White has published widely in academic journals, including *International Journal of Communication, Urban Geography, Communication Culture and Critique*, and *Media Theory* and in popular news platforms such as *The Atlantic, The New York Times, The Root*, and *The Washington Post*. She is a founding executive director of a community nonprofit, SOMA Justice, which organizes for racial, social, and economic justice in New Jersey.

Sadie Dempsey is a PhD candidate in the Department of Sociology at University of Wisconsin–Madison. As a political sociologist, she studies democracy, social movements, and civic life. Her dissertation is an ethnography that explores how engaged citizens experience political institutions and highlights how the political process itself contributes to the degradation of political trust. She is a Knight Fellow at the Center for Communication and Civic Renewal and the graduate student coordinator at the Wisconsin Center for Ethnographic Research and the cofounder of its Qualitative Methods Workshop.

Lewis Friedland is Vilas Distinguished Achievement Professor Emeritus at the University of Wisconsin–Madison, School of Journalism and Mass Communication and Department of Sociology (affiliated). He is a cofounder of the Center for Communication and Civic Renewal. Friedland's scholarship has focused on communication and democracy, the public sphere, and civil society; the critical theory of Jürgen Habermas; communication ecologies and social networks at the local and state levels; public and civic journalism; and civic innovation. Most recently, he has published *Battleground* (2022) on the political communication ecology of Wisconsin (with D. Shah, M. Wagner, C. Wells, K. Cramer, and J. Pevehouse). Friedland also founded Win Wisconsin, which raises funds for field organizing (winwisconsin.org).

He currently advises Civic Media (civicmedia.us), a new Wisconsin alternative talk radio network covering the state, and works with the Democratic Party of Wisconsin and candidates on localized communication strategies. He sits on the advisory board of Filter Labs (Filterlabs.ai). Otherwise, he is working hard to become a decent jazz piano player.

Jay Jennings is a research scientist at the Cline Center for Advanced Social Research, University of Illinois, Urbana-Champaign.

Paul Elliott Johnson is an associate professor in the Department of Communication at the University of Pittsburgh. His research focuses on the American right, in particular its fraught relationship to democracy. He interrogates both the political and cultural forms of this current. He is the author of *I the People: The Rhetoric of Conservative Populism* (2022), and his work has appeared in *Critical Studies in Media Communication, Argumentation and Advocacy,* and *Women's Studies in Communication.*

Dave Karpf is an associate professor in the George Washington University School of Media & Public Affairs. His teaching and research focus on strategic political communication in the digital age. He is the award-winning author of two books: *The MoveOn Effect: The Unexpected Transformation of American Political Advocacy* (2012) and *Analytic Activism: Digital Listening and the New Political Strategy* (2016). His current research is focused on the history of the digital future.

Christy Khoury is a PhD student at the School of Information Studies at Syracuse University. Her research interests center on crisis informatics, online diaspora mobilization, and social network analysis. She has a master's degree in Information Management from Syracuse University, and worked in the industries of cyber security and technology assurance.

Pyeonghwa Kim is a PhD student at Syracuse University's School of Information Studies. Her primary research interests lie in the areas of information systems and human-computer interaction. Her current research focuses on the changing nature of work and skills in the technology-mediated work environments. She holds a B.A. in Media and Communications from Goldsmiths, University of London and an M.S. in Digital Contents and Information Studies from Seoul National University.

Daniel Kreiss is the Edgar Thomas Cato Distinguished Professor in the Hussman School of Journalism and Media at the University of North Carolina at Chapel Hill and a principal researcher of the UNC Center for Information, Technology, and Public Life. Kreiss is the co-author of the forthcoming *Power in Ideas: A Case-Based Argument for Taking Ideas Seriously in Political Communication Research,* first author of *Recoding the Boys' Club: The Experiences and Future of Women in Political Technology* (2020), and author of *Prototype Politics: Technology-Intensive Campaigning and the Data of Democracy* (2016) and *Taking Our Country Back: The Crafting of Networked Politics from Howard Dean to Barack Obama* (2012). Kreiss

xvi CONTRIBUTORS

co-edits the Oxford University Press book series Journalism and Political Communication Unbound and is an associate editor of *Political Communication*. Kreiss is an affiliated fellow of the Information Society Project at Yale Law School and received a PhD in Communication from Stanford University.

Regina Lawrence is associate dean of the School of Journalism and Communication in Portland, research director of the Agora Journalism Center at the University of Oregon, and editor of the journal *Political Communication*. Her research focuses on press-state relations; journalistic norms, routines, and innovations; and the role of the media, gender, and social identity in political communication. She has been chair of the Political Communication section of the American Political Science Association and a fellow at the Shorenstein Center on the Press, Politics, and Public Policy at Harvard University. Her studies have appeared in numerous journals, including *Journalism*, *Perspectives on Politics*, *Political Communication*, *Journalism Practice*, and *Information, Communication & Society*. Lawrence's books include *When the Press Fails: Political Power and the News Media from Iraq to Katrina* (2007, with W. Lance Bennett and Steven Livingston), winner of the 2016 Doris A. Graber Best Book Award from the Political Communication section of the American Political Science Association; *Hillary Clinton's Race for the White House: Gender Politics and the Media on the Campaign Trail* (2009, with Melody Rose); and *The Politics of Force: Media and the Construction of Police Brutality* (2000), which is being reissued in 2022.

Becca Lewis is a Stanford Graduate Fellow and PhD candidate in Communication at Stanford University, as well as a research affiliate at the University of North Carolina's Center for Information, Technology, and Public Life. She researches right-wing media, with a particular focus on the internet. She holds an MSc in Social Science from the Oxford Internet Institute.

Jianing Li is an assistant professor in the Department of Communication at the University of South Florida. Her work examines the intersection of mis/disinformation, contentious politics, and social inequality. She specializes in computational methods, quantitative methods, and mixed methods. Her research asks how people make informed decisions in today's digital media environment, with growing concerns over mis/disinformation, contentious politics, and structural inequalities. Her current work focuses on identifying discourses around and dissemination of mis/disinformation on digital platforms; evaluating strategies to mitigate mis/disinformation, including fact-checking, content flagging, and digital literacy intervention; and studying how the broader communication ecology interacts with identity and social inequality in shaping misperceptions, policy preferences, and support for racial justice movements. Methodologically, she uses experiments (quasi-experiment, web-based dynamic experiment), computational methods (natural language processing, machine learning, network mapping), large-scale panel surveys, mixed-methods approaches, and work on the integration of textual, behavioral, and/or social geographical data. Li's work has been published in *Journal of Communication*, *Human Communication Research*, *Political Communication*, *Mass Communication and Society*, and *Social Media + Society*. Her work also appeared in *The Routledge Companion to Media Disinformation and Populism* (2021), *Cambridge Elements in Politics and Communication* (2022), and *"An Epidemic on My People": Religion in the Age of COVID-19* (forthcoming), as well as in *The Washington Post, Brookings TechStream*, and *MediaWell*. Her research has been funded by the Social Science Research Council, the International Fact-Checking Network, and the Knight Foundation.

Michael Martin is a senior research coordinator at the Cline Center for Advanced Social Research, University of Illinois, Urbana-Champaign.

Alice E. Marwick is an associate professor in the Department of Communication and a principal researcher at the Center for Information, Technology and Public Life at the University of North Carolina at Chapel Hill. She researches the social, political, and cultural implications of social media technologies and is currently interested in disinformation and identity. Marwick is the author of *The Private Is Political: Networked Privacy on Social Media* (2023), *Media Manipulation and Disinformation Online* (2017), and *Status Update: Celebrity, Publicity and Branding in the Social Media Age* (2013), and co-editor of *The Sage Handbook of Social Media* (2017). As an Andrew Carnegie Fellow, she is working on a book about online radicalization.

Shannon C. McGregor is an assistant professor in the Hussman School of Journalism and Media at the University of North Carolina and a senior researcher with UNC's Center for Information, Technology, and Public Life. She is an award-winning and internationally recognized communication scholar whose research addresses the role of social media in political processes. In particular, she examines how social media shapes political communication, journalism, public opinion, and epistemologies of public life in democracies. McGregor's interdisciplinary and mixed-methods research has been published across the fields of communication, political science, and sociology, including in the *Journal of Communication, New Media & Society, Political Communication*, and *Information, Communication & Society*. She is co-editor (with Talia Stroud) of *Digital Discussions: How Big Data Informs Political Communication* (2019). McGregor's writing also appears in *The Washington Post, Wired, Slate*, and *The Guardian*.

Brian McKernan is a research assistant professor in the School of Information Studies at Syracuse University and co-director of the Human-Centered Computing and Design Lab. His research interests include the design and study of innovative applications to strengthen reasoning, increase political transparency, combat harmful misinformation, and promote civic engagement. He has served as key personnel on two research projects focused on developing tools to strengthen reasoning and mitigate cognitive biases. As a lead on the Illuminating Project, he studies and helps develop tools to monitor strategic communication efforts by political actors on social media. His work has been published in such journals as *Digital Journalism, Social Media + Society, Computers in Human Behavior, Games and Culture*, and the *American Journal of Cultural Sociology*.

xviii CONTRIBUTORS

Anthony Nadler is an associate professor of Media and Communication Studies at Ursinus College. He is the author of *Making the News Popular: Mobilizing U.S. News Audiences* (2016) and co-editor with A. J. Bauer of *News on the Right: Studying Conservative News Cultures* (2019). His current research focuses on conservative news, media and populism, and debates surrounding targeted advertising and civic culture in a digital media landscape. He is currently working on a book project focused on how American conservative media portray liberalism and the left. His articles have appeared in a variety of scholarly journals, including *International Journal of Communication, Critical Studies in Media Communication, Journalism, Journalism Studies*, and *Journal of Information Policy*. His writing has also appeared in *L.A. Review of Books, Wired, n + 1, Salon, Columbia Journalism Review*, and other popular venues.

Buddy Peyton is a project coordinator at the Cline Center for Advanced Social Research, University of Illinois, Urbana-Champaign.

Whitney Phillips's writing and teaching focus on political communication, media history, and digital ethics. Phillips is the author of several books on media, culture, and politics: *This Is Why We Can't Have Nice Things: Mapping the Relationship between Online Trolling and Mainstream Culture* (2015); *The Ambivalent Internet: Mischief, Oddity, and Antagonism Online* (2017, with Ryan Milner); and *You Are Here: A Field Guide for Navigating Polarized Speech, Conspiracy Theories, and Our Polluted Media Landscape* (2021, with Ryan Milner). With Milner, Phillips also published a digital ethics guide for young adult readers, *Share Better and Stress Less: A Guide to Thinking Ecologically about Social Media* (2023). Additionally she is the author of the 2018 Data & Society report "The Oxygen of Amplification: Better Practices for Reporting on Extremists, Antagonists, and Manipulators Online." Her current work focuses on the intersection of right-wing media and Evangelicalism. In addition to journal articles and book chapters on a range of communication, technology, and media studies topics, Phillips has written numerous pieces for *The Atlantic, The New York Times, Slate*, and other popular outlets, including the work she published in her *Wired* magazine Ideas column. She regularly provides expert commentary for national and global news stories, as well as ethics consultation for journalism outlets and has been profiled by the *Columbia Journalism Review*, Niemen Journalism Lab, and Knight Commission on Trust, Media, and Democracy, among many others. Phillips is an assistant professor in the University of Oregon's School of Journalism and Communication.

Dan Shalmon was an external engagement coordinator at the Cline Center for Advanced Social Research, University of Illinois, Urbana-Champaign at the time the initial online version of this chapter was written, in January 2021.

Jennifer Stromer-Galley is a professor in the School of Information Studies and senior associate dean for academic and faculty affairs at Syracuse University. She is a former president of the Association of Internet Researchers and is an associate editor for the *Journal of Computer-Mediated Communication*. Her book *Presidential Campaigning in the Internet Age* received the 2015 Roderick P. Hart Top Book Award in the Political Communication Division of the National Communication Association. She has been studying social media since before it was called social media, studying online interaction and strategic communication in a variety of contexts, including political forums and online games. She has published more than 70 journal articles, proceedings, and book chapters and received over $15 million in federal and corporate grants to support her research endeavors. She is principal investigator of the Illuminating Project (illuminating.ischool.syr.edu), a computational social science project to archive and categorize U.S. presidential campaign communication for journalists and the public.

Andrew Ifedapo Thompson is an assistant professor of political science at George Washington University and leads the Digital Democracy research cluster in the Institute for Data, Democracy, and Politics. He specializes in the role of racial threat in driving democratic backsliding and violent attitudes across the U.S. public. In his book, The Big Flip: Racial Demographic Change and the Future of American Democracy, and across a series of articles, he emphasizes the central role that Black Americans have to future ideas of democracy in the mass public. His work has appeared in Political Behavior and Political Science Research and Methods.

Francesca Tripodi is a sociologist and information scholar whose research examines the relationship between search engines, participatory platforms, politics, and inequality. She is an assistant professor at the School of Information and Library Science and a senior researcher at the Center for Information Technology and Public Life at UNC–Chapel Hill. In 2019, she testified before the Senate Judiciary Committee on how search engines are gamed to drive ideologically based queries. This topic is the basis of her book, *The Propagandists' Playbook* (2022), which draws on ethnographic observations, content analysis, media immersion, and web-scraped metadata to provide a detailed analysis of the seven tactics conservative elites use to spread disinformation in pursuit of partisan goals. Her research has been covered by *The Washington Post*, *The New York Times*, *The New Yorker*, NPR, *The Columbia Journalism Review*, *Wired*, *Slate*, *The Guardian*, and the Neiman Journalism Lab.

Rebekah Tromble is director of the Institute for Data, Democracy & Politics and an associate professor in the School of Media & Public Affairs at George Washington University. Her research examines digital political behavior, with a particular focus on the darker sides of online communication, including right-wing extremism, hate speech, and harassment and has been published in journals such as the *American Political Science Review*, *New Media & Society*, and *Political Communication*. Tromble is currently leading a multimillion dollar interdisciplinary, cross-sector project to develop a rapid-response system in support of journalists, scientists, public health officials, and other experts facing campaigns of online harassment. Tromble regularly serves as advisor to policymakers, regulators, and civil society, particularly on topics

xx CONTRIBUTORS

of digital platform accountability, transparency, and responsible data access and use. She is a member of the European Digital Media Observatory's Advisory Board and co-founder and member of the Executive Board of the Coalition for Independent Technology Research (https://independenttechresearch.org/).

Silvio Waisbord is Professor and former Director of the School of Media and Public Affairs at George Washington University. He is the author or editor of nineteen books, as well as articles on journalism and politics, communication studies, media policy, and communication for social change. His most recent books are *Public Scholarship in Communication Studies* (co-edited with T. J. Billard, University of Illinois Press, 2024), *El Imperio de la Utopia* (Peninsula/Planeta, 2020) and *The Routledge Companion to Media, Disinformation and Populism* (co-edited with H. Tumber, Routledge, 2020). He is the former Editor-in-Chief of the *Journal of Communication* and the *International Journal of Press/Politics*. He is President-Elect and Fellow of the International Communication Association.

Yunkang Yang is an assistant professor of communication at the Department of Communication and Journalism at Texas A&M University. He is also a research affiliate at the Institute for Data, Democracy & Politics at George Washington University. His most recent publication on U.S. right-wing media is "Interactive Propaganda: How Fox News and Donald Trump Co-produced False Narratives about the Covid-19 Crisis" (with Lance Bennett) in *Political Communication in the Time of Coronavirus* (2022). In 2022, Yang provided his research and expert opinions to the U.S. House Select Committee on the January 6th Attack as statements of record. His work on U.S. right-wing media, social media, and disinformation has been quoted by various media outlets, including *The New Yorker, The Hill*, NPR, CTV, and AFP.

Dannagal G. Young is a professor of communication and political science at the University of Delaware, where she studies political and media psychology. She has published over 50 academic articles and book chapters on the content, psychology, and effects of political information, satire, and misinformation. Her book *Irony and Outrage* (2020) examines satire and outrage as the logical extensions of the respective psychological profiles of liberals and conservatives, and she has just published her latest book, *Wrong: How Identity Fuels Misinformation and How to Fix It* (2023). Young's 2020 TED Talk, explaining how our psychology shapes our politics and how media exploit these relationships, has been viewed over 1.9 million times. She publishes extensively in *Vox, The Washington Post*, and *The Atlantic*. She has appeared on CNN, PBS Newshour, ABC News, NPR, and various national and international podcasts. As of 2020, her research had been cited in over 70 popular press articles, news stories, and interviews in *The Washington Post, USA Today, Politico, Christian Science Monitor, Variety, The New York Times, The Atlantic*, PBS, *Slate, and Vox*. Young received the University of Delaware Excellence in Teaching Award in 2014, and her popular University of Delaware course "Propaganda and Persuasion" is available on Wondrium from The Great Courses.

1

Understanding Media's Role in January 6, 2021

Khadijah Costley White, Daniel Kreiss, Shannon C. McGregor,
and Rebekah Tromble

The images cast across screens on January 6, 2021, laid bare the fragility of American democracy in a stark and dismaying way. The steps and halls of the U.S. Capitol, one of the institutions at the heart of American democracy, were inundated by a violent band of insurrectionists. Fed by blatant lies and political and racial animus, they sought to halt a procedure enshrined in the U.S. Constitution and overturn a freely and fairly run election. Meanwhile, efforts to obstruct, avoid, and misrepresent the subsequent investigation of the January 6th attack have continued in its wake.

The final congressional investigative report of the Select Committee to Investigate the January 6th Attack on the United States Capitol (U.S. House of Representatives, 2022) details the behind-the-scenes efforts of Donald Trump to hold on to power through false allegations of election fraud. After a thwarted attempt to appoint a new attorney general to overturn the election (p. 54), Trump saw the formal certification of electoral votes by Vice President Mike Pence as his last opportunity to secure the presidency. Pence, Trump concluded, could refuse to count the electoral votes for Joe Biden and declare Trump to be president. On December 18th, four days after the Electoral College vote, Trump applied pressure on Pence by tweeting an invitation to his supporters to join a "Big protest in D.C. on January 6th"—the day that Pence would be undertaking the task to certify votes (p. 55). "Be there," Trump tweeted, assuring his followers that it "will be wild" (p. 55).

Social media accounts from white supremacist and right-wing groups such as the Three Percenters, Proud Boys, and Oath Keepers responded quickly, circulating the president's charge that they come to D.C. and calling

Khadijah Costley White, Daniel Kreiss, Shannon C. McGregor, and Rebekah Tromble, *Understanding Media's Role in January 6, 2021* In: *Media and January 6th*. Edited by: Khadijah Costley White, Daniel Kreiss, Shannon C. McGregor, and Rebekah Tromble, Oxford University Press. © Oxford University Press 2024.
DOI: 10.1093/oso/9780197758526.003.0001

for others to "fill the streets," "revolt," and "invade" the Capitol (U.S. House of Representatives, 2022, p. 56). At the "Save America" rally on January 6th, Trump told the crowd of protestors, "[I]f Mike Pence does the right thing, we win the election." He then urged them to go to the Capitol and "take back" their country (p. 5). "You have to show strength, and you have to be strong," Trump declared. The crowd surged on the Capitol, some chanting "hang Mike Pence" (p. 38).

In the postelection days leading up to the attack on the Capitol, Trump and his supporters aimed their violence at everyone from local election workers to members of Congress. A young tech in Georgia was reportedly threatened with a noose for writing up voter reports. Trump's camp tweeted the private phone number of a Michigan official (Mike Shirkey) who refused to decertify the election, triggering thousands of hate messages (U.S. House of Representatives, 2022, p. 47). Two Michigan election clerks reported death threats; one was threatened by a man outside of her home (p. 304).

The mass mobilization of Trump supporters on January 6th was the culmination of this election violence and intimidation. In preparing for January 6th, members of the Proud Boys discussed plans to attack police, Trump supporter posts on social media called for spilling blood on January 6th (U.S. House of Representatives, 2022, p. 62), and armed militias stored weapons just outside the Capitol to await Trump's orders (p. 501). At Trump's rally, the Secret Service confiscated hundreds of weapons, including knives, cannisters of pepper spray, brass knuckles, tasers, batons, and body armor (p. 68)—and scholars have noted the presence of service members and veterans at the Capitol on January 6th (Schake & Robinson, 2021). A short while later, the attendees marched to attack the Capitol; one woman among them would be shot dead. Trump supporters on January 6th also attacked Capitol police officer Brian Sicknick, who died the next day.

More than two years later, it is not clear that we have absorbed the lessons of January 6th. At a moment when we should be "all hands on deck" to protect and secure elections, democratic institutions, and the rights of all citizens—with a particular determination to protect the rights of those historically prevented from full democratic participation—we have instead seen many political leaders choose inaction. And in far too many instances, those holding political, economic, and media power have made matters worse: continuing the lies, intensifying hostilities, failing to clearly analyze threats to democracy, and even actively working to undermine democratic rights and processes.

As scholars of political communication and behavior, we believe our work can help clarify what happened on January 6, 2021. Our expertise lies in examining why and how January 6th came to be and the centrality of media to the attempted coup. It lies in our visioning of a fair and just path forward for democracy. And yet, as a field, we too have fallen short in our responsibilities. We have long taken democracy for granted. We have allowed biases shaped by American exceptionalism to distort our views of U.S. political institutions, processes, behaviors, and norms—too often viewing them as steadfast and, though perhaps slow and halting, still largely forward-moving. We have long imagined America to be one of the world's oldest democracies, not the exclusionary, antidemocratic set of states it actually was until the 1970s. With a relative dearth of work centering historical and contemporary racial, ethnic, and power dynamics, our field has been caught flat-footed, unprepared to respond to those who actively seek to undermine American democracy.

This edited volume is a first step toward remedying this situation. We have brought together a diverse group of leading scholars in communication, media studies, political science, sociology, and related fields to help us more clearly understand the relationship between media and the events of January 6, 2021. The Capitol insurrection was a politically significant event that laid bare both America's tortured democratic history and the constellation of threats to its future as a multiracial democracy. Our aim, therefore, is also forward-thinking: We seek not only to understand what happened but also to help prevent another attempted coup and bolster multiracial democracy.

In this brief introduction, we discuss the volume's origins and provide detailed chapter overviews. The volume is organized around three key questions: How should we understand January 6, 2021? What should research look like after January 6, 2021? How can we prevent another January 6, 2021? We conclude with an assessment of where we should go from here if we share a commitment to democracy in the United States. As the epilogue to this volume notes, even the official congressional investigation of the Capitol attack released in 2022 fails to substantially take up the role of media in shaping the events of January 6th. We take up that work here.

Origins of the Volume

This edited volume is an outgrowth of a joint conference. The Capitol Coup One Year Later: How Research Can Assess and Counter Threats to

Democracy, hosted by the University of North Carolina at Chapel Hill's Center for Information, Technology, and Public Life and George Washington University's Institute for Data, Democracy, and Politics in January 2022. On the one-year anniversary of the attack on the U.S. Capitol, scholars in political communication, journalism, sociology, rhetoric, and theory came together to discuss the causes and meaning of a day that marked a very visible assault on the heart of American democracy. To our knowledge, it was the *only* event for researchers dedicated to understanding January 6, 2021, as the democratic threat it was.

In a series of panels and keynote talks, participants brought to the forefront key provocations that made clear the important aims of this volume. Scholars discussed how America's relatively new multiracial democracy requires more in-depth historical analysis. And they pointed out how analyses of contemporary politics need to be grounded against America's long antidemocratic past. They discussed the importance of considering the roles of corporations and the press in influencing the framing and outcomes of January 6th and warned against using social media as a way of evaluating and assessing public opinion. Other scholars took up the kinds of research questions scholars ask and the normative commitments that shape how we answer them. Before presuming the stability and importance of democratic ideals, panelists charged that we must investigate American commitments to them and analyze what democracy even means in the U.S. imagination. Scholars also took up the role of digital platforms like Facebook in shaping the political landscape, but clearly centered the importance of political elites and political interests in using them toward antidemocratic ends.

Above all, the assembled researchers shared an orientation toward clearly identifying and calling out the realities of America's past and present. While some scholars believe that they should stay "above the fray," we believe that we are already firmly situated within it and therefore we have a set of responsibilities to clearly identify threats to and defend democratic institutions. Scholars also shared a commitment to public engagement as a way of reaching beyond the ivory tower to tackle the problem of democratic crisis. Such work comes with pitfalls: misquotes in the press, time spent on op-eds that may never be published or distract from other scholarly projects, harassment, and potential retaliation from authoritarian regimes or hostile parties. Presently there is a lack of protections and training for scholars who produce work for audiences outside of the academy, meaning they have both ample opportunity for innovation and challenging terrain to navigate in public scholarship and engagement. Still, speaking directly to the problems of the day in a way that applies our training, expertise, and—yes—our commitment to democracy is crucial work in a fragile time. This volume takes up that work.

Structure of the Volume

The volume centers three core questions, which we group into two main sections of the book. In Part I, authors take up the question of how we should understand January 6, 2021. Part II centers two different but related questions: What should research look like after January 6, 2021? And how can we prevent another January 6, 2021? The authors of this volume come from interdisciplinary backgrounds, including communication, political science, sociology, and media studies but, in keeping with the theme of this volume, share an orientation toward understanding January 6th through the lens of the intersection of politics and communication.

How Should We Understand January 6, 2021?

The January 6th congressional report (U.S. House of Representatives, 2022) and the Dominion Voting Systems defamation lawsuit against Fox News (*Dominion Voting Systems Corp v. Fox News Network LLC*, 2023) clearly reveal that media and communication figured prominently in the Capitol attack. The groundwork for the attempted coup was laid in the media and press, as Trump and his staff created and widely disseminated "official" reports alleging voter fraud, held press conferences about the "stolen election" (U.S. House of Representatives, 2022, p. 111), took out ads asking supporters to call their governors and urge them to recount votes for Trump, and strategized with Fox News anchor Sean Hannity and others about how to publicly portray (and contest) the election outcome. The attempt to overturn the election was a highly profitable one for the sitting president; through his messages about voter fraud and his fight against the "rigged election," Trump raised "roughly one quarter of a billion dollars in fundraising between the election and January 6th" (p. 27).

The chapters in Part I take up the central question of how social scientists, media scholars, policymakers, journalists, and the public should think about

6 MEDIA AND JANUARY 6TH

January 6, 2021. Our aim in selecting these chapters is to provide a shared set of concepts and terms for scholars and journalists to use when discussing the attack on the U.S. Capitol, as well as a framework for understanding why and how it occurred. Taken together, these essays clearly argue (1) that January 6, 2021, was an attempted coup that was (2) grounded in the political interests of the president, his supporters, and members of his party, and (3) that communication, media, and rhetoric were central to laying the groundwork for January 6th. The latter includes the president's and his party's strategic attempts to delegitimize the election and the mobilization and coordination of political insurrectionists through media.

To put all of this in perspective, Part I opens with a team from the Cline Center for Advanced Social Research at the University of Illinois utilizing the most extensive data set in academic research on global coups to determine that the events of January 6, 2021, were an attempted coup by President Trump and his supporters. In Chapter 3, Danielle K. Brown shows how the news media struggled to settle on a label for the events of January 6th and wrote multiple first drafts of history; Brown argues that we need to find "authoritarian words to describe authoritarian-sponsored practices." Khadijah Costley White offers a key historical perspective in Chapter 4, showing how Tea Party backlash during President Barack Obama's first term laid the groundwork for the attempted coup at the U.S. Capitol. In Chapter 5, Francesca Tripodi shows how "Stop the Steal" *continues* a long racial history of election disinformation. Jennifer Stromer-Galley, Brian McKernan, Christy Khoury, and Pyeonghwa Kim reveal in Chapter 6 how Trump long set the stage rhetorically for his supporters to view, or embrace the idea of, the vote being irredeemably corrupted, in turn creating a ready-made justification of political violence at the U.S. Capitol to restore (and protect) their political power.

In Chapter 7 Andrew Ifedapo Thompson argues that there are growing antidemocratic attitudes among Republicans who perceive racial threat, but he offers hope: Since race is a social construct, there are no *necessary* outcomes in the United States. However, in Chapter 8 Dannagal Young reveals why stories of demographic outcomes are so potent and likely will be with us for a long time: Political actors (especially Republicans) articulate strategic political narratives (including disinformation) to help people make sense of their environments, provide them with a sense of agency, and reaffirm their identities and group status toward the ends of political mobilization. In Chapter 9, meanwhile, Paul Elliott Johnson argues that January 6th should be seen as the logical extension of conservative populism's project to secure and maintain political dominance in the United States.

In Chapter 10, Silvio Waisbord argues that we need to understand the antidemocratic nature of January 6, 2021, and the violence at the heart of many democracies, as well as the centrality of digital media to this violence in our time, as "digital fascism"—antidemocratic actions, often facilitated by charismatic leadership communicated directly to the masses, that defend unequal racial and political orders. Also focusing on the digital right wing, in Chapter 11 Alice Marwick argues that political violence on the right has long been mainstream, yet January 6th in particular is the outcome of antidemocratic, illiberal conspiracy movements in the contemporary Republican Party that provide opportunities for the use of disinformation to justify political violence. To close out Part I, in Chapter 12 Becca Lewis empirically analyzes right-wing media in relation to January 6th and finds that these outlets *reversed* the threat of the day, spinning narratives that left-wing activists and liberals were responsible for the threats to democracy on January 6th, not Trump and his Republican supporters.

What Should Research Look Like after January 6, 2021? How Can We Prevent Another January 6, 2021?

The chapters in Part II ask what we can do going forward as researchers if we are concerned with understanding the dynamics at play on January 6th and how can we work toward shoring up the peaceful transfer of power through competitive elections. In Chapter 13 Megan A. Brown focuses on the crucial need for researcher access to platform data to understand events like the January 6th attempted coup. In Chapter 14, Cynthia Burack, who was on the National Mall early on January 6, 2021, takes up the question of how politically left academics can shore up democratic political institutions and urges us to critically examine our own biases and identity-based group commitments in the service of promoting the salience of shared "American" identities.

In Chapter 15 Daniel Kreiss takes a different approach, arguing that media and communication scholars should focus on how people come to see themselves as members of social groups with political interests and analyze when these groups perceive their power and status under such threat that they engage in political violence, such as on January 6th. In Chapter 16

Whitney Phillips and Regina Lawrence use the arresting metaphor of an "antidemocratic agribusiness" to shine a light on the deep networks of domestic extremists, dark money flooding politics, far-right militias, white supremacy, and media environments that amplify antidemocratic extremism and provide the potent soil for antidemocratic crisis. Anthony Nadler argues for the study of "conservative news cultures" after January 6th in Chapter 17, especially the "popular right," the relationship between the media right and the political right, the complex forms of identity work in conservative media, and normative ideas that exist in conservative media.

In Chapter 18 Yunkang Yang engages in a compelling empirical analysis of right-wing media in the wake of January 6, 2021, as a means to set a new research agenda for the field going forward, concluding that it is better to move beyond the "partisan media" idea and understand these entities as political organizations that trade in narratives and symbols and engage in actions designed to achieve political objectives. In Chapter 19 Sadie Dempsey and Jianing Li argue for turning from understanding January 6th as a national and elite phenomenon to focus on the meso-level forms of politics—from political institutions to citizenship practices—that sustained false election claims.

In Chapter 20 Dave Karpf argues for the importance of "norms," which in turn require very real costs—social, professional, and reputational—for violating them. In an impassioned Chapter 21, Lewis Friedland argues that political communication research *must* focus more on states if it is to help stop the slide into authoritarianism and that research agendas should be "ruthlessly practical"—centered on persuasion, winning majorities to protect democracy, and working with groups on the ground to help them win power. Chapter 22 closes Part II with Meredith Clark's strong call for "reparative journalism"—a set of values and practices that center journalists' obligation to lay bare, and make amends for, historical injustices in American society, especially racial injustices.

Where Do We Go from Here?

Our aim in bringing together the scholars in this volume—diverse in identity, perspective, and discipline—to consider the relationship of media to January 6th is to shape research across many fields in the years ahead, as well as to inform policy, platform, media, political, and research responses to the democratic threats that face us today. These scholars provide a robust foundation upon which to ask questions and develop theories, methods, and research designs aimed at centering questions of democracy in academic work and in political and social life.

At the level of national policy, government officials have already begun to lay out a path forward. The January 6th Select Committee report (U.S. House of Representatives, 2022) highlights recommendations for legislation that makes clear that the vice president holds no authority to reject electoral votes, prohibits any change of presidential electors after Election Day, provides more security for electoral vote certification, stiffens consequences for threatening electoral workers, and offers other measures to protect votes and election officials on the ground. Within the congressional analysis, the media figure prominently, concluding that media reports on the election "had the effect of radicalizing their consumers" and "provoking people to attack their own country" (p. 692). Its authors recommend that social and legacy media companies examine their role in the January 6th insurrection. As scholars, we must also take up our own new approaches to tracking, exploring, and defining right-wing and conservative attacks on democracy in our current era.

So where, as a field and as a nation, do we go from here? As a field, we must analyze the interaction of identity (McGregor et al., 2022) and power (Kreiss, this volume). Dempsey and Li's call to engage in research that bridges micro, meso, and macro levels provides one path forward in both regards. Critically interrogating and centering identity not only makes analyses of power both possible and rich; it also means recognizing the historical dominance of particular social groups. For too long, white, Christian, masculine identities have been understood as the default rather than as a focus of research. We must also embrace normativity; it is only by having a commitment to democracy in scholarly works of all kinds that we can work to uphold it (see Nadler, this volume). As a nation, we can also embrace our shared identities—as Americans and as patriots (Burack, this volume). We must vociferously enforce democratic norms through public accountability (Karpf, this volume). We must work to build and uphold media systems that support democracy (Phillips and Lawrence, this volume), like the reparative journalism Meredith Clark outlines (this volume). We must also analyze, identify, and call out systems that allow partisan political organizations to masquerade as media (Yang, this volume).

In ignoring or not acting on the provocations discussed in this volume, we risk not only irrelevance as academics but further democratic crises as a country. Moments of rupture, like that of the attempted coup on January 6th, bring not only cataclysm but also opportunity. As many of these chapters demonstrate, the virulent racism and illiberal philosophies fueling the "Stop the Steal" movement have deep roots in our history. But the violent storming of the Capitol—egged on by elected lawmakers and taking place under the dual banners of Trump and the Confederacy—laid bare the antidemocratic ends of white conservatism and the extreme means to which many are willing to go in order to preserve their own status and power. This volume seeks to critically understand January 6th and the role of various media in fomenting and justifying the attempted coup and, with that foundation, to consider what might be done to prevent what will undoubtedly be future attempts to overturn free and fair elections. Our field—alongside mainstream discourses and histories of the United States—has thus far largely failed to take seriously America's checkered democratic history and the willingness of whites and Christian social groups to use force to maintain their power. But this moment—and we do mean *this* moment, as threats to undermine democratic rights and processes continue in earnest—offers an opportunity for repair. Ignore it at democracy's peril.

References

Dominion Voting Systems Corp v. Fox News Network LLC, C.A. No. N21C-03-257, Superior Court of the State of Delaware (2023).

McGregor, S. C., Coe, K., Saldaña, M., Griffin, R. A., Chavez-Yenter, D., Huff, M., McDonald, A., & Smith, T. R. (2022). Centering identity in political communication research. Paper presented to the Political Communication Division, annual meeting of National Communication Association, New Orleans.

Schake, K., & Robinson, M. (2021). Assessing civil-military relations and the January 6th Capitol insurrection. *Orbis, 65*(3), 532–544.

U.S. House of Representatives. (2022, December 22). *Final report: Select Committee to Investigate the January 6th attack on the United States Capitol*. Retrieved from https://www.govinfo.gov/app/details/GPO-J6-REPORT/context.

PART I
HOW SHOULD WE UNDERSTAND JANUARY 6, 2021?

Part I takes up the question of how we should think about January 6, 2021, as a singular political moment in American history. More specifically, how should we think about *media* in relation to the attempted coup at the U.S. Capitol? Different chapters have different answers to these questions. However, they converge around the observation that the events of January 6th were fundamentally grounded in political *interest* and facilitated by a media environment that created the context for the president, influential members of his party, and networks of supporters to challenge the election and carry out a concerted act of political violence.

The Cline Center opens Part I with a clear statement, grounded in extensive comparative evidence, that January 6th was an attempted coup by a sitting president and his supporters. It was an attempt by these individuals to seize congressional authority and prevent the legitimate, peaceful transfer of power. Starting from this point, a number of chapters in this section analyze the historical, and media-driven, factors that shaped the attempted coup. Khadijah Costley White's historical account finds antecedents of January 6th in the rise of the Tea Party movement as a form of white backlash to President Barack Obama, with its routinization of violence, defense of a white Southern order, and institutionalization of right-wing media such as Fox News that justifies and defends a particular version of the nation (see also Nadler, this volume). Adopting a complementary, historically informed analysis, Francesca Tripodi documents Stop the Steal's much longer origin story than is conventionally recognized, revealing that it was originally the product of the 2016, not the 2020, election. Right-wing actors set up this specific narrative in the face of an expected Trump loss in 2016, but the candidate's surprise victory meant it did not have to be used to contest the election. More proximately, Jennifer Stromer-Galley, Brian McKernan,

Christy Khoury, and Pyeonghwa Kim empirically document how Trump and his allies rhetorically embraced "Stop the Steal" months before the election across platforms to encourage supporters to see *any* result that was not a Trump win as illegitimate.

Similar to chapters across this volume that document the underlying racial dynamics at play on January 6th, and the contemporary right wing more generally as a form of white backlash, Tripodi shows how Stop the Steal was articulated on racial and ethnic terms. A number of contributors in both Part I and Part II reveal how America's racial ideologies connect January 6th to antidemocratic and racial violence during the post-Reconstruction era (Lassiter and Crespino, 2009; Mickey, 2015). The upshot, as Tripodi affirms alongside Costley White, is that January 6th is not so much a break with the past as a continuation of how white Americans have subverted democracy at key moments in their attempts to preserve their political, social, and economic power. It is then not surprising, as a number of contributors to this section point out, that lies that the election was stolen were asserted, believed, or simply acted on by so many on the right—it would have been surprising if they were not.

As contributors across the volume suggest, January 6th was *not* an aberration but the continuation of political movements, partisan dynamics, and white political interests that stretch throughout U.S. history and had their contemporary alignment after the civil rights movement, and especially the election of the country's first Black president. For example, Paul Elliott Johnson reveals the very real political interests at play on January 6th. Through analysis of invocations of a restricted "people" that defines Americanness on white racial, masculine, and Christian grounds, Johnson shows how the insurrectionists of January 6th sought to defend a very particular and circumscribed vision of America. Building on his book on conservative populism, Johnson shows how an antidemocratic orientation is a fundamental part of contemporary conservatism. This provides the key to understanding how patriotism and the deification of law enforcement can sit alongside and be reconciled with an assault on a sacred national site. Through analysis of footage of January 6th, Johnson shows how conservative populism advances the idea that American democracy *requires* political violence in defense of this narrowly defined "people."

These appeals and constructions of "the people" take shape across the media ecosystem and platforms and are propagated by many actors, including new networked social movements. Silvio Waisbord provides a deep analysis of how connective, digital fascist action looks on the right and how it took shape on January 6th. Just as racial ideologies animate American history in ways that do not break with the past, so the attempted coup in many ways was the culmination of a broad turn toward what scholars have understood as "connective action," or the new possibility of organizing collective action at scale through social and affective ties on digital networks (Bennett & Segerberg, 2013; Papacharissi, 2015). The presumption of many scholars in an earlier era was that connective action would expand democracy. Following the election of Barack Obama and the Arab Spring, scholars even went so far as to see connective action as *inherently* democratizing in lowering the costs of political and collective action and expanding participation. While digital media clearly have vastly expanded the public sphere and given voice to new protest movements centered on political and social equality (Jackson et al., 2020), as Waisbord argues, the ends toward which digital action is directed are not predetermined. The surge in far-right and right-wing groups over the past decade in the United States is a case in point. The same platform affordances that fueled Black Lives Matter organizing also facilitate right-wing recruitment, mobilization, and action in the streets.

Indeed, building on an extensive exegesis of the idea of "extremism," Alice Marwick shows how January 6th was about the mainstreaming of online conspiracy propagated by online movements such as QAnon, which provided an actionable set of narratives and symbols for Trump and his supporters to take up in their efforts to undermine democratic accountability and prevent the peaceful transfer of power. Becca Lewis meanwhile shows how right-wing media created an antidemocratic feedback loop in relation to January 6th, continually redirecting the threat of the attempted coup to Black Lives Matter. These outlets blamed the racial equity movement for provoking the attempted coup and castigated mainstream media for having a double standard in their (lack of) coverage of the supposed violence of Black Lives Matter and coverage of the actual violence on January 6th. As Lewis shows, right-wing media strategically leveraged the discourse of polarization (see Kreiss, this volume) to blame Democrats seeking to understand what happened on January 6th or condemning the assault on the Capitol, calling them divisive or merely out for partisan advantage.

Taken together, these efforts at reversal, deflection, and accusation were strategic, mediated efforts to undermine inquiries into January 6th and limit accountability for the Republican actors involved. These efforts by right-wing media were especially important as journalists adopted multiple labels to conceptualize January 6th for their audiences (see Zulli et al., 2022). Danielle K. Brown reveals how in their documentation of the attempted coup, journalists tried out various labels for what they were witnessing—including "riot," "mob," "insurrection," and "coup," the most prominent being that those at the Capitol were "rioters." Drawing on her extensive work studying the structure of media protest coverage and public participation in protest events, Brown argues that across U.S. history, professional journalism has transformed Black racial justice protests into *riots*. In the process, this media frame has a corrosive effect on the legitimacy of racial justice protests in the minds of the public. Indeed, it is hard to see the same label of "riot" applying to Black people in the streets urgently protesting murder amid repressive police presences and white people having the time and safety to shit and piss unmolested in the halls of the U.S. Capitol. In the end, Brown argues that democracy needs "authoritarian words to describe authoritarian-sponsored practices."

Communication can also be about rethinking who we are and the forms of solidarity we can create (see also Burack, this volume). Using a psychological approach, Andrew Ifedapo Thompson analyzes January 6, 2021, against the backdrop of the changing racial landscape of the United States. Elites who propagate strategic narratives of demographic change, white status threat (see Kreiss, this volume), and racialized stolen elections help create the sense of an "existential threat" among whites—where their way of life will fundamentally change and they can no longer win fair elections. As such, some whites embrace antidemocratic actions, including political violence, that they believe will preserve their group's status and power. Thompson demonstrates this through a series of experiments that manipulate narratives about demographic change benefiting or harming the in- or out-party. He finds that when Republicans learn of the benefits of racial demographic change they express more pro-democratic views. Thompson concludes on the more optimistic note that racial categories can shift as can party coalitions—and with a clear warning that scholars should be careful about how they discuss the inevitability of racial and social change.

The challenge is that Republican elites continue to find electoral and political gains in articulating narratives of racial and political threats for the social groups they represent. Dannagal Young's chapter reveals just how central social identity is to the acceptance of the story of a stolen election. Young focuses on how comprehension (the understanding of our environments), control (or agency), and community (having fellowship with others) condition the acceptance of mis- and disinformation. Political actors craft strategic political narratives, including blaming and crafting threats from out-groups. While it is tempting to see this as a generalized political phenomenon, like many chapters in this volume, Young shows that these dynamics are more pronounced among Republicans, a party that has a tight alignment between a few salient racial (white) and religious (Christian) identities, but also party members with psychological profiles that facilitate beliefs in group threat. Meanwhile, media reinforce these dynamics, distilling disparate political and social identities into pure and emotionally responsive forms. Young ends by arguing that media should dilute, as opposed to distill, identities to help prevent future antidemocratic actions and political violence.

References

Bennett, W. L., & Segerberg, A. (2013). *The logic of connective action: Digital media and the personalization of contentious politics.* Cambridge University Press.

Jackson, S. J., Bailey, M., & Welles, B. F. (2020). *# HashtagActivism: Networks of race and gender justice.* MIT Press.

Lassiter, M., & Crespino, J. (Eds.) (2009). *The myth of Southern exceptionalism.* Oxford University Press.

Mickey, R. (2015). *Paths out of Dixie: The democratization of authoritarian enclaves in America's Deep South, 1944–1972.* Princeton University Press.

Papacharissi, Z. (2015). *Affective publics: Sentiment, technology, and politics.* Oxford University Press.

Zulli, D., Coe, K., & Isaacs, Z. (2022). News framing in the aftermath of the January 6 attacks on the US Capitol: An analysis of labels, definitional uncertainty, and contextualization. *American Behavioral Scientist, 67*(6), 702–720.

2

It Was an Attempted Coup

The Cline Center's Coup d'État Project Categorizes the January 6, 2021, Assault on the U.S. Capitol

Scott L. Althaus, Joseph Bajjalieh, Jay Jennings, Michael Martin, Buddy Peyton, and Dan Shalmon

The Cline Center's Coup d'État Project[1] has categorized the storming of the US Capitol Building on January 6, 2021 as an attempted coup.[2] Labels matter when it comes to political violence, because each type has distinctive consequences and implications for societal stability. Coups and attempted coups are among the most politically consequential forms of destabilizing events tracked by the Cline Center for Advanced Social Research.

How the Cline Center Defines Coups d'État

The Cline Center's Coup d'État Project is the world's largest global registry of failed and successful coups. The Cline Center defines a coup as an "organized effort to effect sudden and irregular (e.g., illegal or extra-legal)

---

[1] The Cline Center's Coup d'État project page can be found at https://clinecenter.illinois.edu/proj ect/research-themes/democracy-and-development/coup-detat-project Chapter authors are listed alphabetically, and all were members of the Cline Center research staff at the time this statement was originally issued.

[2] Two days after the storming of the Capitol, the Cline Center initially released a provisional statement describing the categories of political violence that might be used to characterize the event. At that time, evidence relevant to two of the five Coup d'État Project event criteria was ambiguous. On January 27, 2021, the Cline Center released a second statement incorporating new evidence reported in multiple news sources, including court documents and firsthand accounts, that further clarified what happened on January 6th. The present statement incorporates additional new information that has come to light since that time, including notably the sworn testimony of numerous witnesses appearing before the U.S. House Select Committee to Investigate the January 6th Attack on the United States Capitol.

Scott L. Althaus, Joseph Bajjalieh, Jay Jennings, Michael Martin, Buddy Peyton, and Dan Shalmon, *It Was an Attempted Coup* In: *Media and January 6th*. Edited by: Khadijah Costley White, Daniel Kreiss, Shannon C. McGregor, and Rebekah Tromble, Oxford University Press. © Oxford University Press 2024. DOI: 10.1093/oso/9780197758526.003.0002

removal of the incumbent executive authority of a national government, or to displace the authority of the highest levels of one or more branches of government." To be categorized as a coup, an event must meet the following criteria (which are detailed at greater length in the Coup d'État Project codebook):[3]

1. There must be some person or persons who initiated the coup.
2. The target of the coup must have meaningful control over national policy.
3. There must be a credible threat to the leaders' hold on power.
4. Illegal or irregular means must be used to seize, remove, or render powerless the target of the coup.
5. It must be an organized effort.

These events fall into three categories. Coups that are planned but thwarted before action is taken are *coup conspiracies*. Once action is taken against a target, it may fail, in which case it is an *attempted coup*. If the authority of a target is seized, or removed, it is a *successful coup*.

Some social scientists define coups d'état in ways that require the perpetrators to hold formal positions within the existing national government. We do not. In the Cline Center's approach, the relationship between the perpetrators and the government determines only the type of coup. Coup d'État Project data includes events initiated from both within and outside the government. Other researchers might classify efforts to overthrow a government by nongovernmental actors as insurgencies or civil conflict events rather than coups. We allow data users to decide whether the broader or narrower definition is appropriate for their purposes.

Observers watching the unfolding event live on January 6th could see that the storming of the U.S. Capitol clearly met the first three criteria: one or more persons posed a credible threat to the power of the legislative branch to determine national policy. However, it was unclear at that time whether the attackers were trying to merely disrupt the process of governing or were attempting to change who controls the government. It was also unclear whether the assault on the Capitol was spontaneous or had been organized

---

[3] The Cline Center's Coup d'État Project codebook (Peyton et al., 2023) can be found at https://doi.org/10.13012/B2IDB-9651987_V6

in advance. By late January 2021, Cline Center researchers reviewing voluminous reports about the event, including official documents, quotes from participants, and analysis of details in videos and images, concluded this additional evidence clearly demonstrated that the two remaining criteria were also met.

One or More Groups Planned to Storm the U.S. Capitol

The fifth criterion for categorizing coups excludes purely spontaneous acts that are not intentionally organized in advance. It is clear that those assembled on January 6th possessed a variety of motives and expectations. Those who stormed the U.S. Capitol Building—as well as those who merely joined in the peaceful protests that preceded it—included a diverse mix of groups and unaffiliated individuals. But one or more of the groups within the ranks of those who entered the Capitol Building had carefully planned, equipped, and organized themselves for violent action.

One or More Groups Intended to Usurp Congressional Authority to Certify the 2020 Presidential Election

The "Save America March" rally that immediately preceded the attack on the U.S. Capitol Building was thematically focused on changing the outcome of the 2020 U.S. presidential election. That alone does not mean the people who stormed the building intended any more than temporarily disrupting the normal operations of the U.S. Congress. Cline Center researchers paid careful attention to evidence that might clarify the intentions of those involved in assaulting the Capitol. Our team concluded from publicly available reports that one or more groups attempted to intervene in the presidential transition in order to extend President Trump's time in office past the constitutionally imposed limit of January 20, 2021. Ample evidence demonstrated that one or more groups within the ranks of those who illegally entered the Capitol intended to usurp congressional authority to certify the election, arrogating control of the transition to themselves or to the executive branch. This would change who controls the federal government rather than merely disrupt the process of governing.

What Type of Coup Attempt Was It?

If a failed act of insurrection was planned, organized, and implemented in such a way that it posed a short-term credible threat to overthrow the legitimate authority of a policymaking branch of national government, it is an attempted coup d'état under Cline Center definitions. But which type of attempted coup it might be depends on its circumstances and initiators. At the time of this writing, the Cline Center has concluded that available evidence supports two types of event classification for the January 6th assault on the Capitol.

First, some of the groups and individuals known to have organized and planned this coup attempt fall clearly into the category of "dissidents." In the Cline Center typology, a *dissident coup* is initiated by a small group of discontents that can include former government officials, religious leaders, business owners, or civilians.

Second, ongoing investigations by members of the U.S. Congress, legal authorities, and news organizations have revealed credible additional evidence that President Trump was actively involved in attempting to displace the authority of the legislative branch, which also makes the events of January 6 an attempted auto-coup. Under Cline Center definitions, an auto-coup occurs when "the incumbent chief executive uses illegal or extra-legal means to assume extraordinary powers, seize the power of other branches of government, or render powerless other components of the government such as the legislature or judiciary."

The Coup d'État Project codebook contains more detailed definitions of the various types of coups in the data set. Cline Center researchers will continue to assess whether any additional coup categories should be applied to this event.

Summary

Using the Cline Center's Coup d'État Project definitions, the storming of the Capitol on January 6, 2021, was an attempted coup d'état: an organized, illegal attempt to intervene in the presidential transition by displacing the power of the Congress to certify the election. In terms of the type of coup attempt, the complex nature of this event leads it to be categorized as both an *attempted auto-coup* and as an *attempted dissident coup*, reflecting the separate activities of distinctive actors involved in the event.

About the Cline Center and the Coup d'État Project

The Cline Center for Advanced Social Research[4] is a nonpartisan research center at the University of Illinois, Urbana-Champaign, with over a decade of experience in systematically categorizing acts of protest and political violence around the world. Since its initial public release in 2013, the Cline Center's Coup d'État Project has aimed to document every coup, attempted coup, and coup conspiracy anywhere in the world since 1945. Version 2.1.2 of the data set encompasses 981 events, including 441 realized coups, 349 attempts, and 191 conspiracies that occurred between 1945 and 2022. It is the largest global registry of these destabilizing events.

To build the data set, Cline Center researchers began with the excellent work of other scholars, including the Center for Systemic Peace[5] (Marshall & Marshall, 2007), the *World Handbook of Political and Social Indicators* (Taylor & Jodice, 1983), Luttwak's (1979) *Coup d'État: A Practical Handbook*, Powell and Thyne (2011),[6] and unpublished data sets compiled by Svolik and Akcinaroglu (2006). The Coup d'État Project team refined and then expanded on existing data sets using the Cline Center Global News Index,[7] events from the Social, Political, and Economic Event Database Project,[8] and other open-access resources. For more details, see the Coup d'État Project codebook (Peyton et al., 2023).

References

Luttwak, E. (1979). *Coup d'état: A practical handbook*. Harvard University Press.
Marshall, M., & Marshall, D. (2007). *Coup d'état events, 1960–2006*. Center for Systemic Peace.

---

[4] https://clinecenter.illinois.edu/.
[5] https://www.systemicpeace.org/inscrdata.html.
[6] https://www.jonathanmpowell.com/coup-detat-dataset.html.
[7] https://clinecenter.illinois.edu/project/data-science/global-news-index.
[8] https://clinecenter.illinois.edu/project/human-loop-event-data-projects/SPEED.

Peyton, B., Bajjalieh, J, Shalmon, D., Martin, M., Bonaguro, J., & Althaus, S. 2023. "Cline Center Coup d'État Project Dataset Codebook." *Cline Center Coup d'État Project Dataset*. Cline Center for Advanced Social Research. V.2.1.2. February 23. University of Illinois Urbana-Champaign. doi: 10.13012/B2IDB-9651987_V6

Powell, J. M. & Thyne, C. L. (2011). Global instances of coups from 1950 to 2010: A new dataset. *Journal of Peace Research, 48*(2), 249–259.

Svolik, M., & Akcinaroglu, S. (2006). *Government change in authoritarian regimes* [Unpublished data sets]. University of Illinois at Urbana-Champaign.

Taylor, C. L., & Jodice, D. A. (1983). *World handbook of political and social indicators*. Yale University Press.

3

What January 6th Was Not

Danielle K. Brown

Leading up to January 6, 2021, the news media rumbled with headlines speculating what readers might see at the day's original leading event, the "Save America Rally," also known as the "March for Trump" and the "Stop the Steal Rally." A few news organizations signaled that events could be dangerous, leading with headlines like "Nation's Capitol Braces for Violence as Extremist Groups Converge to Protest Trump's Election Loss" (Carless, 2020).

Having spent most of my research career examining the news media's relentless hype of social movements, I've repeatedly found that speculative news narratives about social movements are often unfounded and unfulfilled. Moreover, the news media have a penchant for stereotyping demonstration efforts and the people that engage in them (Brown, 2021b; Carney & Kelekay, 2020; Jackson, 2020). Rarely are those representations fully realized quite like they were on January 6, 2021.

On that particular day, I was in a Zoom meeting discussing a research project when I got a notification: "Shot fired at the capital." I spent the remainder of the day glued to my television, stunned by the unfolding events. Honestly, I had never seen anything quite like this—not just the actions of thousands of people storming the U.S. Capitol but also the unfolding and quickly changing media narrative that described the day's events, sympathizing media channels excluded (Brown, 2021a).

As the afternoon dragged on, news narratives evolved. Having earlier described the event as the "Save America Rally," the news media quickly switched to calling it a protest. Then images began to emerge of the massive crowds barreling through doors and windows, the gallows erected on the Capitol lawn, and the man with a horned helmet carrying a spear yelling in a Capitol corridor. The narrative then shifted again. With an abundance of caution, words like "riot," "attempted coup" (d'état), "siege," and "insurrection" were used to describe the unfolding events (e.g., Diaz et al., 2021; *Washington Post*, 2021).

Danielle K. Brown, *What January 6th Was Not* In: *Media and January 6th*. Edited by: Khadijah Costley White,
Daniel Kreiss, Shannon C. McGregor, and Rebekah Tromble, Oxford University Press. © Oxford University Press 2024.
DOI: 10.1093/oso/9780197758526.003.0003

UNDERSTANDING JANUARY 6, 2021

We've often seen calls from academics and public figures for the media to "call it like it is." Many have debated the appropriate term for describing these events. Singh (2021) wrote, "Definitions matter because they direct our attention toward key people or groups and suggest effective responses. The wrong definition obscures our understanding and directs us away from the critical parts of the problem." However critical such definitions are, in the interest of protecting some of the fundamental and oft-overlooked facets of democratic governmental structures, I argue it is equally important to identify and define what January 6th was not.

January 6th Was Not a Protest

Sure, at a purely fundamental level, protests are acts of dissent, and January 6th could fit this description. But the function of protest within the context of democracy and democratic systems is much more robust. Protests provide opportunities for people to air their grievances, signal their strength (Tufekci, 2017), and engage more directly in the political process beyond voting. Protests offer an essential function in democracy, providing citizens with an outlet (other than voting) to elevate concerns. Protests are used to signal concerns to the public and politicians alike and motivate awareness of a group of the electorate that feels unheard or underconsidered. Protests fight to work within the democratic system, not to overthrow it. Hinck (2023) argues that the academic structures that have been dominantly used to understand citizen protests lack the same utility when used to analyze the events of January 6th. We need different terms to describe antidemocratic behavior.

Such a distinction is critical for constructing knowledge within the general public. In the United States, most citizens don't engage in protests at all. Every protest participation survey I've put in the field since 2015 suggests that only about 5% of people participate in protest activities, even against data that suggest protest activity has been on the rise. Without direct experience in protests or encounters with them, how people understand protests is still largely dependent on the narratives they are introduced to rather than direct engagement in or with such activities. Therefore, what most people know about protests comes from media narratives, conversations with friends, and a bit of imagination. Among peers, protests are often labeled with political ideologies and attached to political parties (Gillion, 2020). In the news media, most protests have been stunted by sensational and speculative narratives that reduce their legitimacy in the eyes of the public. In the United States specifically, protests of racial injustice are among the most delegitimized by news media narratives. Since the antiracism movement was reenergized in the early 2010s after the death of Trayvon Martin and Michael Brown, media narratives have focused excessively on the sticks and stones of protest activity, fires, property destruction, emotional outrage, and criminalizing descriptions of victims of police violence and the protests that follow their deaths. Such was the case in analyses of national and local media coverage of the killing of Michael Brown, Eric Garner, and Tamir Rice. And again, after the death of Sandra Bland, Freddie Gray, Alton Sterling, Philando Castile, and Stephon Clark. The trend of associating Black civil rights with riots has historical roots. The 1960s "race riots" and the peaceful actions of Black civil rights leaders were also delegitimized, demonized, and associated with violence. However, those historical moments are often memorialized and sterilized as the civil rights movement (Jackson, 2020). Riots stand separately from these depictions. For example, the 1990s riots in Los Angeles occurred only after video evidence documented the modern-day torture of Black Americans by police (Richardson, 2020). Those protests are now often referred to as the LA riots, not the 1990s Black civil rights movement. Notably, the association with Black civil rights and riots is ingrained in U.S. culture. One Black resident of Minnesota recently told me in an interview, "Sometimes it seems like we [are] the only ones that ever riot. . . . We go out to the streets; people start feeling threatened. . . . They don't even want us to say [anything]." The association with civil rights for Black people and riots is a common theme in the public discourse. Few, if any, other movements in the United States have been given a similar designation.

That is, until January 6, 2021. As rally attendees made their way to the Capitol that day, media narratives evolved rapidly. At first, participants were dominantly described as protesters. Later some news organizations escalated the description, using terms like "rioters" and "mobs." Most news organizations simply waited for official sources and political partisans to make public statements and used their words (often in quotations) to deflect the responsibility of naming the group an "out of the ordinary" term. Later, narratives flirted with words like "siege," "insurrection," and "coup" (Brown, 2021a). Still, the most dominant description in news discourse one year later typically describes these entities as "Capitol rioters." According to *NewsWhip's Analytics* archive of online news, digital coverage was 1.5 times more likely to describe the events as a riot than an insurrection. Table 3.1 shows frequencies

Table 3.1 Total Numbers of Event Descriptors in Digital Coverage of January 6

Keyword	Article Count	Percentage
Riot	172,440	48.9
Insurrection	117,372	33.2
Siege	28,115	9.0
Rally	21,254	6.0
Protest	9,673	2.7
Coup	4,107	1.2
Total	*352,861*	*100*

Note: Coverage totals from January 7, 2021, to January 6, 2022.

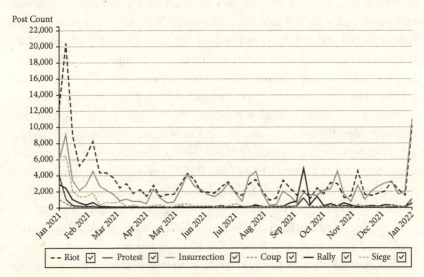

Figure 3.1 Over time comparison of event descriptors from January 6 coverage.

of keywords used in the coverage of January 6th, while Figure 3.1 shows shifts in keywords over time. Those tuned in to initial coverage were likely to encounter a flurry of descriptors, but the most common throughout the year at most points was the description of the events as a riot.

As I mentioned before, my objective in this chapter is not to argue for the exact term that should be used—a task that is undertaken by others in this volume. Instead, I argue that to fully understand January 6, 2021, we must create discourse about what January 6 was not.

January 6th Was Not Simply a Riot

If January 6th had been simply a protest-turned-riot, then we can make a case for comparison between it and other events we associate with protests and riots, like Black Lives Matter protests.

However, in times of political instability, this comparison is inaccurate, and it is critical to understand what a protest is by its normative function within a democratic government. In the United States, protests are protected by the First Amendment of the Constitution, which provides a framework for understanding the political purpose of protest within the country's democratic systems. Protests can petition the government for a redress of grievances—grievances effectively left unaddressed within the existing governmental structure. From this democratically centered perspective, protests like those related to excessive force by police against Black people in 2020 were protests: assemblies of people calling to redress the long-standing grievances about police brutality, killings, and murders that have gone unaddressed by the existing governmental system. They also served as an uprising against oppressive government institutions that literally kill people, triggered by the filmed murder of George Floyd.

Contrarily, January 6th can be described as a protest only under the following circumstances: (1) We privilege all acts of congregation as protest, (2) we accept false and deceptive narratives of rampant election fraud as legitimate grievances, and (3) we deny that a political leader organized the crowd. Accepting such assumptions will only further fuel the mis/disinformation conundrum we currently face globally. Led by the president of the United States, the participants of January 6th were not engaged in civil or uncivil protests. *They were rallying—quite literally coming together after a (proven) defeat to regroup.* Many in the group chose authoritarian-like strategies to attempt to take down the (mostly) democratic infrastructure of the United States. The erection of gallows and the smashing of Capitol windows during a procedural election confirmation for the president of the United States are not the equivalent of a broken CVS window and a burned gas station in downtown Minneapolis (though indeed, the 2020 protests, demonstrations, and riots sparked after the murder of George Floyd were much more complex than this). We need authoritarian words to describe authoritarian-sponsored practices. January 6th was not a protest.

Despite the fact that January 6th was most commonly described as a riot, we fall short if we define this event by riotous behavior alone, given the long-standing imbalances in discourse that have criminalized civil rights protests by privileging narratives that present those protests as riots. We cannot negate that there was property destruction and violence during civil rights protests; otherwise, however, they have few substantial commonalities with the January 6th Capitol events, where individuals assembled while destroying barricades, defecating in the halls, and searching for the whereabouts of political opponents as a response to a democratic election outcome.

Rather than using familiar and comfortable language, we must understand January 6th in terms that make sense for the reality we're facing within a faltering democratic system threatened and empowered by authoritarian, politically supported people and behavior. Just as we've developed language to differentiate among democracies, anocracies, autocracies, and authoritarian regimes, we must also refine the language we use to describe citizens' actions within evolving governmental and societal realities. Separating citizen-sponsored protest activity within the normative democratic framework from January 6th is vital for maintaining protests' integrity within democratic systems. Put another way, we need protests. But January 6th was not a protest. By associating those events with protests, we threaten all legitimate protest activity.

Language and narratives inevitably serve to keep records, shape cultures, and influence policy. Narratives can embrace and erase ideas, experiences, and progress. How we frame and tell a story can influence human behavior and encourage or discourage people to connect, share, and mobilize. What exists in the dominant narrative can define how society works by defining the problems and solutions and influencing ethical judgments (Entman, 1993). The path forward requires us to explicate, with precision, terms that deviate from normative democratic positionalities while also incorporating clear boundaries that align with governmental systems embraced by power entities. The hard line of definitional boundaries can serve as a protective mechanism we need as knowledge creators and writers to stave off regressive tactics at their most basic level. Just as boundaries are essential to healthy relationships, boundaries enable us to tackle the abuse of words and actions that is evident in the "post-truth" era and distinguish variations in citizen involvement in government in equitable ways. Our understanding of January 6th must come with boundaries that separate the events from citizen-led protest movements. Such boundaries are essential for protecting legitimate protests, a democratic behavior indispensable for the well-being, maintenance, and development of democratic governments.

References

Brown, D. K. (2021a, Jan. 7). The insurrection at the Capitol challenged how US media frames unrest and shapes public opinion. *The Conversation*. https://theconversation.com/the-insurrection-at-the-capitol-challenged-how-us-media-frames-unrest-and-shapes-public-opinion-152805

Brown, D. K. (2021b). Police violence and protests: Digital media maintenance of racism, protest repression, and the status quo. *Journal of Broadcasting & Electronic Media*, 65(1), 157–176.

Brown, D. K., Mourão, R. R., & Sylvie, G. (2019). Martin to Brown: How time and platform impact coverage of the Black Lives Matter movement. *Journalism Practice*, 13(4), 413–430.

Carless, W. (2020, Jan. 4). Nation's capital braces for violence as extremist groups converge to protest Trump's election loss. *USA Today*. https://www.usatoday.com/story/news/nation/2021/01/04/january-6-dc-protests-against-election-certification-could-violent/4132441001/

Carney, N., & Kelekay, J. (2022). Framing the Black Lives Matter movement: An analysis of shifting news coverage in 2014 and 2020. *Social Currents*. 9(6), 558–572. https://doi.org/10.1177/23294965221092731

Diaz, J., Chappell, B., & Moore, E. (2021, Jan. 7). Police confirm death of the officer injured during attack on Capitol. NPR. https://www.npr.org/sections/insurrection-at-the-capitol/2021/01/07/954333542/police-confirm-death-of-officer-injured-during-attack-on-capitol

Entman, R. M. (1993). Framing: Toward clarification of a fractured paradigm. *Journal of Communication*, 43(4), 51–58.

Gillion, D. Q. (2020). *The loud minority: Why protest matters in American democracy*. Princeton University Press.

Hinck, R. S. (2023). US hypocrisy and the end of American exceptionalism? Narratives of the January 6th attack on the US Capitol from illiberal national media. *American Behavioral Scientist*, 67(6), 807–836. https://doi.org/10.1177/00027642221096335.

Jackson, S. J. (2020). The news narratives that are covering up police violence. *The Atlantic*. https://www.theatlantic.com/culture/archive/2020/06/george-floyd-protests-what-news-reports-dont-say/612571/.

Jackson, S. J. (2021). Making #BlackLivesMatter in the shadow of Selma: Collective memory and racial justice activism in US news. *Communication, Culture and Critique*, 14(3), 385–404.

Richardson, A. V. (2020). *Bearing witness while Black: African Americans, smartphones, and the new protest# journalism*. Oxford University Press.

Singh, N. (2021, Jan. 9). Was the U.S. Capitol riot really a coup? Here's why definitions matter. *Washington Post*. https://www.washingtonpost.com/politics/2021/01/09/was-us-capitol-riot-really-coup-heres-why-definitions-matter/

Tufekci, Z. (2017). *Twitter and tear gas: The power and fragility of networked protest*. Yale University Press.

Washington Post. (2021, Jan. 7). Woman dies after shooting in the U.S. Capitol; DC National Guard activates after mob breaches building. https://www.washingtonpost.com/dc-md-va/2021/01/06/dc-protests-trump-rally-live-updates/

4

Remembering January 6th

An Insurrection, the Media, and the Shadow of the Tea Party

Khadijah Costley White

> I saw friends with blood all over their faces. I was slipping in people's blood. You know, I—I was catching people as they fell. It was carnage. It was chaos. I can't even describe what I saw. Never in my wildest dreams did I think that, as a police officer, as a law enforcement officer, I would find myself in the middle of a battle.
>
> —Officer Carolyn Edwards, recounting the attack on the Capitol on January 6, 2021 (National Public Radio, 2022)

It is easy to forget the horror of the January 6th attack on the U.S. Capitol in the midst of the conservative endeavor to reclaim and rebrand the attempted coup in the media. Exactly a year after the attempted overthrow, the detailed accounts of deaths and violence fade in the background of national news coverage that offer alternative interpretations and narratives of the insurrection attempt that led to the deaths of several people, hundreds of injuries, and nearly 900 people charged with related crimes, including physical attacks on members of the media and police and stated intentions to assassinate the vice president of the United States (Hall et al., 2022; Linderman & Mendoza, 2021; U.S. Attorney's Office, 2022). The violent invasion of the country's Capitol by largely white domestic terrorists marked the end of the presidential reign of Donald Trump and demanded investigation, interrogation, and explanation in the American public sphere.

In my general observations of the national commemoration of the January 6th invasion, I have taken note of news narratives repeating previous media patterns in reporting on conservative movements and white supremacist

Khadijah Costley White, *Remembering January 6th* In: *Media and January 6th*. Edited by: Khadijah Costley White, Daniel Kreiss, Shannon C. McGregor, and Rebekah Tromble, Oxford University Press. © Oxford University Press 2024. DOI: 10.1093/oso/9780197758526.003.0004

rhetoric. In particular, the news coverage of January 6th is reminiscent of the reporting on the Tea Party, which roared onto the political scene at the beginning of the presidency of Barack Obama in 2009, the first Black president in American history. Such intersections necessitate further discussion.

Institutional actors already connect the Tea Party and January 6th outside of their news stories: major Tea Party organizers poured funds into coordinating the January 6th coup attempt, and Tea Party leaders, such as Trump White House chief of staff Mark Meadows, advised the president inside the White House while the attack happened (Chavez, 2021). A Tea Party organizer named Amy Kremer started the influential "Stop the Steal" Facebook group and held the government permit for the rally that occurred before the march to the Capitol on January 6th (Tolan, 2022). According to one CNN reporter, the Capitol insurrection was the "evolution of the Tea Party" (Tolan, 2022).

Despite the stretch of a dozen years, I reflect here on how the media's first-anniversary commemoration of the attempted January 6th coup (and Trumpism more generally) shares key similarities with the first reporting on the Tea Party, which I write about in my book *The Branding of Right-Wing Activism: The News Media and the Tea Party* (Costley White, 2018). In covering the rise of the Tea Party, the news media across the political spectrum downplayed white violence and helped promote, defend, legitimize, and establish the Tea Party in ways that actively undermined the democratic function of the press and American political institutions (Costley White, 2018). The news media has treated its coverage of the Capitol attack in similar ways.

Race, class, and gender shape the news reporting on both the "Stop the Steal" and Tea Party movements, particularly in minimizing the impact of their actions and goals and the threats that each movement posed to a multiracial democracy. Here, I will walk through two major themes in news coverage that come from my previous work examining the news reporting on the Tea Party and highlight how they connect with the January 6th anniversary coverage: (1) the mainstreaming of whiteness/white supremacy and (2) the news media's function as citizen-activist. The term "citizen-activist" to describe some of the news coverage speaks to a dynamic in which some members of the press act outside of their traditional role as reporter to defend or promote a political cause in ways that undermine their 'fourth estate' responsibility to educate and serve the public; that is, the substance of their work prioritizes activism over journalism. As a part of this reflection I aim to answer these broader questions: Have the news media learned or changed

32 UNDERSTANDING JANUARY 6, 2021

anything about covering white conservative movements since the Tea Party? And, if not, what might be done about it?

Mainstreaming of Whiteness/White Supremacy

In covering the Tea Party, the news media frequently helped establish white aggression and violence as part of the Tea Party brand through narratives that focused on class, race, and gender. For example, many news stories on the Tea Party featured "Mama Grizzlies," a term coined by Tea Party leader Sarah Palin to reference the conservative women political candidates she supported. "Mama Grizzlies" invoked the idea of women (specifically, white women) fighting for their children in the political battleground the way that a mama bear would naturally (and violently) fight for the safety of her own cubs (Costley White, 2018). Ironically, a substantial number of Palin's "Mama Grizzly" candidates were not mothers at all. "Mama Grizzly" was used as an affective extension of the Tea Party's rebellious and populist brand because it provoked feelings related to motherhood, softened anger and rage by conveying the women as legitimate defenders of self and family, justified harsh political attacks on opponents as maternal instinct, and connected easily with people.

A similar pattern of using white femininity to downplay the threat and severity of white mob violence emerged in some of the memorializing news coverage of the January 6th coup attempt. In one example on the first anniversary of the January 6th insurrection, a *CBS This Morning* (2022) segment told the story of the Capitol attack primarily from the perspective of an older white grandmother with a genteel southern accent and warm smile, scenes of her baking with a grandchild, posing with her sixth grade students, and family photos interspliced with footage from January 6th:

REPORTER: As people stormed the Capitol one year ago today, Sharon Storey[1] and her husband Victor did not follow the crowd inside.
WOMAN: People started singing the national anthem. And it came all across all of us. And everyone, once they started hearing it, was participating. And it was just exciting.

---

[1] The names of the women in this segment are spelled here phonetically and based on the pronunciation in the report, but I was unable to confirm the spellings as the written names did not appear in the show.

REPORTER: But this grandmother of ten—who had driven all the way from Gaffney, South Carolina, to be there—firmly believes that the American democracy she used to teach about in her sixth grade classroom is on the edge of collapse.

REPORTER: Do you think a civil war is possible in your lifetime?

WOMAN: I think if they push people too far against the wall, especially the southerners, they're not going to take it.

REPORTER: . . . That feeling of fraud, if only a feeling, is what led so many to Washington on January sixth to, in their minds, defend democracy.

REPORTER: The words that come to mind for you to describe the feelings and the atmosphere there, what are they?

WOMAN: Patriotic, unity, hope.

This CBS segment focuses on this elderly white woman rather than her husband, who was also in attendance at the Capitol attack. The framing allows her to offer an alternative and softer rendition of the murderous riot[2] filmed on live TV. In this version of the Capitol attack, she is a teacher and protector of American democracy, a person who cares for children, and someone who simply and peacefully sang her country's national anthem at the Capitol. Her threat of violence embedded in reference to "southerners" getting "push[ed] too far" is framed as self-defense rather than an intentional strike on the U.S. government to stage a coup and overturn a presidential election. The seven people who died and others injured are not mentioned in this particular story about January 6th. In this way, this CBS news segment presents the views of the Capitol riot participants as gentle, pleasant, patriotic, relatable, and nurturing, while displacing the explicit violence of the attack.

The lesson of January 6th as framed in this CBS news story is one about general distrust of government rather than the threat of white supremacy and violence. The segment continues by weaving in an interview with Alicia Sedassee, a Black woman bartender and Bernie Sanders supporter from Brooklyn who is still disappointed by his 2016 primary loss to Hillary Clinton. The news segment juxtaposes her left-wing mistrust of government

---

[2] People in the crowd who broke into the Capitol that day have been charged for threats to kill Vice President Mike Pence, House Speaker Nancy Pelosi, and Congresswoman Alexandria Ocasio-Cortez. The crowd was recorded chanting "Hang Mike Pence" as they stormed the Capitol and constructed a gallows outside of the building (Kristan, 2021; Leonard, 2021; Reuters, 2021).

34 UNDERSTANDING JANUARY 6, 2021

with Sharon Storey's right-wing participation in a march to attack members of Congress, deftly implying their political equivalence:

REPORTER: Besides their differences, both women see themselves as defenders of the same underlying principles.
REPORTER: You consider yourself to be a patriot?
STOREY: Yes.
REPORTER: Are you proud to be an American?
STOREY: Yes.
SEDASSEE: I think I am a patriot because I'm fighting for what our constitutional rights are supposed to be and what this country says it is.

After the segment ends, the reporter acknowledges that "putting these two voters together" does suggest "equivalence" and pointedly remarks that only one political party is responsible for the attacks on the integrity of the 2020 election and the U.S. Capitol. But which political party he is referring to is left unnamed, and the larger imbalance in terms of time and framing of the story remains. The Black Sanders supporter is not depicted with any family during her interview or asked about her perspective on the attack, portraying her as less humanized and empathetic to the viewing audience. The story, too, leaves unchallenged the peaceful description of the January 6th rally, despite the large mob carrying Confederate flags, spewing racial slurs at police, holding nooses, and threatening lynchings of political foes (Austin-Hillary & Strang, 2022).

The Fox News coverage of the January 6th insurrection, which was reported across the national news media, also actively downplayed or ignored the threat of white supremacy and white violence on that day. For example, Fox News anchors during the anniversary coverage of January 6th vehemently refuted the argument that the Capitol insurrection was an act of terrorism. After Senator Ted Cruz was criticized for condemning the Capitol attack as terrorism, he went on Tucker Carlson's (Carlson, 2022) show to take back his comments:

CRUZ: The way I phrased things yesterday, it was sloppy and it was frankly dumb.
CARLSON: I don't buy that. Whoa! Whoa! Whoa! Whoa! I don't buy that! . . . You repeated that phrase. I do not believe you used that accidentally. I just don't.

CRUZ: . . . What I was referring to are the limited number of people who engaged in violent attacks against police officers. I think you and I both agree that if you assault a police officer, you should go to jail. . . . I wasn't saying that thousands of peaceful protestors supporting Donald Trump are somehow terrorists. I wasn't saying that the millions of patriots across the country supporting President Trump are terrorists and that's what a lot of people have misunderstood.

CARLSON: Whoa, wait a second! Even what you just said doesn't make sense. So if somebody assaults a cop, he should be charged and go to jail. I couldn't agree more, we've said that for years. But that person is still not a terrorist. How many people have been charged with terrorism? (Carlson, 2022)

This exchange refuting the Capitol attack as terrorism was highlighted in reporting across a range of national news outlets, including the *New York Times, Politico*, the *Washington Post*, and AP News[3] (Blake, 2022; Colvin, 2022; Savage, 2022; Ward, 2022). The *Politico* coverage included a quote from Carlson that Cruz had "told a lie on purpose." The Associated Press headline announced, "Cruz Apologizes for Describing Jan. 6 Attack as Terrorism (Colvin, 2022)." The point here is that conservative media have not only covered political events and officials in ways that minimize, legitimize, or defend white violence (or threats thereof), but are also able to advance those views in other media through provocation and sensationalism. In particular, Fox News is able to push these ideologies that become circulated and embedded in the media ecosphere with a focus on political conflict and emotion rather than policy and action. While Fox News led in producing these frames, other outlets followed in platforming, circulating, and mainstreaming them.

Similarly in the news coverage of the Tea Party, CNN and other news outlets highlighted and featured interviews with a Tea Party leader named Mark Williams who dismissed explicit racist signs and other discourse at Tea Party events as "fringe." Later, Williams was forced to resign as a leader of a major Tea Party PAC (Tea Party Express) after penning a public letter calling for the return of Black slavery in the United States, which he called "satire." Throughout the media coverage of the Tea Party, news reporters across outlets treated this overt racism as marginal, not central, to Tea Party

---

[3] Notably, a few of these stories explained that the crimes some Capitol attackers were charged with could, in fact, count as terrorism under federal law.

36 UNDERSTANDING JANUARY 6, 2021

sentiment and motivations. Reporters highlighted the presence of guns openly carried at Tea Party protests at state capitals and other events, but frequently downplayed the threat of violence that the weapons implied. As in the January 6th insurrection, the media minimized the racist threat of the Tea Party and the symbolic (and actual) violence of a conservative white movement.

Fox News: The News Media's Function as Citizen-Activist

Fox News played a specific media function that moved beyond standard reporting in both the January 6th Capitol invasion and the rise of the Tea Party. In analyzing the Tea Party, members of the news media across outlets were more than just conduits for the Tea Party message and publicity, as is typical of most reporting (though they were that, too). Reporters and anchors explicitly positioned themselves as *citizen-activists* in relation to the Tea Party: they started the Tea Party (with CNBC reporter Rick Santelli kicking it off on live television), they shaped the Tea Party narrative, explored its meaning and significance, defended it, promoted it, gave it a platform, helped manage its branding, and provided it with leadership (Costley White, 2018). But Fox News in particular took on a strategic and participatory role in the Tea Party and an advisory role on January 6th and a defender in its commemoration. Fox News anchors and reporters articulated their role as citizen-activists; that is, they used their visibility as reporters to actively promote, advocate for, advise, and appeal to supporters of the Tea Party. Similarly, the anniversary coverage of January 6th showed Fox News defending, reframing, and supporting the coup attempt and the idea that the 2020 election was stolen.

In one example of Tea Party coverage, Fox News took out an ad in the *Washington Post* to provoke other news networks to cover the Tea Party. Rather than ignore the provocation, CNN responded by pointing to their extensive coverage of the Tea Party and committing to covering the Tea Party, affirming the idea of the Tea Party's political importance. Later, CNN broadcast the "Tea Party State of the Union" address in 2011 and became the first television network to air a third party's rebuttal to the president's annual speech. The regular reporting and provocations from Fox resulted in other networks legitimizing and circulating conservative talking points, campaigns, and misinformation.

As I wrote in my book, "Fox News functions more like a political third party than the Tea Party ever did /(Costley White, 2018: p. 179)." As *citizen-activists* during the Tea Party's rise, Fox News anchors headlined Tea Party events, promoted rumors and stories shared by Tea Party leaders and supporters, provided maps and locations for viewers to attend Tea Party events, cheered on the Tea Party, defended it from negative criticism in other news outlets, highlighted Tea Party candidates, and regularly provided a platform for Tea Party leaders to share their viewpoints and ideas. This activism and relationship to elected conservatives was simply amplified in the Trump years, as shown in the January 6th and 2020 election reporting and investigation.

Fox News anchor Sean Hannity was particularly important to the events of January 6, advising the White House on how to handle the unfolding coup attempt. Text communications between Hannity and Trump staffers show that Hannity received updates about what was happening in the White House at the time and held key information about conflict among Trump lawyers and appointees over undermining the election (while failing to report that information to his viewing audience) (U.S. House of Representatives, 2022). In one text, Hannity advised that Trump "make a statement asking people to leave the Capitol" (U.S. House of Representatives, 2022).

Fox News host Laura Ingraham also advised Trump during the Capitol attack. She told a staffer in a text message that "the president needs to tell people in the Capitol to go home," both implying that Trump held influence over the crowd and the Capitol attackers, and demonstrating her advisory role to the administration. On air, however, Ingraham claimed that people who attacked the Capitol "were likely not all Trump supporters" (Beer, 2021). Angelo Carusone of Media Matters notes that these Fox News anchors "simultaneously were facilitating the coup" and secretly working against it at the same time (Media Matters Staff, 2022).

The amplified relationship of Fox News as a conservative media propaganda outlet and strategic advisor for conservative politicians undermines the news media role as the "fourth estate"—separate from government officials and providing vital information to update and protect the wider public. This erosive dynamic creates major problems for journalistic protections at large as Fox News uses First Amendment rights as cover for other political activity and knowingly advances misinformation to aid a specific political party (Dominion Voting Systems Corp v. Fox News Network LLC, 2023).

The way the Fox News participation in January 6th weakens journalistic protections is shown clearly in this exchange between MSNBC news host Chris Hayes and Representative Adam Schiff discussing Sean Hannity's role in January 6 and the House investigation of the attack (Hayes, 2022). In the interview, Hayes asks Schiff why the constitutional protection guaranteeing freedom of the press does not apply to the Fox News host:

HAYES: But one can argue that you're slicing the bologna pretty thin. If some government body got a hold of my texts with sources and said "Well, in this one you're being an advisor, and in this one you're being a reporter"— and by the way, my texts don't sound anything like that. . . . There is an argument to be made here that this is the kind of stuff that a robust free press should be able to protect from the prying eyes of government.

SCHIFF: Well, first of all we're asking him [Hannity] to come in voluntarily. And, of course, there's nothing about his responsibilities with his show that would preclude him from coming in and say "I can certainly answer these questions—these questions come from my role as an advocate, someone who the president would rely on for advice, and nothing to do with anything journalistic." So, there's nothing precluding him from coming in.

Notably, throughout this interview Schiff carefully refers to Fox News anchors as "Fox personalities" instead of reporters or journalists. The contradictory function of these anchors reporting on a live story while advising elected officials on how to handle it undermines their role as reporters and their ability to fully inform the public on current events.

A Distinction: News Reporters Tackling Race and Racism

One clear departure from the news coverage of the Tea Party versus the attack on the Capitol and the Tea Party supporters was a shift from the popular media portrayal of diehard right-wing voters as working class and uneducated. Frequently in Tea Party news coverage featuring anger, aggression, and explicit displays of racism, reporters and writers described Tea Party supporters as economically marginalized and downtrodden. Polls at the time showed, however, that those who did identify as Tea Party supporters were older white Americans who were just as educated and made just as much money as the rest of the population. Trump supporters have also been portrayed as populist and working poor.

The characteristics of Tea Party supporters revealed in polls also mirror those of folks who have been arrested for the January 6th insurrection. Rather than using class as a proxy for explaining, downplaying, or marginalizing the violence of the Capitol attack, reporters and commentators have explicitly discussed race, and not class, as a key feature of the rioting crowd. Cynthia Miller-Idriss (2022) noted in a *New York Times* essay that a majority of the arrested January 6 attackers were employed, some of them teachers, chief executives, veterans, doctors, and lawyers. A number of police officers and military reservists and business owners have also been arrested for attacking the Capitol. As one *New York Times* columnist put it a few weeks after the Capitol attack:

> These were not just the Trump loyalists of lore, that economically marginalized, over-elegized white working class of the heartland. No, the crowd that stormed the Capitol was a big tent of whiteness, a cross-section of American society bridging divisions of class, geography and demography. They were doctors and lawyer, florists and real estate agents, business executives, police officers, military veterans, at least one elected official and an Olympic gold medalist. They'd all come to coup for America. (Manjoo, 2021)

The frame of right-wing white activism as connecting to issues of class, rather than race, was a sticking point for the Tea Party news narratives that appears to have changed in the post-Trump-era violence of the Capitol attack participants.

News stories related to the Capitol riot attempted to challenge the working-class right-wing frame and advanced whiteness as key to both Trump fervor and supporter violence. This shift from class-based Tea Party news coverage to emphasizing race as the mobilizing connection of the Right is important and reflects the change to openly covering and discussing race and racism in the years between the rise of the Tea Party (Obama's presidency) and the end of the Trump presidency.

Conclusion: Need for New Cooperative Journalistic Standards

In considering the news coverage of right-wing and white supremacist violence, two key contemporary issues plague our current political media ecosystem, which allows stories, frames, and misinformation from the far right to circulate and become legitimized in mainstream news and the larger political sphere. First, as a key source of right-wing government propaganda, misinformation, and disinformation, Fox News is not a credible news network, but rather a political entity that serves as a communications and advisory arm for the leading conservative political party. Other news networks need to treat it as such, avoiding Fox News provocation to cover its stories and explicitly refusing to hire Fox News talent and reporters to establish base ethical guidelines, standards, and norms for contemporary journalists. Second, there is a need to address the lack of a true political spectrum in the news media; there is no progressive or left-wing alternative to the conservative-dominated Fox News. For example, MSNBC's anchor line-up includes Republicans and business reporters; on CNBC, a reporter launched the Tea Party on live TV. This dearth of progressive reporting on mainstream and cable news outlets impacts the scope and insights of political debate and imagination within the public sphere.

In an era of far-right dominance in mainstream politics, the fight against disinformation and the power of white supremacy has to be explicit within news platforms, similar to efforts recommended in digital spaces like Facebook and Twitter. News networks need agreements that limit or ban the quoting or interviewing of guests that have a verifiable history of lies and disinformation. Even before Twitter suspended Trump's account two days after the January 6th attack, ABC, CBS, CNN, and other news networks should have deplatformed Trump within their own news reports based on the sheer number of his tabulated public lies—over 30,000 false claims or lies according to the *Washington Post*—removing his ability to speak directly to a national audience (Kessler et al., 2021).

For example, MSNBC host Rachel Maddow has covered the Trump presidency by describing him rather than sharing misleading soundbites or videos of Trump on her show, effectively deplatforming him. In instances when she had to cover him during a live event, such as the 2020 Republican National Convention, she immediately fact-checked his speech live on air (Lincoln and Owen, 2020). These are important illustrations of how to stanch the spread of misinformation in news outlets and through the portrayal and interviews of conservative pundits and officials. Refusing to repeat and spread known lies is vital to the function of the press in a struggling democracy.

The news media's downplaying of the January 6th attack contributes to the larger public blind spot for white terrorism and violence as displayed in the government's seeming inability to investigate and thwart these threats—as Miller-Idris (2022) points out, the United States has "foiled only 21 of the 110 known domestic terrorist attacks and plots in 2020."

In regard to the role of scholars, there are efforts to be made in the space of political journalism that centers ethics and good faith dialogue and judiciously informs the public. We can push back at folks who give speeches on campus that advance disinformation, homophobia, transphobia, sexism, and white nationalism. As political scholars, we need to openly acknowledge and critique white supremacy and other challenges to a multiracial democracy on our campuses, drawing on our own institutional credibility and knowledge. For example, Kathleen Searles, Daniel Kreiss, Michael Wagner, and other scholars created the Election Coverage and Democracy Network in 2020 to collectively advise on and prepare for any attempt by Trump to retain power in the face of electoral loss, engaging beyond the campus to actively combat misinformation and antidemocracy schemes (Media for Democracy, 2023). Additionally, journalists, political communication and journalism scholars need to take account of the overwhelming whiteness of the experts centered and included as key voices in our field.

In looking at the news media's reports about the rise of the Tea Party alongside the anniversary reporting on January 6th, political news continues to be negatively impacted by the mainstreaming of whiteness and white supremacy. Additionally, the news media's function as citizen-activists in misleading and misinforming the public in service of conservative platforms and ideologies also stand out. As we wrestle with the aftermath of an attempted coup by the 45th president of the United States—with the evidence showing Trump's attempt to both actively and institutionally overturn the outcome of the election that Biden won—we understand the stakes. Without more efforts to shift a promotional and white supremacist media and scholarly ecosystem, the potential for democracy and social change is left unrealized.

References

Austin-Hillary, N., & and Strang, V. (2022, Jan. 5). Racism's prominent role in January 6 US Capitol attack. Human Rights Watch. https://www.hrw.org/news/2022/01/05/racisms-prominent-role-january-6-us-capitol-attack

Beer, T. (2021, Jan. 7). Fox News host who called BLM "poison" says pro-Trump mob made up of "solid Americans." *Forbes.* https://www.forbes.com/sites/tommybeer/

2021/01/07/fox-news-host-who-called-blm-poison-says-pro-trump-mob-made-up-of-solid-americans/?sh=758149996829

Blake, A. (2022, Jan. 6). Ted Cruz grovels to Tucker Carlson over Jan. 6 "terrorist attack" remark. *The Washington Post*. https://www.washingtonpost.com/politics/2022/01/06/ted-cruz-grovels-tucker-carlson-over-jan-6-terrorist-attack-remark/

CBS This Morning. (2022, Jan. 6). January 6th. CBS.

Calson, T. (host) (2022, Jan. 6). *Tucker Carlson Tonight*. Fox News.

Chavez, A. (2021, Jan. 13). Here are the donors to tea party group that helped organize pre-riot rally. *The Intercept*. https://theintercept.com/2021/01/13/capitol-riot-donors-tea-party-patriots/

Colvin, J. (2022, Jan. 8). Cruz apologizes for describing Jan. 6 attack as terrorism. *NBC News* and *Associated Press*. https://nbcmontana.com/amp/news/nation-world/cruz-apologizes-for-describing-jan-6-attack-as-terrorism-01-08-2022

Costley White, K. (2018). *The branding of right-wing activism: The news media and the Tea Party*. Oxford University Press.

Dominion Voting Systems Corp v. Fox News Network LLC, C.A. No. N21C-03-257, Superior Court of the State of Delaware, Feb 27. 2023.

Hall, M., Gould, S., Harrington, R., Shamsian, J., Haroun, A., Ardery, T., & Snodgrass, E. (2022, Aug. 9). At least 889 people have been charged in the Capitol insurrection so far. This searchable table shows them all. *Yahoo News*. https://news.yahoo.com/most-arre sts-capitol-riots-misdemeanor-225235647.html

Hayes, C. (2022, Jan. 4) Interview with Adam Schiff. *The Chris Hayes Show*. [Television broadcast]. MSNBC.

Kessler, G., Rizzo, S., and Kelly, M. (2021, Jan. 24). Trump's false or misleading claims total 30,573 over four years. *The Washington Post*. https://www.washingtonpost.com/polit ics/2021/01/24/trumps-false-or-misleading-claims-total-30573-over-four-years/

Kristan, B. (2021, Feb. 11). Would the Capitol mob have killed Mike Pence? *The Week*. https://theweek.com/articles/966155/capitol-mob-have-killed-mike-pence

Leonard, B. (2021, Jan. 23). Feds: Texas man charged in Capitol riots threatened to kill Alexandria Ocasio-Cortez. *Politico*. https://www.politico.com/news/2021/01/23/ale xandria-ocasio-cortez-capitol-riot-461661

Lincoln, R.A. and Owen, P. (2020, Aug. 28). Watch Rachel Maddow's rapid fire fact-check of Trump's RNC speech. *Yahoo News*. https://www.yahoo.com/video/watch-rachel-maddow-rapid-fire-041656575.html

Linderman, J., & Mendoza, M. (2021, Mar. 10). Officers maced, trampled: Docs expose depth of Jan. 6 chaos. AP News. https://apnews.com/article/docs-expose-depth-janu ary-6-capitol-siege-chaos-fd3204574c11e453be8fb4e3c81258c3

Manjoo, F. (2021, Jan. 13). The Capitol was just the start. *The New York Times*.

Media for Democracy. (2023). Recommendations to journalists covering the pre- and post-Inauguration period. https://mediafordemocracy.org/

Media Matters Staff (2022, Jan. 04). Angelo Carusone: Sean Hannity's text messages ex-pose his role as an adviser and "obliterates this idea that somehow he was engaging journalism." *Media Matters for America*. https://www.mediamatters.org/january-6-insurrection/angelo-carusone-sean-hannitys-text-messages-expose-his-role-advi ser-and

Miller-Idriss, C. (2022, Jan. 9). America's most urgent threat now comes from within. *The New York Times*. https://www.nytimes.com/2022/01/07/us/politics/jan-6-terrorism-explainer.html

National Public Radio. (2022, June 10). Here's every word of the first Jan. 6 Committee hearing on its investigation. https://www.npr.org/2022/06/10/1104156949/jan-6-committee-hearing-transcript

Reuters. (2021, Jan. 15). Capitol rioters planned to capture and kill politicians, says prosecutors. *The Guardian*. https://www.theguardian.com/us-news/2021/jan/15/capitol-rioters-planned-capture-kill-officials-say-prosecutors

Savage, C. (2022, Jan. 7). Was the Jan. 6 attack on the Capitol an act of "terrorism"? *The New York Times*. https://www.nytimes.com/2022/01/07/us/politics/jan-6-terrorism-explainer.html

Tolan, C. (2022, Jan. 26). The operative. CNN. https://www.cnn.com/interactive/2021/06/us/capitol-riot-paths-to-insurrection/amy-kremer.html

U.S. Attorney's Office, Department of Justice. (2022, Dec. 30). One year since the Jan. 6 attack on the Capitol. https://www.justice.gov/usao-dc/one-year-jan-6-attack-capitol

U.S. House of Representatives. (2022, Dec. 22). Final report: Select Committee to Investigate the January 6th attack on the United States Capitol. https://www.govinfo.gov/app/details/GPO-J6-REPORT/context

Ward, M. (2022, Jan. 6). Ted Cruz walks back Jan. 6 "terrorist" remark in heated exchange with Tucker Carlson. *Politico*. https://www.politico.com/news/2022/01/06/ted-cruz-jan-6-terrorist-tucker-carlson-526725

5

"Stop the Steal" and the Racial Legacy of Election Disinformation

Francesca Tripodi

Rallying around false cries of a stolen election, thousands of Trump supporters convened in Washington, D.C., the morning of January 6, 2021. The day included a speech by President Donald Trump, who credited his supporters with inventing the phrase "Stop the Steal" before encouraging attendees at the Save America Rally to march in unison down Pennsylvania Avenue to the Capitol building and take *their* country back. In Trump's own words: "To use a favorite term that *all of you people really came up with*, we will stop the steal. . . . We must stop the steal and then we must ensure that such outrageous election fraud never happens again" (author's emphasis).

Much of Trump's speech that day was inaccurate. The election had not been stolen. Vice President Mike Pence did not have the legal authority to decertify votes and overturn the election. In fact, Trump was even wrong in his claim that the mantra "Stop the Steal" had been created by "all of you people" in response to the 2020 election outcome. Historical accounts of the tagline reveal that "Stop the Steal" was part of a strategic disinformation campaign surrounding Trump's 2016 run for office.

Claiming his supporters created the phrase may seem like a minor falsehood in the sea of disinformation uttered that day. But this chapter explains how the phrase activated the false legacy of fraudulent elections in the United States. By unpacking that history and tracing its roots, this chapter uncovers the origins and impacts of contemporary strategic disinformation campaigns designed to delegitimize democratic outcomes.

"Disinformation" refers to false claims purposefully spread with the goal of advancing political or ideological aims (Freelon & Wells, 2020), but researchers have also noted that these narratives build on preexisting frames frequently rooted in racial inequality (Freelon et al., 2020; Kuo & Marwick, 2021; Ong, 2021; Tripodi, 2022). Activating racialized disinformation

Francesca Tripodi, *"Stop the Steal" and the Racial Legacy of Election Disinformation* In: *Media and January 6th*.
Edited by: Khadijah Costley White, Daniel Kreiss, Shannon C. McGregor, and Rebekah Tromble, Oxford University Press.
© Oxford University Press 2024. DOI: 10.1093/oso/9780197758526.003.0005

narratives is central to identity-based hierarchies, which aid in the spread of these lies (Kreiss et al., 2021). Drawing on previous research, journalist accounts of the 2016 election, archived Tweets, and Google Trends data, I demonstrate the longevity of the trope that fueled the Capitol insurrection. Moreover, I explain how disinformation surrounding "stolen elections" has played a historical role in disenfranchising Black persons in the United States and the implications these narratives have on restricting voting rights.

#StopTheSteal

When Trump first ran for president of the United States in 2016, he was considered the underdog (Milligan, 2015). Many news outlets discounted his chances of winning the primary, let alone beating Hillary Clinton in the general election (Goldmacher & Schreckinger, 2016). To preemptively discount what was predicted as a Trump loss, lies of a stolen election began to surface. The day after Clinton officially became the Democratic nominee, Roger Stone appeared on Milo Yiannopoulos's show to warn that Clinton would use "widespread voter fraud" to steal the election from Trump (Mercieca, 2020, p. 195). Shortly thereafter, Alex Jones hosted Stone on his show, where they both agreed that if Clinton were to effectively "steal" (not win) the election, they would "challenge her being sworn in" (p. 196). Before appearing on *InfoWars*, Stone had already set up a website called Stop the Steal (Mercieca, 2020). As Mercieca describes, "Stop the Steal" bounced with ease throughout the right-wing media ecosystem, going from fringe spaces like *InfoWars* and *Brietbart* to more widespread circulation like *The Sean Hannity Show* and *Christian Times*, an example of what Marwick and Lewis (2017) refer to as "trading up the chain." After gaining momentum through media coverage, Stone encouraged self-appointed "poll watchers" to engage with voters in contested areas as they left the polls to ensure no fraud had been committed (Kruzel, 2016). This slogan gained traction again during the 2018 Florida gubernatorial election when Ron DeSantis was running against Andrew Gillum, but quickly lost traction when DeSantis won the race (Hayden, 2020).

Archived Twitter posts document how the lie spread across platforms. One Tweet even included an advertisement for a company called Trump Ballot Security along with the email stopthesteal@gmail.com.[1] Calls to "stop the

---

[1] Archived tweets are available at https://archive.li/UiiQI.

steal" were also laden with explicit racism and anti-Semitism, and archived Twitter posts affiliated with the #StoptheSteal document this connection (Hayden, 2020). For example, some Tweets claimed that "illegal aliens" were trying to steal the election or that George Soros had paid to rig the 2016 election in his favor (i.e., for Clinton). Soros is a Hungarian-born billionaire of Jewish descent who has donated a significant amount of his wealth to philanthropic aims. However, Soros is also a common "dog whistle" in conservative conspiracy theories—a way of speaking in code to a target audience that conjures racialized stereotypes meant to activate white grievances (Lopez, 2014). Since Soros is Jewish it activates the white supremacist conspiracy that Jewish people dominate the media, political, and economic systems. While Jewish people are often white, civil rights researchers have explained that because the civil rights movement was inconceivable to white supremacists who believed that Black Americans were intellectually incapable of organizing a social movement, they used Jews as the "evil racialized other" behind what they conceived to be white dispossession (Ward, 2017).

In addition to journalistic accounts, Google Trends data can provide a visual representation of these peaks in "Stop the Steal" search traffic, documenting its origins long before Trump lost the 2020 presidential election. The results of Google Trends can be viewed at any time by anyone at trends.google.com. The data represent an unbiased sample of the billions of queries that the search engine handles daily to normalize search data and make comparisons possible. Each data point is divided by the number of total searches based on geographic location and time. A corresponding number is then scaled on a range of zero (minimum search interest) to 100 (maximum search interest) based on a topic's proportion in relation to all other searches on all topics at the time. It is a powerful tool for understanding how people are searching in reaction to what is going on around them.

Data via Google demonstrate that prior to 2016 there was minimal, if any, search traffic about Stop the Steal and that queries quickly declined once Trump won the 2016 election. It again emerged in the months leading up to the 2018 elections, but presumably petered out after Rick Scott and Ron DeSantis narrowly won their respective races (Sheth & Barber, 2022). Search traffic around the concept of stolen elections lay dormant again until October 2020. According to Google Trends, the highest spike in searches around the phrase began shortly after Joe Biden was declared the winner on November 7, 2020, and lasted for roughly a week following the outcome of the election. It did not surface again until January 2021 in the days surrounding the Capitol insurrection. (See Figure 5.1.)

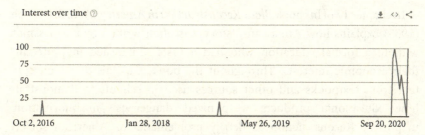

Figure 5.1 Google Trends data of #stopthesteal Over Time

Trump helped keep the mantra circulating. When the Capitol was stormed, Trump did eventually call for law and order, but not before he posted a video to Twitter reiterating the lie that the election was rigged: "We had an *election that was stolen* from us. It was a landslide election, and everyone knows it, especially the other side."

"Stolen Elections" and Other Racist Lies

The "Stop the Steal" narrative was alive and well as early as 2016. Yet allegations of stolen elections go back considerably further than this. Indeed, the phrase is the cornerstone of a disinformation campaign that has been recycled for centuries, one predicated on the idea that Black people are subhuman—a white supremacist narrative that has been used to justify racial subordination and the violation of human rights.

The Reconstruction period in the United States encompassed the turbulent decade following the end of the Civil War, in which millions of newly freed Black people, and the Southern states of the Confederacy, were integrated into American life. The Reconstruction Act of 1867 outlined the terms for readmission, dividing the former Confederate states into five military districts, and was contingent on the ratification of the Thirteenth and Fourteenth Amendments. Ratifying these amendments provided inroads for newly freed Black Americans to take part in the electoral process. In the decade that followed, voters elected a record number of Black men to serve in the U.S. Congress (Pruitt, 2020). As Black Americans used their voting rights to ascend the ranks of political office, disinformation campaigns surfaced accusing African Americans of corruption and insinuating that they were unfit to participate in the democratic process (Sokol, 2006, p. 238).

48 UNDERSTANDING JANUARY 6, 2021

In chapter 17 of his book *Black Reconstruction in America,* W. E. B. Du Bois (1935) explains how American history was often written by businessmen without a formal education who had a vested interested in protecting their economic interests. Throughout the book, Du Bois draws on content from textbooks and other sources used in schools to demonstrate how educational products weaponized dangerous "misinformation" to portray Reconstruction as deeply problematic for American society (p. 714). Allegations that Du Bois surfaced from these texts include language describing Black people as ignorant, lazy, dishonest, and responsible. Authoritative encyclopedic texts, like *Encyclopedia Britannica,* tried to frame democratic wins that granted Black men the right to vote as a failure of "Negro ignorance and corruption," undermining their ability to organize (Du Bois, 1935, p. 713). Repeatedly these texts argued that Black peoples' participation in the democratic process was problematic because they lacked political honesty, did not have the capacity to govern, and were intellectually inferior (Du Bois 1935).

Such accusations rely on a historical legacy of disenfranchisement in the United States, whereby Black people were first brought to the United States to work in indentured servitude and then were repeatedly robbed of their rights under the auspices of intellectual inferiority. Those who founded the United States knew that human slavery was morally wrong and economically retrogressive, yet these truths were often neglected as a form of absolving guilt (Du Bois, 1935). Instead, white supremacist frameworks tried to "sort" racial groups by genetic inferiority or superiority to rationalize chattel slavery, maintain segregation, ensure wealth gaps, illegally detain immigrants, and restrict human rights (Mejia et al., 2018). These eugenics policies were so effective they were publicly endorsed by the American Eugenics Society in 1933, paving the way for future Nazi laws (Powell, 2002).

In the early 20th century, disinformation surrounding intellectual fortitude was used in the United States to sterilize "genetically inferior" people without their consent (Powell, 2002). These practices have been upheld at the highest level, when the U.S. Supreme Court struck down the case of Carrie Buck, a Virginia woman fighting for her right to reproduce. In its remarks, the Court elevated eugenic prejudices to constitutional status, proclaiming:

It is better for all the world, if instead of waiting to execute degenerate offspring for crime, or let them starve for their imbecility, society can prevent

those who are manifestly unfit for continuing their kind. . . . Three generations of imbeciles are enough. (Powell, 2002, p. 502)

Even though the U.S. Supreme Court overturned *Roe v. Wade* on June 24,
2022, under the auspices of protecting life, cases like *Buck v. Bell*—fueled on
disinformation regarding genetic and intellectual inferiority—have yet to be
overturned.

By looking both contextually and historically at the lie that the 2020 election was stolen, we can see how the central goal in this disinformation narrative is to reproduce *whiteness* in the United States (Kuo & Marwick, 2021,
emphasis theirs). Without considering how Black rights in the United States
are embedded inside a hegemonic narrative surrounding Black Americans'
participation in the democratic process, "Stop the Steal" seems like an
anomaly, a fresh tagline invented by Trump supporters. By engaging with
sociologists like Du Bois and contextualizing how disinformation is rooted
in systems of power (Kuo & Marwick, 2021), we can see why such an egregious lie, supported by no evidence, could become so plausible, spurring
thousands of (white) American voters to engage in democratic destruction.

A "stolen" election resonates with white voters drawn to Trump from the
outset because it activates a narrative of white diminishment—even though
white people control an overwhelming majority of powerful positions and
land wealth in the United States (Moss et al., 2020). Feelings of abandonment
and distrust in government help to legitimate candidates like Trump who try
to blame feelings of neglect in white, rural communities on people of color
(Cramer, 2016). These "deep stories" are narratives often rooted in race, for
example, the story that frames immigrants as "line cutters" or blames affirmative action for economic loss (Hochschild, 2016). By framing social justice as a
zero-sum game, it positions civil rights *gains* for Black and brown Americans
as a *loss* for white Americans (Butler, 2021; Carter, 2000; Sokol, 2006). These
worldviews are then supported by disinformation that Black people abuse their
office, are incapable of political participation, and are intellectually inferior.
What results are restrictive policy measures meant to prevent further gains.

Voter Suppression and Redistricting Efforts

Despite the century-old lie that "others" steal *their* elections, conservative elites have wielded their power and political advantage to rig election

outcomes through redistricting efforts and bills designed to suppress voter turnout. For example, following the 2020 U.S. presidential election, Georgia's legislature passed significant restrictions that impact voter participation. This includes strict new identification requirements for absentee ballots, less time to request absentee ballots, and expanded early voting for small rural towns but not for more populous metropolitan areas. The new restrictions also make it illegal for election officials to mail absentee ballot applications to all registered voters. These laws are clearly aimed at reducing the already precarious voting rights of Black Georgians given that Black voters used mail-in ballots in far higher rates than white voters in the 2020 presidential election (Morris, 2021).

The motivations behind these policies are often barred from public view, but a leaked video from the Heritage Foundation, a conservative public policy think tank, explicitly states the impetus behind these aims. In the video, conservative elites boasted about the organization's ability to draft and pass model legislation suppressing voter access in states like Georgia and Iowa (Benen, 2021). Efforts to redistrict states are also tied to Trump's push to add a citizenship question to the 2020 U.S. Census. Doing so could have reduced the response rate in heavily Latino communities, leading to an undercount of the population in areas that tend to vote Democratic and losses in representation and federal funding (Wines, 2019).

While many efforts to curb the participation of brown and Black constituents have largely been conducted behind the scenes, other historical attempts are much more visible. For example, in 1981 the Republican National Committee created the National Ballot Security Task Force to patrol polling sites in traditionally Black and Hispanic neighborhoods. These volunteers were frequently off-duty police officers who would come armed to polling stations (Sullivan, 1993).

Some might be surprised that a party committed to constitutional principles would fervently support laws designed to disenfranchise voters. Yet Tripodi (2022) documents that conservatives engage in a close reading of documents like the Constitution (a practice she refers to as *scriptural inference*) to conclude that the Constitution supports their understanding of the United States as a *republic*, not a democracy. Through ethnographic research of a college Republican group and a women's Republican group, she found that conservative media (from books like *The 5000 Year Leap* to digital-first content like PragerU videos) advocate for a model of democratic participation that dilutes the value of the popular vote (Tripodi, 2022). Likewise, regulations put into place to protect the electoral college are of high priority to conservative politicians and pundits.

Election Denial as a Political Platform

Some might argue that protecting the electoral college is not necessarily a threat to the democratic processes. While regulations that impact voter participation is a more clear-cut example of how the lie of "stolen" elections infiltrates participatory outcomes, states like Georgia have still been able to overcome suppression tactics through grassroots voter organization (Baltimore Sun Editorial Board, 2021). Nonetheless, these efforts must still be validated by a governing body that certifies the results. What is particularly concerning about the 2022 primary cycle is that the mantra of "Stop the Steal" has made its way into election platforms and seems to be working. Take Kari Lake, who ran for governor of Arizona on the lie that Trump was cheated out of a second term of office (Epstein, 2022). Even though Lake lost the general election (by a mere 7,116 votes), U.S. congressmen like Kevin McCarthy and Steven Scalise, who openly denied the results of the 2020 election, were both reelected by their constituents and then elected by their peers to prominent positions like Speaker of the House and House majority leader. The Congressman who recently replaced McCarthy as speaker—Mike Johnson—was among the handful of elected representatives to vote against certifying Biden's win *after* the January 6 attack (Riccardi, 2023).

By unpacking what seems like a recent disinformation phenomenon, we can trace the origins of the Big Lie back centuries, demonstrating that it is embedded in voting rights and predicated on nefarious falsities meant to deny Black people equal rights. Understanding how attacks on the Capitol are connected to Reconstruction provides an important lens by which we can truly understand our past, our present, and, more important, our future.

References

Baltimore Sun Editorial Board. (2021, Jan. 8). Stacey Abrams showed there's still power in grassroots organization. *The Baltimore Sun.*

Benen, S. (2021, May 14). Group quietly boasts about crafting GOP's voter-suppression bills. MSNBC.

Butler, A. (2021). *White evangelical racism: The politics of morality in America*. University of North Carolina Press.

Carter, D. (2000). *The politics of rage: George Wallace, the origins of the new conservatism, and the transformation of American politics*. Louisiana State University Press.

Cramer, K. (2016). *The politics of resentment: Rural consciousness in Wisconsin and the rise of Scott Walker*. University of Chicago Press.

Du Bois, W. E. B. (1935). *Black reconstruction: An essay toward a history of the part which Black folk played in the attempt to reconstruct democracy in America, 1860–1880*. Harcourt, Brace and Company.

Epstein, R. J. (2022, Aug. 4). Kari Lake, backed by Trump, wins Arizona's G.O.P. governor primary. *The New York Times*. https://www.nytimes.com/2022/08/04/us/politics/kari-lake-arizona-governor.html

Freelon, D., & Wells, C. (2020). Disinformation as political communication. *Political Communication, 37*(2), 145–156.

Freelon, D., Bossetta, M., Wells, C., Lukito, J., Xia, Y., & Adams, K. (2020). Black trolls matter: Racial and ideological asymmetries in social media disinformation. *Social Science Computer Review, 40*(3), 560–578. https://doi.org/10.1177/0894439320914853

Goldmacher, S., & Schreckinger, B. (2016, Nov. 9). Trump pulls off biggest upset in U.S. history. *Politico*.

Hayden, M. E. (2020, Nov. 6). Far right resurrects Roger Stone's #StopTheSteal during vote count. *Hatewatch*. Southern Poverty Law Center

Hochschild, A. R. (2016). *Strangers in their own land: Anger and mourning on the American right*. New Press.

Kreiss, D., Marwick, A., & Tripodi, F. (2021, Nov. 10). The anti–critical racy theory movement ill profoundly affect public education. *Scientific American*.

Kuo, R., & Marwick, A. (2021). Critical disinformation studies: History, power, and politics. *Harvard Kennedy School (HKS) Misinformation Review*.

Kruzel, J. (2016, Nov. 7). Controversial pro-Trump group warns members to avoid election day meddling. ABC News.

Lopez, I. H. (2014). *Dog whistle politics: How coded racial appeals have reinvented racism and wrecked the middle class*. Oxford University Press.

Marwick, A., & Lewis, B. (2017). Media manipulation and disinformation online. Data & Society Research Report. https://datasociety.net/library/media-manipulation-and-disinfo-online/

Mejia, R., Beckermann, K., & Sullivan, C. (2018). White lies: A racial history of the (post) truth. *Communication and Critical/Cultural Studies, 15*(2), 109–126.

Mercieca, J. (2020). *Demagogue for president*. Texas A&M University Press.

Milligan, S. (2015, Aug. 28). The year of the underdog? *U.S. News & World Report*. https://www.usnews.com/news/the-report/articles/2015/08/28/2016-may-be-the-year-of-the-underdog-with-trump-sanders-and-carson

Morris, K. (2021). Georgia's proposed voting restrictions will harm Black voters most. Brennan Center for Justice. https://www.brennancenter.org/our-work/research-reports/georgias-proposed-voting-restrictions-will-harm-black-voters-most

Ong, J. C. (2021, Feb. 4). The contagion of stigmatization: Racism and discrimination in the "Infodemic" moment. MediaWell Social Science Research Council. https://mediawell.ssrc.org/event/the-contagion-of-stigmatization-racism-and-discrimination-in-the-infodemic-moment-digital-society-network/

Moss, E., McIntosh, K., Edelberg, W., & Broady, K. (2020, Dec. 8). The Black-white wealth gap left Black households more vulnerable. *The Brookings Institute*

Naylor, B. (2021). Read Trump's Jan. 6 speech, a key part of impeachment trail. *National Public Radio*. https://www.npr.org/2021/02/10/966396848/read-trumps-jan-6-speech-a-key-part-of-impeachment-trial

Powell, L. (2002). Eugenics and equality: Does the Constitution allow policies designed to discourage reproduction among disfavored groups? *Yale Law & Policy Review, 20*(2), 481–512.

Pruitt, S. (2020). When did African Americans actually get the right to vote? History. https://www.history.com/news/african-american-voting-right-15th-amendment

Riccardi, N. (2023). New US House speaker tried to help overturn the 2020 election, raising concerns about the next one. *Associated Press* https://apnews.com/article/congress-house-speaker-2024-election-certification-8cd7c5a9e6ae69635bbb4624cc78e5c5

Sheth, S., & Barber, C. R. (2022, Nov. 11). "Bogus," "ridiculous," and "made-up crap": DOJ veterans throw cold water on Trump's claim that he "sent in the FBI" to help Ron DeSantis. *Business Insider*.

Sokol, J. (2006). *There Goes My Everything: White Southerners in the Age of Civil Rights, 1945–1975*. Alfred A. Knopf.

Sullivan, J. F. (1993, Nov. 11). Florio's defeat revives memories of GOP activities in 1981. *New York Times*.

Tripodi, F. (2022). *The propagandists' playbook: How conservative elites manipulate search and threaten democracy*. Yale University Press.

Ward, E. K. (2017). Skin in the game: How antisemitism animates white nationalism. PoliticalResearch.org.

Wines, M. (2019, July 2). 2020 census won't have citizenship question as Trump administration drops effort. *The New York Times*.

6

"Fake and Fraudulent" vs.
"An American Right"

Competing Imaginaries of the Vote in the 2020 U.S. Presidential Campaign

Jennifer Stromer-Galley, Brian McKernan, Christy Khoury, and Pyeonghwa Kim

The attack on the Capitol on January 6, 2021, was not a surprise event. We contend in this chapter that President Trump used the massive exposure social media platforms offer to produce and amplify false and misleading claims about election fraud. His arguments laid the groundwork for members of the public to mistrust the election results, which in turn created the conditions for the attack on the Capitol. Our conclusions are based on an in-depth thematic analysis of President Trump's Twitter and Facebook posts on his personal social media accounts, which doubled as his reelection campaign accounts. We also analyzed President Trump's campaign ads on Facebook and Instagram. We contrast the analysis of Trump's messaging with that of Trump's general election campaign rival, Joe Biden.

When rioters attacked the U.S. Capitol on January 6, 2021, they did so under the mistaken belief that the electoral process was fraudulent and believing that Donald Trump had been robbed of the presidency. Epistemic philosophy from Berger and Luckman (1966) to Taylor (2004) advances the idea that knowledge is socially constructed. As Taylor explains, our understanding of democracy today is based on groundwork laid over three centuries, driven by theories articulated from Locke and Rousseau, among others, that advance as a *social imaginary* the idea that people have a natural right to self-govern and that elections are "the only source of legitimate power" (p. 110). This is a core tenet of the social imaginary embraced in the United States of the governance structure of democracy, specifically that free and fair elections are bedrock to a functioning republic. But this social

Jennifer Stromer-Galley, Brian McKernan, Christy Khoury, and Pyeonghwa Kim, *"Fake and Fraudulent" vs. "An American Right"* In: *Media and January 6th*. Edited by: Khadijah Costley White, Daniel Kreiss, Shannon C. McGregor, and Rebekah Tromble, Oxford University Press. © Oxford University Press 2024. DOI: 10.1093/oso/9780197758526.003.0006

imaginary is not a given, and without continued ritualistic reaffirmation of the ability of the people to self-govern through the exercise of the vote, the core tenet of democracy is undermined. We argue that Trump's rhetoric during and after the election undermined that affirmation, thereby putting our system of representative governance at risk.

It is important to note that the 2020 presidential campaign and voting process was radically altered because of the COVID-19 pandemic that swept through the United States starting in mid-March 2020. State legislatures quickly passed measures to allow for mail-in balloting, to expand absentee balloting, and to position special ballot boxes for voters to drop their ballots in without standing in long lines with other people. This dramatic shift in the processes and policies around voting further opened lines of argument for Trump to question election outcomes in key states (such as Pennsylvania).

For this analysis, we examined all of Trump's and Biden's campaign-account Facebook posts and tweets from September 1, 2020, to January 6, 2021, and all of their paid ads on Facebook and Instagram from August 15, 2020, to November 15, 2020. These were collected using the Twitter Research API, Crowdtangle for Facebook, and the Facebook Ad Library API. We examined all of the messages and inductively developed themes on several dimensions, such as messages around election integrity—including attacks and defenses of voting mechanisms, voting more broadly, vote counting, and the people and offices that oversee elections. As we examined the election integrity theme during and after the general election, the first author went back and read the tweets and Facebooks posts and watched the Facebook and Instagram ads from Trump during the primaries. The aim was to better contextualize the general election messaging by understanding Trump's framing and themes during the primaries.

Trump

Our analysis of Trump's social media messages during the campaign suggests that Trump used his heavily followed social media accounts to sow distrust of the vote process and doubt about the accuracy of the vote count starting in March 2020. The imagery that Trump invoked in his campaign rhetoric was of chaos on Election Day because of the fallibility of particular voting systems, especially mail-in balloting. He used his Twitter and Facebook accounts and ran targeted ad buys on Meta (on the platforms of Facebook

56 UNDERSTANDING JANUARY 6, 2021

and Instagram) to make arguments and amplify attacks on mail-in ballots, which he alleged were being indiscriminately mailed to people and houses. He described mail-in ballots as a hoax, as creating chaos, and declared fraud. For example, Trump tweeted, "Wow! 100,000 Mail In Ballots in New York City a total MESS. Mayor and Governor have no idea what to do. Big Fraud, Unfixable! Cancel Ballots and go out and VOTE, just like in past decades, when there were no problems!" (September 30, 2020). Note that he references "just like in past decades," which insinuates that the changes in election laws to allow for social-distanced voting were leading to fraud.

Trump alleged in his social media advertisements that an unnamed "they" were going to try to "take away" the votes of the targets. The Trump campaign aired a large set of ads (74 unique variations) targeted primarily to Michigan, a critical state that was decisive in his win in 2016, between October 26 and November 2 that hinted at election fraud. In each ad, Trump stands in the garden of the White House and extemporaneously talks on a variety of topics, including heralding his policy positions and attacking Biden's competence. At the end of each ad a voice-over of Trump accompanies text on the screen: "Go to the voting booth and vote early and in person. Don't let them take your vote away, the most important election we've ever had." This tag line underscored the importance of in-person voting, and it insinuated election fraud through the command "Don't let them take your vote away." This tactic employs enthymematic argumentation, wherein the target fills in the unstated elements of the argument. This was a common style of argument by Trump (Stromer-Galley, 2020). That is, the target can complete the argument with whoever "they" are and using whatever actions they imagine.

Trump repeatedly expressed doubt in the validity of the election results, and he did so well before general election votes were cast. For example, on September 17, nearly two months before the election, he tweeted:

> Because of the new and unprecedented massive amount of unsolicited ballots which will be sent to "voters," or wherever, this year, the Nov 3rd Election result may NEVER BE ACCURATELY DETERMINED, which is what some want. Another election disaster yesterday. Stop Ballot Madness!

By advancing arguments months before the actual election, he laid the groundwork for doubt, which he then further amplified on and after November 4. The steady stream of attacks on the integrity of the results made it easier for Trump to declare in the days and weeks after the election that his prognostication had been realized.

The extent of Trump's often baseless attacks on perceived opponents during his campaign in 2016 and throughout his presidency is widely acknowledged. Such attacks continued during his 2020 campaign. He specifically accused Democrats and the Democratic Party of attempting to steal the election. He was especially fixated on something he called "ballot harvesting." He tweeted:

> California hired a pure Sleepy Joe Democrat firm to count and "harvest" votes. No way Republicans get a fair shake. Lawyers, get started!!! @ GOPLeader California is in big trouble. Vote Trump and watch the greatest comeback of them all!!! Also, New York and Illinois—go for it! (October 13, 2020)

This line of argumentation before the election further advanced his argument after the election that it was "stolen" from him, underpinning the slogan "Stop the Steal."

Immediately after the election on November 3, Trump repeatedly declared that he was the true winner and that his underperformance at the polls was illusory. He cited several different causes for not having enough votes to win, including voting machine errors—malfunctions and deliberate tampering—and widespread fraudulent voting. On Twitter Trump was especially obsessed with what he described as "late ballots" that he insisted were not received until after the election and thus not valid, for example:

I easily WIN the Presidency of the United States with LEGAL VOTES CAST. The OBSERVERS were not allowed, in any way, shape, or form, to do their job and therefore, votes accepted during this period must be determined to be ILLEGAL VOTES. U.S. Supreme Court should decide! (November 6, 2020)

In this tweet, he spins a tale of conspiracy in which unknown "observers" in unspecified states were prevented by unknown others to ensure a free and fair election. He then leaps to the conclusion that the situation means that there were necessarily illegal votes cast, which is why he underperformed at the ballot box. In Trump's imaginary, no other conclusion made sense.

He continued his relentless attack on mail-in ballots in the days after the election. He claimed on Twitter, for example, that these mail-in ballots appeared to be overwhelmingly for Biden, asking, "How come every time they count Mail-In ballot dumps they are so devastating in their percentage and power of destruction?" (November 4, 2020). His question here is revealing for what it insinuates. First, he described mail-in ballots as "dumps," which tied into his claims during the campaign that mail-in ballots were being sent indiscriminately. In one Facebook advertisement that ran for a week in the summer, he falsely claimed in a video that ballots were being mailed to vacant houses and warehouses, allowing anyone to cast a vote. He also described the increase in absentee ballots for Biden as evidence of fraud, when in fact he knew and was told there would be a "red mirage" as Republicans opted more frequently to vote in person on election day given Trump's attacks on mail-in voting. Democrats, by contrast, chose more convenient and safer options (given the pandemic), such as absentee and mail-in voting, which meant more absentee and mail-in ballots were tallied for Biden (U.S. House of Representatives, 2022).

As the January 6th Committee investigation identified clearly, Trump was responsible for the attacks on the Capitol. What we observed in reading through all of Trump's messages is that his conspiracist ideation and false narratives about the vote during the campaign framed his argument after the election, including the calls for his supporters to act. Some of these messages were vague on what supporters should do, such as Trump tweeting, "STOP THE FRAUD" and "STOP THE COUNT!" on November 5, 2020. On December 12, 2020, he tweeted and posted to Facebook, "Wow! Thousands of people forming in Washington (D.C.) for Stop the Steal. Didn't know about this, but I'll be seeing them! #MAGA." Trump went from establishing an alternative imaginary, a conspiracy, of nefarious actors stealing the election to mobilizing his supporters to take matters into their own hands, leading to the violent events on January 6, 2021.

Biden

Biden's rhetoric, by contrast, exemplified what is historically normal discourse around elections and the vote. Biden's campaign messages communicated support for the public to vote using any available means. He urged voters to make a plan to vote, and he urged voting by mail-in, by absentee, and by in-person ballot. For example, he tweeted, "If you can still vote early, then vote early today. If you haven't returned your absentee ballot yet, then return it today. If you're voting in-person tomorrow, then make your plan today. Let's end this—today" (November 2, 2020). Unlike the Trump arguments, Biden did not differentiate among forms of voting or deprecate one form of voting over another. Instead, he underscored the sovereign right all Americans have to vote. On Facebook, he posted, "The right to vote is the most sacred American right there is—exercise it. Make your voice heard this November" (September 9, 2020). Some of Biden's ad buys on Facebook and Instagram provided a "fact check" on false claims by Trump about voting, even stating that Trump was spreading lies about mail-in balloting.

After the election, the majority of Biden's messages pertained to the electoral count process and the election outcomes. Biden's messages included calls to make sure all the votes were counted and messages of optimism about the eventual result. On Facebook a day before the attack on the Capitol, Biden posted a message identical to one of his tweets: "In America, politicians can't assert, take, or seize power. It has to be given by the American people. We can't ever give that up. The will of the people must always prevail" (January 5, 2020).

Conclusion

Our analysis suggests Biden and Trump offered competing imaginaries of the vote. Biden's rhetoric portrayed an image of America where the democratic process is sacred and was ultimately followed in the 2020 election despite the clear threat Trump posed. In contrast, Trump's rhetoric portrayed an image of America where democratic institutions had been completely corrupted, the electoral process could not be trusted, and "true" Americans must thus exert their will through violence. These imaginaries matter. For some members of the public Trump's vision of reality was compelling and believable enough for them to act. The consequences of Trump's imaginary will be long-lasting.

References

Berger, P. L., & Luckmann, T. (1966). *The social construction of reality: A treatise in the sociology of knowledge*. Doubleday.

60 UNDERSTANDING JANUARY 6, 2021

Stromer-Galley, J. (2020). Vulgar eloquence in the digital age: A case study of candidate Donald Trump's use of Twitter. In R. Davis & D. Taras (Eds.), *Power shift? Political leadership and social media* (pp. 33–49). Routledge.

Taylor, C. (2004). *Modern social imaginaries*. Duke University Press.

U.S. House of Representatives. (2022, Dec. 22). *Final report: Select Committee to Investigate the January 6th Attack on the United States*. 117th Congress Second Session House Report 117-663. U.S. Government Printing Office.

7

The Changing American Racial Landscape and January 6th

Andrew Ifedapo Thompson

The United States is undergoing a grand racial demographic transition that it has never experienced before. The white American population is in decline, while the number of Americans of color, en masse, is increasing. Although the actual date is debated, at some point in the next few decades, white Americans could become a numerical minority for the first time in U.S. history. To many Americans, this indicates progress or simply innocuous change. But Pew Research finds that most Americans view both the declining white population and the racial majority-minority flip as neither good nor bad for American society (Krogstad et al., 2021; Parker et al., 2019).

Despite these more pervasive neutral views about the demographic changes, a sizable portion of the public views them as an existential crisis (Belew, 2019). These Americans feel that their sense of the world is under threat—their sense of being American is tied to white identity (Jardina, 2019). Importantly, the projected changes and fears about them do not capture how white identification is bound to change as the United States diversifies. In earlier eras, the ideas of whiteness have changed and expanded with the influx of Irish and Italian immigration (Ignatiev, 2008; Painter, 2010). These historical examples have led demographers and others to contest that we can even predict how racial demographic change might affect American society (Levy & Myers, 2021; Sohoni, 2022). Despite these historical examples and the experts' ambivalence about how racial demographic change might pan out within the United States, many white Americans still express fear about and feel threatened by these changes (Craig & Richeson, 2014; Craig et al., 2018).

Those sentiments about racial demographic change have existed in the public for some time, but they have steadily become more unified with the formal political process. That is, Americans have previously felt threatened,

Andrew Ifedapo Thompson, *The Changing American Racial Landscape and January 6th* In: *Media and January 6th*. Edited by: Khadijah Costley White, Daniel Kreiss, Shannon C. McGregor, and Rebekah Tromble, Oxford University Press. © Oxford University Press 2024. DOI: 10.1093/oso/9780197758526.003.0007

but their sense of threat has become more steadily aligned with their political identity (Brown et al., 2022; Jardina, 2021). Elite messaging about race has worked to inflame these sentiments consistently over time (Druckman & Green, 2021; Mendelberg, 2001; Newman et al., 2021; Thompson & Busby, 2021). Racial demographic change has become more consistently tied to American politics. So when Americans think about how the country is going to look in the future, they also imagine how politics will be affected.

The culmination of racial threat from demographic change and the formal political process was the insurrection on January 6, 2021. As a political event, it was not a flash-in-the-pan moment, however. The lead-up to the insurrection sheds light on the motivations of insurrectionists, and also unveils the ideas that likely will continue to inflame antidemocratic views. We should be equally concerned with extremist political attitudes *and* extremist political actions. Extremist ideas create an environment that can facilitate actions and explain away actions, which then shifts norms in further antidemocratic directions.

In the months leading up to the 2020 presidential election there were clear indicators that racial threat was a key motivator of antidemocratic attitudes regarding the election. Scholars demonstrated that, compared to support for the Republican Party, support for President Trump, economic conservativism, cultural conservatism, and political cynicism, threat from racial outgroups was the strongest predictor of Republicans' support for antidemocratic ideas (Bartels, 2020). They also showed that Republicans were significantly more supportive than Democrats of political violence and preventing political opposition from winning office (Kalmoe & Mason, 2022; Thompson, 2022).

These background conditions in the mass public were accompanied by consistent rhetoric about the country "changing," the implication of racial demographic change. This idea was then connected to notions of the 2020 presidential election being stolen because immigrants and other "undeserving Americans" (e.g., people of color who support the Democratic Party) committed some form of election fraud (Jacobson, 2021). The use of people of color and immigrants as scapegoats helped to sow seeds of discontent with the electoral process.

The consistent prodding of this point did more than just get out the vote among the most aggrieved Republican voters. It had a staying power in their minds. After Biden's victory, many Republicans believed that the election had been stolen. One poll that was run in the days following the election found that 70% of Republicans did not believe the election was free and fair (Kim, 2020). This lack of trust in the electoral process led to the rally on January 6. In a study among insurrectionists, racial threat from changing local racial demographics was the strongest predictor of insurrectionist participation (Pape, 2021).

Mounting evidence supports racial demographic change as a key feature of American democratic backsliding. It is causing concern among Americans, many of them white and Republican, about the future of the country. Recent homegrown terrorist events lend even more credence to this connection, for example, the Buffalo mass shooting of mostly African Americans that was found to be motivated by the Great Replacement conspiracy theory. The logic behind these concerns about the future of the country is complex, and for that reason, I will flesh them out. The heart of the matter is the perception that the demographic change poses an existential threat to conventional ways of American life.

Existential Racial Threat and American Democracy

Threat can help to lend credence to antidemocratic views, but the motivation behind these attitudes varies quite widely. As I mentioned, racial threat as it relates to American politics has become increasingly tied to partisan politics. We have seen this emerge in discussions of threat coming primarily from Republican elites. So it appears that Republican voters are the Americans who are primarily concerned about racial demographic change affecting their ideas about the future of the country. There is a great deal of evidence that there have been long-standing inferences made about how racial demographic change will come to affect the future of American party politics. Simply put, Republicans for years have assumed that more Americans of color will benefit the Democratic Party more than the Republican Party. One important and public assertion of this perceived GOP disadvantage to racial demographic change came in the "GOP autopsy" after the 2012 presidential loss to Obama. The party elites who wrote this assessment of the state of Republicans declared:

> The nation's demographic changes add to the urgency of recognizing how precarious our position has become. America is changing demographically, and unless Republicans are able to grow our appeal the way GOP governors

have done, the changes tilt the playing field even more in the Democratic direction. (Barbour et al., 2013)

At this time, the perception was that the party needed to pivot its strategy in order to expand and compete with Democrats on a national stage. The more recent interpretation of racial demographic change is less about changing party strategy and more about shifting institutions in an antidemocratic direction. I argue that the intention behind this shift is the perception that Americans of color are perceived to identify more as Democrats who will *not* shift in the political identification. The conclusion from this perception is that the GOP cannot sway these voters, and instead must behave in antidemocratic ways in order to keep power. Racial demographic change therefore represents an existential threat to the Republican Party.

To test how Republicans process information about racial demographic change, I conducted a set of experiments wherein I framed racial demographic change as benefiting either the Republican or the Democratic Party, then measured Republicans' antidemocratic views.

Reversing Racial Threat and Support for Authoritarianism

In a set of two survey experiments, I reframed the discussion of racial threat into the context of partisan politics. I ran this test with a diverse sample of Democrats and Republicans. As the baseline, I described the majority-minority flip: that Americans of color are projected to be the majority by midcentury, and that white Americans in a coextensive fashion will become the numerical minority. In addition, I used a set of partisan frames that simply added partisan benefits to the discussion of the majority-minority flip. These conditions explicitly state that racial minorities are projected to mostly identify as Republicans *or* Democrats. This articulates the idea that the respective party in the frame will be more likely to electorally benefit from the diversifying United States. I then compared the Democratic- and Republican-advantage frames to the baseline condition where there is not explicit mention of political parties.

Following the treatments, I analyzed how priming the partisan frame affects support of antidemocratic ideas among both Republicans and Democrats. The antidemocratic support that I looked into encompassed specific policy proposals, ranging from reducing polling stations in areas where the outparty is dominant, to banning far-right and far-left parties from participating in politics. My major expectation in this study was that when Republicans learned their party would benefit from racial demographic change—which is the opposite of the ideas that motivate existential racial threat—they would express more pro-democratic views. This is exactly what I found, as shown in Figure 7.1.

In direct comparisons with Democrats and narratives about Democrats being advantaged (the existential racial threat narrative for Republicans), the only idea that ended up affecting any of their antidemocratic support was when Republicans learned that the GOP will positively benefit from racial demographic change.

When they received the narrative that contests existential racial threat, Republicans expressed more pro-democratic attitudes across all of the policy proposals. This is a clear, *causal* demonstration of racial threat contributing to democratic backsliding, but in a way that suggests there are potential ways to mitigate it. More specifically, discussion that mitigates racial threat actually leads to more pro-democratic support among Republicans. Additionally, I showed that these sentiments exist primarily among Republicans because the equivalent frames for Democrats, regardless of race, did not move their pro- or antidemocratic attitudes.

Implications from Racial Demographic Change

I turn now to describing the implications that this growing sense of pervasive racial threat has on the future of American democracy. Focus has, understandably, been on preventing a repeat of January 6, yet in many respects, this misses the mark of the normative implications of racial demographic change and its role in democratic backsliding within the United States.

Existential racial threat is a strong driver of attitudes that lead to backsliding. It causes Americans to become concerned about the future of the country and feel as though their entire sense of being is under attack. These sentiments lead to relaxing attachment to democratic norms in order to protect this sense of life by any means necessary. Antidemocratic beliefs and actions then become more permissible. The more this threat is prodded in the public, the more support there is for antidemocratic beliefs. Connecting this directly to January 6th, the more racial threat is felt, the

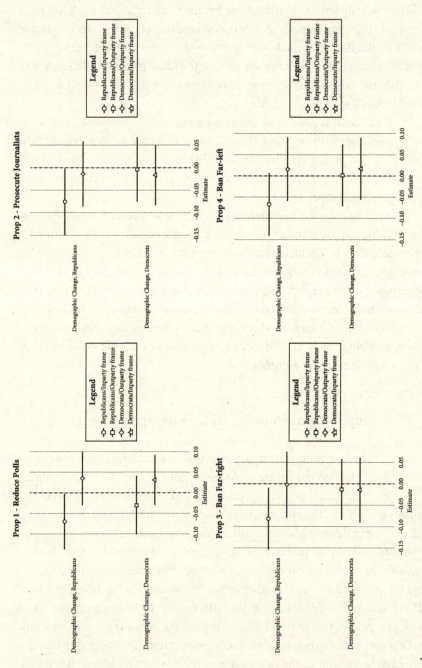

Figure 7.1 Experimental results

more likely events like January 6th are bound to occur along with the interpretation among supporters that they are normal.

Importantly, the sense of threat that occurs from racial demographic change is a *perception*. It has little grounding in reality. Demographers currently contest that a majority-minority flip is bound to happen in the United States because of the unique way that race functions (Alba, 2018; Alba et al., 2018). Because of its operation as a social construct, there is little way that we can anticipate or predict it changing in the future. At this point, mixed-race identities are already in flux, so much so that some Americans who are mixed race identify as white. These behavior decisions are contingent on many factors, thus nearly impossible to predict in the long run. That is the case *only* with racial identity. When adding in partisanship, prediction and anticipation become essentially impossible. There is no way to anticipate how the major political parties will adjust their platforms, or how racial groups will come to identify with them over time. From this point, we can extrapolate the idea that we *should not* aim to predict how the political and social landscape of the country might change in light of racial demographic change because it will remain an open question. It is purely conjecture to anticipate that racial minorities will identify with the Democratic Party more than the Republican Party—this rests at the heart of existential fears among Republicans, as I show in my studies.

One fruitful path forward is reiterating that speculation about future racial demographic change and how it might shape American society is a form of misinformation. It does little to explain the world and lacks grounding in articulating how race and politics work in the United States. These forms of misinformation lead to the fear and threat that manifested on January 6, and they also can work to shape interpretations of antidemocratic events like it.

Moving forward, scholars, media, and all Americans interested in racial demography of the country ought to be careful how they articulate the ongoing changes. Because for better or for worse, this information has grand implications for the global function of American democracy.

References

Alba, R. (2018). What majority-minority society? A critical analysis of the Census Bureau's projections of America's demographic future. *Socius*, *4* (Jan.), 2378023118796932. https://doi.org/10.1177/2378023118796932

Alba, R., Beck, B., & Sahin, D. B. (2018). The rise of mixed parentage: A sociological and demographic phenomenon to be reckoned with. *Annals of the American Academy of Political and Social Science, 677*(1), 26–38. https://doi.org/10.1177/0002716218757656

Barbour, H., Bradshaw, S., Fleischer, A., Fonalledas, Z., & McCall, G. (2013). Growth and Opportunity Project. https://www.wsj.com/public/resources/documents/RNCreport03182013.pdf

Bartels, L. M. (2020). Ethnic antagonism erodes Republicans' commitment to democracy. *Proceedings of the National Academy of Sciences, 117*(37), 22752–22759. https://doi.org/10.1073/pnas.2007747117

Belew, K. (2019). *Bring the war home: The white power movement and paramilitary America*. Reprint ed. Harvard University Press.

Brown, X., Rucker, J. M., & Richeson, J. A. (2022). Political ideology moderates white Americans' reactions to racial demographic change. *Group Processes & Intergroup Relations, 25*(3), 642–660. https://doi.org/10.1177/13684302211052516

Craig, M. A., & Richeson, J. A. (2014). On the precipice of a "majority-minority" America: Perceived status threat from the racial demographic shift affects white Americans' political ideology." *Psychological Science, 25*(6), 1189–1197. https://doi.org/10.1177/0956797614527113

Craig, M. A., Rucker, J. M., & Richeson, J. A. (2018). The pitfalls and promise of increasing racial diversity: Threat, contact, and race relations in the 21st century." *Current Directions in Psychological Science, 27*(3), 188–193. https://doi.org/10.1177/0963721417727860

Druckman, J. N., & Green, D. P. (2021). *Advances in experimental political science*. Cambridge University Press.

Jacobson, G. C. (2021). "Donald Trump's big lie and the future of the Republican Party." *Presidential Studies Quarterly, 51*(2), 273–289. https://doi.org/10.1111/psq.12716

Ignatiev, N. (2008). *How the Irish became white*. Routledge. https://doi.org/10.4324/9780203473009

Jardina, A. (2019). *White identity politics*. Cambridge University Press.

Jardina, A. (2021). In-group love and out-group hate: White racial attitudes in contemporary U.S. elections. *Political Behavior, 43*(4), 1535–1559. https://doi.org/10.1007/s11109-020-09600-x

Kalmoe, N. P., & Mason, L. (2022). *Radical American partisanship: Mapping violent hostility, its causes, and the consequences for democracy*. University of Chicago Press.

Kim, C. (2020, Nov. 9). Poll: 70 percent of Republicans don't think the election was free and fair. *Politico*. https://www.politico.com/news/2020/11/09/republicans-free-fair-elections-435488

Krogstad, J. M., Dunn, A., & Passel, J. S. (2021, Aug. 23). Most Americans say the declining share of white people in the U.S. is neither good nor bad for society. Pew Research Center (blog). https://www.pewresearch.org/fact-tank/2021/08/23/most-americans-say-the-declining-share-of-white-people-in-the-u-s-is-neither-good-nor-bad-for-society/

Levy, M., & Myers, D. (2021). Racial projections in perspective: Public reactions to narratives about rising diversity. *Perspectives on Politics, 19*(4), 1147–1164. https://doi.org/10.1017/S1537592720003679

Mendelberg, T. (2001). *The race card: Campaign strategy, implicit messages, and the norm of equality*. Princeton University Press.

Newman, B., Merolla, J. L., Shah, S., Lemi, D. C., Collingwood, L., & Ramakrishnan, S. K. (2021). The Trump effect: An experimental investigation of the emboldening effect of racially inflammatory elite communication. *British Journal of Political Science*, *51*(3), 1138–1159. https://doi.org/10.1017/S0007123419000590

Painter, N. I. (2010). *The history of white people*. W. W. Norton.

Pape, R. A. (2021, Jan. 6). The Jan. 6 insurrectionists aren't who you think they are. *Foreign Policy* (blog). https://foreignpolicy.com/2022/01/06/trump-capitol-insurrection-january-6-insurrectionists-great-replacement-white-nationalism/

Parker, K., Morin, R., & Horowitz, J. M. (2019, Mar. 21). 3 views of demographic changes. Pew Research Center's Social & Demographic Trends Project (blog). https://www.pewresearch.org/social-trends/2019/03/21/views-of-demographic-changes-in-america/

Sohoni, Deenesh. (2022). The coming majority-minority state?: Media coverage of US Census projections, demographic threat, and the construction of racial boundaries. *The Sociological Quarterly*, *63*(1), 94–113.

Thompson, A. I. (2022, June 8). The partisan utility of racial demographic change and democratic backsliding in the American public. APSA Preprints. https://doi.org/10.33774/apsa-2022-544lb

Thompson, A. I., & Busby, E. C. (2021, Nov.). Defending the dog whistle: The role of justifications in racial messaging. Political Behavior. https://doi.org/10.1007/s11109-021-09759-x

8

Asymmetrical Identity-Driven Wrongness in American Politics

Dannagal G. Young

On January 6th, after listening to speeches from several hours of warm-up acts, attendees at the "Stop the Steal" rally got to hear from President Trump himself. In his signature style—off-the-cuff and impassioned—the president claimed that the presidential election result was wrong, that there had been widespread voter fraud, that the voting machines were rigged against him, and that the announcement of Biden's victory showed that the system as a whole was rigged to silence the voices of his supporters and steal their political victory. But, more important, his words offered the populist pairing of both flattery and deference:

> You're stronger, you're smarter. You've got more going than anybody, and they try and demean everybody having to do with us, and you're the real people. You're the people that built this nation. You're not the people that tore down our nation. (Jacobo, 2021).

Then, at the behest of Trump himself, the energized and angry crowd proceeded to "walk down Pennsylvania Avenue" toward the U.S. Capitol building, where many of them pushed through police barriers, some destroyed windows, and a few beat police officers with hockey sticks and American flags. Rioters broke into the halls of Congress, wielding flags of the Confederacy and of Donald Trump, and wandered the halls chanting "Execute the traitors" and "Hang Mike Pence." By day's end, five people, including Capitol police officer Brian Sicknick, would be dead. In the weeks and months that followed, another four officers would commit suicide (Breuninger & Mangan, 2021).

As hours passed and the rioters continued to ransack the Capitol, Trump finally released a video statement encouraging his supporters to go home in

---

Dannagal G. Young, *Asymmetrical Identity-Driven Wrongness in American Politics* In: *Media and January 6th*.
Edited by: Khadijah Costley White, Daniel Kreiss, Shannon C. McGregor, and Rebekah Tromble, Oxford University Press.
© Oxford University Press 2024. DOI: 10.1093/oso/9780197758526.003.0008

peace. But he didn't condemn them. Rather, he identified with them, praised them, validated their sense of betrayal, and repeated the claim that the election had been "stolen" and that "everyone knows it."

"I know your pain, I know you're hurt," Trump told his supporters. "There's never been a time like this where such a thing happened where they could take it away from all of us—from me, from you, from our country." And again Trump expressed his affection: "We love you. You're very special."

Later that evening in the aftermath of the insurrection, Jenny Cudd, a rioter who had breached the Capitol, streamed a video on Facebook live saying, "Fuck yes, I am proud of my actions. I fucking charged the Capitol today with patriots today. Hell yes, I am proud of my actions." (Tillman, 2021).

I highlight these anecdotes about that day to bring our attention *not* to the content of the lie itself, not to the details of the false claims of "fraud" or "rigging," but to the social, emotional, and threat-related aspects of Trump's message—and the accompanying social, emotional, and threat-related motivations for those participating in the insurrection. In that moment, as salient to Cudd as the "reason" for the insurrection was her performance of her political identity in solidarity with a group of people she admired and to whom she felt emotionally connected.

The Three Cs of "Identity-Driven Wrongness"

Cudd's attitudes and behaviors on January 6th reflect the essence of "identity-driven wrongness," attitudes and behaviors that are largely devoid of empirical meaning. They have little to do with the specific claims themselves. Instead, their meaning derives from individual needs that take shape through the lens of our social identities: our needs for *comprehension, control*, and, most of all, *community*. We seek to understand our worlds (*comprehension*), have agency over our lives (*control*), and feel part of a social group (*community*). Making efficient sense of the world (comprehension) enables us to act quickly, efficiently avoiding or neutralizing threats. Agency (control) provides us a sense of purpose and direction, protects our ego, and makes us feel safe. And being a part of a community was (and is) a necessary precursor to survival. Because historically these three Cs have aided in our survival and well-being, they continue to be fundamental needs that shape how we think and act.

Researchers studying belief in misinformation have found that each of these three Cs also contributes to our belief in misinformation (van Prooijen, 2018; van Prooijen & Acker, 2015; van Prooijen & Douglas, 2018). False information offers a causal mechanism to help us *comprehend* seemingly chaotic events (e.g., "Vaccinations cause autism"). Misinformation might provide a feeling of safety or *control* (e.g., "COVID is no worse than the flu"). And, when shared with others, it might provide a sense of social connection and *community* (e.g., being an active member of an anti-vaxx Facebook group). In the case of conspiracy theories—stories of secret plots by a handful of powerful elites harming people while benefiting themselves—the nature of the conspiracy theory narrative satisfies *all three Cs* (van Prooijen & Douglas, 2018). They feature a protagonist responsible for causing chaotic or unexpected events (aiding comprehension). They provide an answer to who to blame and who to "stop" to end the harm (offering a sense of control). And because the bad actors in the conspiracy theory are powerful elites harming some group of people, they activate a sense of in-group threat (reinforcing our connection to our community). Finally, when conspiracy theories are shared and discursive communities grow around them, as was the case with "Stop the Steal" communities, they help generate tangible social connections based on a shared-identity threat. Crucially, the specific shape each of these three Cs takes—that is, how we *comprehend* events, what we need *control* over, and how we think about our *community*'s norms—is largely informed by our *social identity*, or how we categorize ourselves as part of a social group.

Overlapping Identities in the U.S. Fuel the Three Cs

In the U.S. context, changes in the sociodemographic and cultural composition of our political parties have served as an accelerant for political identity-driven dynamics. Over the past 40 years, the two political parties have become increasingly distinct in terms of race, religion, culture, and even geography (Mason, 2018). Not only have party members become more like-minded, but especially within the Republican Party they also became more like-looking, like-worshiping, like-living, and like-valuing. As these different group categorizations come to overlap, Americans' political "mega-identities" increasingly encapsulate different ways of being, living, and knowing, especially on the political right.

The asymmetrical nature of this sorting is noteworthy, with Republicans' sociodemographic categories and ideological beliefs very well-aligned (Mason, 2018; also see Grossmann & Hopkins, 2015, 2016). While the Democratic Party has become more diverse, secular or agnostic, and culturally liberal, the Republican Party has become homogeneously white, evangelical, rural, and culturally traditional. As Ezra Klein writes, "sorting has made the Democrats into a coalition of difference and driven Republicans further into sameness" (2020, p. 231). The alignment of sociodemographic and ideological categories means lots of Republicans look like what most Republicans look like, they worship like most Republicans worship, they live where most Republicans live, and they value what most Republicans value. In the language of social identity theory, Republicans have very strong "group fit" (Hogg & Reid, 2006; Oakes, 1987). When people "fit" nicely into their social category, their identity as a member of that group becomes salient in their minds. And when a group identity (being Republican) is salient, it shapes (1) how we interpret the world (what we *comprehend*) (see Van Bavel & Packer, 2021), (2) the domains in which we want to feel agency (what we want to feel *control* over), and (3) our need to connect with that social group (how we perform the role of member of our *community*).

Scholars have also documented an ideological asymmetry in susceptibility to, spread of, and supply of misinformation (Garrett & Bond, 2021; van der Linden et al., 2021). While some of this asymmetry undoubtedly stems from the sociodemographic homogeneity upon which GOP elites capitalize in their identity-based rhetoric, social and cultural conservatives may be more susceptible to misinformation and conspiracy theories in general (Jost, van der Linden, Panagopoulos, & Hardin, 2018). They are also more approving of the spread of misinformation by their party's political elites (Roets, 2019). Surveys of the misinformation landscape show misinformation from the ideological right is more prevalent than misinformation from the left (Benkler et al., 2018; Freelon et al., 2020; Grinberg et al., 2019; Guess et al., 2019). Political psychologists suggest that part of this asymmetry stems from the unique psychological profile of individuals who tend to hold culturally conservative views (Jost, 2017). Individuals who are prone to monitor for interpersonal and physical threats in their social environments tend to be conservative on cultural issues relating to crime, race, and sexuality. Meanwhile, their threat monitoring also informs how they make sense of the world—tending toward efficiency, using cognitive shortcuts like emotions and source cues to make judgments quickly. These patterns may be responsible for the greater susceptibility to misinformation on the cultural right than the left (Jost & Krochik, 2014). In keeping with this framework, my colleagues and I have found that Americans who valued intuition and emotions while rejecting evidence and data were more favorable toward President Trump. These gut-guided, evidence-rejecting Trump supporters were also more likely to believe *both* the Big Election Lie underlying January 6th's attacks *and* misinformation about COVID-19 (Young et al., 2022).

Asymmetrical Identity Distillation Fueling the Three Cs

These asymmetrical identity-reinforcing processes are occurring in a media system whose economic model makes efficient use of—and reinforces—mega-political identities. The economics of social media are predicated on acquiring user data that facilitates the microtargeting of advertising messages to users. The machinery of social media thus rewards content that elicits emotional responses (likes, reactions, and shares), responses that shed light on a user's interests and passions. Some of the most effective content at eliciting such responses is identity-based "moralized emotional content," that is, emotional posts about what *should* or *should not* be happening and that reflect our social group's fundamental values and beliefs (Brady et al., 2017, 2020).

Because advances in data analytics allow the observation and analysis of viewer and user behaviors and preferences in real time (Karpf, 2017; Kelly, 2019; McGregor, 2019), the logics of our mediated world draw upon and reinforce the overlapping sociodemographic and cultural categories described earlier—all of which are more aligned and homogeneous on the right than the left. However, since the participants in America's mediated political world are exceptionally politically interested and partisan, and since American partisans have more "aligned" social and cultural categories, these media metrics aren't capturing the responses of average Americans, but of a hyperpolitical subset of Americans whose exceptional "fit" makes them especially high in *political identity salience*. And as regular apolitical people use social media to connect with friends and family, it is the hyperpartisan "good fit" folks who generate most of the political content online, giving their less political friends a skewed perception of what regular Americans care about (see Settle, 2018). This ongoing process—which operates even more efficiently on America's political right—primes, reinforces, and distills our political, racial, religious, and cultural identities in ways that chronically inform how we *comprehend* the world, what aspects of the world we feel we need to *control*, and how we define our *communities*. All in terms of rival identity-based factions.

In Sum

What we witnessed on January 6th was the culmination of these phenomena: a complex and uniquely American engine that integrates conservatives' ideological, racial, religious, and cultural identities, puts them through a distillation apparatus, then draws upon the resulting emotionally responsive mega-identities again and again. The result is salient partisan mega-identities on the right informing the largely white, Christian, ideologically and culturally conservative crowd's needs for *comprehension, control,* and *community*. The Big Lie offered all three. As Republicans sought to *comprehend* why some states' election results shifted from Republican leads to Democratic ones over time, the Big Lie attributed it to election rigging instead of the reality that mail-in ballots that took longer to count were used by more Democrats than Republicans. As Trump supporters sought *control* over their dismay at the prospect of an electoral defeat, the Big Lie proposed that they hadn't lost at all—that they *were* the legitimate winners and that their victory, and very way of life, had been stolen from them. And as they yearned for *community*, the Big Lie provided that, too. With a salient outgroup threat in the form of mainstream media and Democrats, Republicans had a shared fate, shared enemy, and shared course of action: to "fucking charge the Capitol with patriots."

It goes without saying that Trump and conservative media personalities deliberately cultivated the Big Lie in the months before January 6th (see Inskeep, 2021). But the upstream factors that activated, reinforced, and distilled partisan mega-identities are what allowed these tactics to succeed in the first place. In my book-length work on this topic, *Wrong: How Media, Politics, and Identity Drive Our Appetite for Misinformation* (Young, 2023), I unpack these dynamics and propose various ways of reducing partisan-identity salience. Although the easiest lever to pull to change *all of this* would be for political elites on the right to shuffle their partisan mega-identities and model a shared American identity (Levitsky & Ziblatt, 2018), at present I fear the political incentives are simply too great. Thus far, tapping into and reminding Republicans of threats to their white, Christian, rural, conservative identity has proved a winning strategy for Republicans. However, there are levers that media organizations could pull to disrupt this balkanization. Local journalism that emphasizes community identity over partisanship (Darr et al., 2021), self-transcendent media experiences that elevate our collective identity as human beings (Janicke-Bowles et al., 2021), social media platforms' increasing transparency to facilitate the spread of counterspeech and identity-diluting narratives (Kreiss & McGregor, 2019), news organizations abandoning conflict norms and "both-sidesism" in favor of democracy-focused journalism (Young, 2017): there are so many ways that media organizations could help dilute partisan mega-identities rather than distill them. Sure, we would still have our needs for *comprehension, control,* and *community* that might lead us astray, but being reminded of a shared social identity committed to democratic values and human dignity might disrupt these dynamics of partisan mega-identity-driven wrongness.

References

Benkler, Y., Faris, R., & Roberts, H. (2018). *Network propaganda: Manipulation, disinformation, and radicalization in American politics.* Oxford University Press.

Brady, W. J., Crockett, M. J., & Van Bavel, J. J. (2020). The MAD model of moral contagion: The role of motivation, attention, and design in the spread of moralized content online. *Perspectives on Psychological Science, 15*(4), 978–1010.

Brady, W. J., Wills, J. A., Jost, J. T., Tucker, J. A., & Van Bavel, J. J. (2017). Emotion shapes the diffusion of moralized content in social networks. *Proceedings of the National Academy of Sciences, 114*(28), 7313–7318.

Breuninger, K., & Mangan, D. (2021, Aug. 3). Two more officers die by suicide after defending Capitol during riot by pro-Trump mob, tally now 4. CNBC. https://www.cnbc.com/2021/08/02/3rd-police-officer-gunther-hashida-kills-himself-after-capitol-riot-by-trump-mob.html

Darr, J. P., Hitt, M. P., & Dunaway, J. L. (2021). *Home style opinion: How local newspapers can slow polarization.* Cambridge University Press.

Freelon, D., Bossetta, M., Wells, C., Lukito, J., Xia, Y., & Adams, K. (2020). Black trolls matter: Racial and ideological asymmetries in social media disinformation. *Social Science Computer Review, 40*(3), 0894439320914853.

Garrett, R. K., & Bond, R. M. (2021). Conservatives' susceptibility to political misperceptions. *Science Advances, 7*(23), eabf1234.

Grinberg, N., Joseph, K., Friedland, L., Swire-Thompson, B., & Lazer, D. (2019). Fake news on Twitter during the 2016 us presidential election. *Science, 363*(6425), 374–378.

Grossmann, M., & Hopkins, D. A. (2015). Ideological Republicans and group interest Democrats: The asymmetry of American party politics. *Perspectives on Politics, 13*(1), 119–139.

Grossmann, M., & Hopkins, D. A. (2016). *Asymmetric politics: Ideological Republicans and group interest Democrats*. Oxford University Press.

Guess, A., Nagler, J., & Tucker, J. (2019). Less than you think: Prevalence and predictors of fake news dissemination on Facebook. *Science Advances, 5*(1), eaau4586.

Hogg, M. A., & Reid, S. A. (2006). Social identity, self-categorization, and the communication of group norms. *Communication Theory, 16*(1), 7–30.

Inskeep, S. (2021, Feb. 8). Timeline: What Trump told supporters for months before they attacked. National Public Radio. https://www.npr.org/2021/02/08/965342252/timel ine-what-trump-told-supporters-for-months-before-they-attacked

Jacobo, J. (2021, January 7). This is what Trump told supporters before many stormed Capitol Hill. *ABC News*. https://abcnews.go.com/Politics/trump-told-supporters-stor med-capitol-hill/story?id=75110558

Janicke-Bowles, S. H., Raney, A. A., Oliver, M. B., Dale, K. R., Jones, R. P., & Cox, D. (2021). Exploring the spirit in US audiences: The role of the virtue of transcendence in inspiring media consumption. *Journalism & Mass Communication Quarterly, 98*(2), 428–450.

Jost, J. T. (2017). Ideological asymmetries and the essence of political psychology. *Political Psychology, 38*(2), 167–208.

Jost, J. T., & Krochik, M. (2014). Ideological differences in epistemic motivation: Implications for attitude structure, depth of information processing, susceptibility to persuasion, and stereotyping. In A. J. Elliot (Ed.) *Advances in Motivation Science: Vol. 1* (pp. 181–231). Elsevier.

Jost, J. T., van der Linden, S., Panagopoulos, C., & Hardin, C. D. (2018). Ideological asymmetries in conformity, desire for shared reality, and the spread of misinformation. *Current Opinion in Psychology, 23*, 77–83.

Karpf, D. (2017). Digital politics after Trump. *Annals of the International Communication Association, 41*(2), 198–207.

Kelly, J. P. (2019). Television by the numbers: The challenges of audience measurement in the age of Big Data. *Convergence, 25*(1), 113–132.

Klein, E. (2020). *Why we're polarized*. Simon and Schuster.

Kreiss, D., & McGregor, S. C. (2019). The "arbiters of what our voters see": Facebook and Google's struggle with policy, process, and enforcement around political advertising. *Political Communication, 36*(4), 499–522.

Levitsky, S., & Ziblatt, D. (2018). *How democracies die*. Broadway Books.

Mason, L. (2018). *Uncivil agreement: How politics became our identity*. University of Chicago Press.

McGregor, S. C. (2019). Social media as public opinion: How journalists use social media to represent public opinion. *Journalism, 20*(8), 1070–1086.

Oakes, P. J. (1987). The salience of social categories. In J. C. Turner, M. A. Hogg, P. J. Oakes, S. D. Rieche, & M. S. Wetherell (Eds.), *Rediscovering the social group: A self-categorization theory* (pp. 117–141). Blackwell.

Roets, A. (2019). Is there an ideological asymmetry in the moral approval of spreading misinformation by politicians? *Personality and Individual Differences, 143*, 165–169.

Settle, J. E. (2018). *Frenemies: How social media polarizes America*. Cambridge University Press.

Tillman, Z. (2021, Jan. 21). "Everything we fucking trained for": The Capitol mob, in their own words. BuzzFeed News. https://www.buzzfeednews.com/article/zoetillman/capt iol-rioters-charged-social-media-posts-violence

Van Bavel, J. J., & Packer, D. J. (2021). *The power of us: Harnessing our shared identities to improve performance, increase cooperation, and promote social harmony*. Little, Brown Spark.

van der Linden, S., Panagopoulos, C., Azevedo, F., & Jost, J. T. (2021). The paranoid style in American politics revisited: An ideological asymmetry in conspiratorial thinking. *Political Psychology, 42*(1), 23–51.

van Prooijen, J. W. (2018). *The psychology of conspiracy theories*. Routledge.

van Prooijen, J. W., & Acker, M. (2015). The influence of control on belief in conspiracy theories: Conceptual and applied extensions. *Applied Cognitive Psychology, 29*(5), 753–761.

van Prooijen, J. W., & Douglas, K. M. (2018). Belief in conspiracy theories: Basic principles of an emerging research domain. *European Journal of Social Psychology, 48*(7), 897–908.

Young, D., Maloney, E., Bleakley, A., & Langbaum, J. B. (2022). "I feel it in my gut": Epistemic motivations, political beliefs, and misperceptions of COVID-19 and the 2020 US presidential election. *Journal of Social and Political Psychology, 10*(2).

Young, D. G. (2017). Stop covering politics as a game. NiemanLab Predictions for Journalism 2018. https://www.niemanlab.org/2017/12/stop-covering-politics-as-a-game/

Young, D. G. (2023). *Wrong: How media, politics, and identity drive our appetite for misinformation*. Johns Hopkins University Press.

9

January 6th as Logical Extension of Conservative Populism

Paul Elliott Johnson

When coupists charged into the U.S. Capitol building on January 6, 2022, they sought to interrupt the transition of presidential power from Donald J. Trump to Joseph R. Biden. While January 6 was about keeping Trump in power, we should read the day not only in terms of the reality star's charismatic power. The events of the day are the logical consequence of a long-term conservative argumentative and political strategy. For decades conservatives argued and acted as if they had been locked out of the power structures of U.S. politics and culture. The coup attempt follows from decades of conservative populism, a rhetorical strategy used by right-wing forces to obtain political dominance in the last third of the 20th century. By "conservative populism" I mean a way of arguing and imagining which claims "the people," attempts to monopolize their definition, defines them in opposition to others socially constructed as derelict, and invests in this opposition at the expense of some positive shared program (say, establishing a single-payer healthcare system or abolishing prisons). They paint themselves, to borrow former vice-presidential candidate Sarah Palin's formulation, as *real Americans*, the legitimate owners of the nation, but also somehow simultaneously excluded from the United States (Johnson, 2022, pp. 3–5).

From the 1960s onward, conservatism mainstreamed itself by mendaciously narrating the story of the postwar moment as one characterized by a feminizing, and "Blackening" radicalization of U.S. society and institutions: Richard Nixon affirmed the "silent majority" over noisy urban rioters, while Ronald Reagan praised white suburbanites for their commitment to family and attacked Black "welfare queens." Both opposed what they saw as "original sins" of Black radicalization, progressivism, and a tyranny of social difference rooted in the 1960s. If the 1960s had found "nascent conservatives" interpreting the decade's disorder as a sign of the "constitutive

Paul Elliott Johnson, *January 6th as Logical Extension of Conservative Populism* In: *Media and January 6th*.
Edited by: Khadijah Costley White, Daniel Kreiss, Shannon C. McGregor, and Rebekah Tromble, Oxford University Press.
© Oxford University Press 2024. DOI: 10.1093/oso/9780197758526.003.0009

80   UNDERSTANDING JANUARY 6, 2021

exclusion of both white personhood and conservative views from the political center" (Johnson, 2022, p. 7), then the summer 2020 protests against racist police and vigilante killings similarly threatened conservative orthodoxy. The protests followed from the proximate events of the police killings of George Floyd and Breonna Taylor and the racist vigilante murder of Ahmaud Arbery and put in relief the struggle for Black life which has subtended the history of the United States. Rhetorical scholar Louis Maraj (2020, p. 15) calls this moment "post-Ferguson" to mark the Missouri uprising which contested the police's right to kill following Darren Wilson's shooting of Michael Brown.

Understanding the post-Ferguson context of the January 6 coup attempt can help resolve what might seem to be a stunning contradiction at the heart of the events of January 6: How do so many people describe themselves as patriots and proud Americans, yet nevertheless occupy, destroy, and defame a sacred national space, the U.S. Capitol? In the rest of this chapter, I analyze the language used during the coup to show that the day's plotters were defending a historically legible idea of the United States within the conservative tradition.

Context

The summer 2020 protests are one of the key contexts both for Trump's campaign for reelection and the attempt by his supporters to keep him in power. One should not underestimate the degree to which the election was a referendum on the wave of summer 2020 protests and the legitimacy of white grievance politics. On January 6, rioters invoked "Black Lives Matter" and "Antifa" (short for "antifascism," which designates a method for fighting against political injustice but which conservatives assert is a coherent social movement, with *antifascists* a class of people analogous to other leftists). Such invocations carried forward the sentiment of Trump's 2020 campaign, which sought to conflate Black Lives Matter and Antifa in the public eye and paint both as threats to the United States (Shanahan & Wall, 2021, p. 73). On various occasions, Trump and associates called both Black Lives Matter and Antifa terrorists. When he visited Kenosha, Wisconsin, on September 1, 2020, he invoked "domestic terror" (Miller & Lemire, 2020) to describe the protestors. Following demonstrations in Washington, D.C., Trump spoke about "acts of domestic terror," acknowledging the protests were done in response to the murder of George Floyd but insisting that Antifa and others were engaging in "savage violence" (C-SPAN, 2020). Researcher Charisse Burden-Stelly (2020, p. 5) has noted that anti-Blackness manifests by reducing Blackness "to a categorical abjection and subjection" through the use of essentializing language, that is, taking a complicated phenomenon and reducing it to a single—often unsavory or off-putting—element, for example reducing the Black Radical Tradition to only calls for terrorism or violence. In this vein, ads like "Break In" and "Defund the Police" sought to frame the protests in the summer of 2020 not as signs of a democracy trying to right itself but as sources of danger and violence. The 2020 election was a referendum on the protests, positioning Trump as the defender of white order against a racialized insurgency.

Analysis of Footage

I pay particular attention to how the coupists invoke the concept of home and the salience of racism in understanding their rhetoric, drawing mostly on video evidence compiled by ProPublica from videos taken from the right-wing social media site Parler. I focus on two themes: rhetoric of "the house" and talk about left radical organizations. Invoking the house expands the imagined space of the ideal home, in which the (white and male) head of household assumes an authoritarian relationship over spouse, offspring, and extended family, illustrating how ownership over the nation mirrors the model of white patriarchal authority (Young, 2003, p. 2). Meanwhile, racializing radicals offer a stabilizing principle that keeps consistent the linkage between earlier moments of conservatism and the January 6 coup, figuring conservatism's "people" as oriented toward the preservation of white rule.

Home as Possession

The coupists' insistence on claiming the Capitol as their property, with references to it as their house, implies the potential threat to white and masculine rule posed by democracy, literally the "House," as the House of Representatives is called to vote to certify the results of the presidential election. As the crowd gathers outside of the Capitol and starts to menace the

Capitol police, a feminine voice starts leading a chant, "Who's house? Our house! Who's house? Our house!," before Capitol police, struggling to fend off members of the crowd pushing against barriers in front of the steps to the building, disperse an explosive projectile—either tear gas or a flashbang—into the crowd, to which a deeper voice yells, "You pussies!" Here "house," a place of masculine prerogative and rule, can take precedence over democracy, while the contrast between a feminine voice claiming ownership and a masculine voice offering up the vagina as a form of epithet for weakness exemplifies two levels to how the masculine politics of the mob operate: particular feminized figures might have a place in the riot, but the abstracted genitalia are an insult.

The "Our house!" language also shows up elsewhere, as the mob makes its case to be "the people" in charge of deciding who is and is not allowed into the House, and therefore the nation. The coupists aim to assert their control over who is and is not "the people." Reporter Luke Mogelson (2021) documented people breaching one of the windows and entering the building, capturing video of one participant asking, "Whose house?" and another person responding, "Our house." Though the U.S. political system is not democratic in structure, the House of Representatives is one of its most democratic elements. Boasting 538 members and without the arcane antimajoritarian traditions of the Senate, the House stands for shared power. The call and response, which asks and answers the question of ownership of the House, rehearses the potential of democracy, in that ownership of the nation is an open question. But the response closes down other potentials for ownership, a proxy reply to the answer that had been given by "the people" in the 2020 election.

The chant embodies many key elements of conservative populism. "Who's house? Our house" as call and response is consistent with the white and masculine prerogative that holds among the right and poaches from left-wing vocabularies. As the white and male head of household is imagined to govern the family with a firm hand, so the nation is to be ruled by a similar logic, insofar as the input of the other family members—in the case of the election the American "people" who voted for Joe Biden—is at best advisory, with the "real Americans" demanding to maintain their monopoly on determining the course of the nation. In seeking to gatekeep the contours of their imagined nation, conservative understandings of "the people" cannot entertain the possibility that those who voted for Joe Biden might really be Americans. Complementary to this prerogative is the idea that the election's verdict turning against conservatives amounts to some kind of world-historical trauma. Antiracist protestors chanted "Whose streets? Our streets" when they marched following Darren Wilson's killing of Michael Brown in Ferguson, a phrase that became popular enough that filmmakers Sabaah Folayan and Damon Davis made it the title of their documentary about the Ferguson uprising (Cornish, 2017). The imagination of the white man as being subjected to subjugating violence is characteristic of the white victimhood central to conservative populism. This chant communicates an understanding on the right that they have suffered a grievous trauma, and therefore democratic imperatives will not impede their ownership of the nation.

Race

Members of the crowd repeatedly invoke antiracist slogans like Black Lives Matter and subversive forces like antifascists (shortened to "Antifa" in the right's vocabulary to produce the illusion of a unified social organization rather than the pro-democracy ethos which antifascism names) to contrast themselves with those whom they hold to be *illegitimate* civil protestors. The repeated invocation of these figures works to remind those on the right that, in their imaginations, it is *they* who are on the margins of the U.S. power structure, while Black people and left-wingers control the nation by sowing discord.

Sometimes members of the crowd invoke Black Lives Matter in order to try to calm things down. Right-wing radio host Alex Jones, for example, tried to calm the crowd by saying that the people gathered on the Mall were different from Black Lives Matter and Antifa: "We're not like them." Another clip, from outside the Capitol around 2:40, shows police marching to the building, while a woman's voice says "They don't care about us but they'll protect Black Lives Matter." In each case Black Lives Matter builds conservative identity, both with Jones's invocation, which draws on a long tradition of pathologizing Blackness by associating it with disorder and civil unrest, and with the woman who identifies Black Lives Matter as a privileged class enjoying police protection.

The routine invocations of Black Lives Matter and the police on January 6 are attempts to demarcate both the mob's virtue and Americanness via racism, acknowledging the assembled mob's resemblance to the masses on the streets of cities in the summer of 2020 and say: What is happening here is different, that is, not Black. Read closely, the sentiment behind Jones's comment is more unsettling, reading literally as: We *are not* Black Lives Matter, that is, we are not Black. Even if his intent was to calm things down, in saying it he underscores the white right to riot, reminding the crowd that they could do whatever they wanted while trusting that they would face only modest, if any, consequences.

Similarly, the accusations that the police and establishment were siding with Black Lives Matter and Antifa should not be read as casual mendacity. Rather, the belief that the U.S. political establishment and its agents are captured by a progressive liberalism has long been a core sentiment for many conservatives. When Ronald Reagan argued that the expansion of the welfare state would pathologize the U.S. population, his argument held that no citizens, not even white citizens, could survive being entangled with a "Blackened" political apparatus, conflating progressive advances in policy with federal action on civil rights to delegitimate the whole bundle of liberal democratic government by associating it with Black radicals (Johnson, 2022, p. 38).

For conservatives, the temptation to interpret the summer of 2020 as a rerun of the protests and riots which had emboldened the "silent majority" was irresistible. Many members of the mob on the Mall sincerely believe that the political and policing apparatus is beholden to an alliance of radicals whose political success will threaten white America's power. In one video compilation of the day, as people walk inside the Capitol shortly before occupying the legislative room, one invader says, "You were afraid of Antifa? Well, guess what: America showed up." Certainly, there are echoes of the "Great Replacement" logic here, an ethic which imagines that white Americans are being zeroed out as a coalition of "un-American" people take root in the United States. There is also a racist envy at work, which observes the hypervisibility of Black people in U.S. culture and—despite the fact that this hypervisibility indexes Black vulnerability to violence, commodification, and objectification—sees it as a sign of privilege and power (Story, 2017, p. 409).

Conclusion

I have shown how the reactionary threads of U.S. conservatism remain consistent between earlier periods in U.S. history and the present. January 6 deserves to be understood as a moment of continuity with previous U.S. conservatism rather than some break. Of course, there are differences, particularly in style: While there has always been violence on the right, that violence was either episodic during periods of emerging conservative hegemony—think the hard hat riots during Nixon's presidency and the bombing of schools in West Virginia—or more capable of being plausibly (if not accurately) separated from the mainstream right, as in the case of Timothy McVeigh and Terry Nichols's bombing of the Alfred P. Murrah Federal Building in Oklahoma City in 1993. In January 6 we have a moment of convergence between a national presidential election and the open sense of aggrievement and entitlement central to conservative political mobilization. I did not comment at length upon some of the more openly disturbing elements of the January 6 invasion, like the display of Confederate flags. Their significance is obvious. But it bears mentioning that the co-presence of such symbols alongside other, more coded rhetoric should not be interpreted as the sign of latent tensions that will eventually destroy right-wing solidarity. Rather, it is evidence of shared, durable sentiment that underwrites American conservatism.

References

Burden-Stelly, C. (2020). Modern US racial capitalism. *Monthly Review, 72*(3), 1–14.

Cornish, A. (2017, Aug. 9). "Whose streets?" follows unrest in Ferguson after Michael Brown's death. National Public Radio. https://www.npr.org/2017/08/09/542468258/whose-streets-follows-unrest-in-ferguson-mo-after-michael-browns-death

C-SPAN. (2020, June 1). President Trump delivers remarks on protests and civil unrest. https://www.c-span.org/video/?472684-1/president-deploy-military-states-halt-violent-protests

Johnson, P. (2022). *I the people: The rhetoric of conservative populism in the United States.* University of Alabama Press.

Maraj, L. (2020). *Black or right: Anti-racist campus rhetorics.* Utah State University Press.

Miller, Z., & Lemire, J. (2020, Sept. 1). Trump visits Kenosha, calls violence "domestic terror." Associated Press. https://apnews.com/article/virus-outbreak-election-2020-ap-top-news-politics-shootings-4a58a15c9955bb6312c1fbe42215110d

Mogelson, L. (2021, Jan. 17). A reporter's footage from inside the Capitol scene. *The New Yorker.* https://www.youtube.com/watch?v=270F8s5TEKY

Shanahan, J., & Wall, T. (2021). "Fight the reds, support the blue": Blue Lives Matter and the US counter-subversive tradition. *Race & Class, 63*(1), 70–90.

Story, K. A. (2017). Fear of a Black femme: The existential conundrum of embodying a Black femme identity while being a professor of Black, queer, and feminist studies. *Journal of Lesbian Studies, 21*(4), 407–419.

Young, I. M. (2003). The logic of masculinist protection: Reflections on the current security state. *Signs: Journal of Women in Culture and Society, 29*(1), 1–25.

10

Antidemocratic Publics

The January 6th Mob and Digital Organizing

Silvio Waisbord

Violent mobs have been central to antidemocratic movements, as illustrated by the 1923 Beer Hall putsch and the failed military uprising of July 1936 in the history of Nazism and Spanish fascism, respectively. The January 6th insurrection against U.S. democracy may have similar significance for U.S. far-right politics. If the 2017 deadly march in Charlottesville was the "coming-out party" of the far right (DiMaggio, 2021), January 6th was the materialization of violent white identity in the heart of U.S. politics.

As in other fascist movements, violence and hate were distinctive elements of January 6th. A mob entered the U.S. Capitol by force in order to halt the democratic process. As reported by the *Washington Post* on January 8, 2021, "[m]embers of the mob scaled walls, smashed doors and windows, vandalized works of art, and stole laptops, correspondence and personal items from offices, forcing the emergency evacuation of lawmakers and staff" (Brooks 2021). Five people died as a consequence of the attack. Prominent politicians, notably President Donald Trump, social media influencers, and right-wing media personalities from Fox, *Breitbart, Infowars,* and far-right bloggers (Atlantic Council's DFRLab, 2021) urged participants to block the certification of the 2020 election results (Szilagyi et al., 2022). Trump had infamously predicted that the "Stop the Steal" rally would "be wild." The postrally assault on the Capitol was aimed at forcing Vice President Mike Pence to derail the certification. At the time of this writing, a congressional investigation is under way, and more than 775 people have been arrested in cases related to the breach of the Capitol. Members of the white supremacist groups Proud Boys and Oath Keepers were charged with sedition for their role in the assault.

It is hard to imagine what happened on January 6th without the use of digital platforms for participation and coordination in public affairs (Munn,

Silvio Waisbord, *Antidemocratic Publics* In: *Media and January 6th*. Edited by: Khadijah Costley White, Daniel Kreiss, Shannon C. McGregor, and Rebekah Tromble, Oxford University Press. © Oxford University Press 2024.
DOI: 10.1093/oso/9780197758526.003.0010

2021). While the full story is not public yet, as the United States House Select Committee to Investigate the January 6th Attack on the United States Capitol continues its deliberations and holds hearings, some key elements are clear. According to the U.S. Department of Justice, the Oath Keepers and the Proud Boys had used digital platforms to plan violent actions for that day (Bump, 2022a). During the event, digital communication was essential as the crowd gathered at Trump's rally proceeded with the violent assault on the Capitol, as well as during the attack.

The event was the culmination of escalating online and offline violence by far-right groups in previous years. The January 6th mob had used digital platforms to voice demands, find and recruit sympathizers, nurture ideologies, coordinate plans, and act locally and nationally (Rondeaux et al., 2022). In several states, the Proud Boys and other organizations had staged violent protests against various issues, including the removal of Confederate statues, COVID-related mask mandates, and the "imposition of Sharia law" (MacFarquhar, 2021). In many cases, they assaulted citizens and public officials. These offline actions were directly connected to digital activities, full of hateful rhetoric and support for violence as a legitimate form of political action.

In this chapter, I argue that January 6th not only reveals the centrality of digital organizing for contemporary U.S. right-wing politics, but it also complicates early arguments about the consequences of digital politics. January 6th demonstrates the significance of digital organizing in right-wing populism and antidemocratic publics and raises questions about comparative aspects of digital mobilization among different ideological movements.

Connective Actions: For What?

January 6th reminds us that digital participation does not necessarily contribute to expanding democracy. It should not be seen as inherently good in normative terms. Nothing about citizens expressing and organizing online necessarily leads to virtuous outcomes. What can be seen as democratic from a standpoint focused on citizen participation in public affairs may lead to overthrowing democracy and fostering hate. Citizens may participate to contribute to the public good or to impose their will by force, to promote emancipation and critical reasoning, or to spread hate and violence.

While this point may seem obvious, it is a necessary corrective to early, exuberant optimism about digital participation in contemporary politics. A decade ago, scholars generally hailed digitally enabled protests in democratic and nondemocratic regimes as new opportunities for self-governing (Diamond & Plattner, 2012). This line of argument had a distinctive hopeful tone about the impact of digitally enabled actions, grounded in the experience of pro-democracy and progressive movements around the world. Movements like U.S. Occupy, Spain's Indignados, and "the Twitter revolutions" in the Arab world were seen as representative of the emancipatory potential of digital politics. According to this argument, digital platforms, including social media, blogging, and websites, facilitate "connective actions" (Bennett & Segerberg, 2012). This concept refers to the ability of groups to organize and coordinate actions without utilizing traditional, brick-and-mortar associations. Citizens can bypass conventional organized politics and engage in direct forms of participation. Digital technologies offer radically different opportunities for citizen organization because they lower the costs of participation and organization (Bimber et al., 2005). Connective actions represent new forms of organizing in terms of recruiting and joining movements, coordinating logistics, and producing and sharing messages.

The current spirit is quite different. Gone is the air of hope and endless possibilities. Notwithstanding the contributions of specific movements, such as Black Lives Matter and #MeToo, to expanding expression and public debate (Chandra & Erlingsdóttir, 2020; Jackson et al., 2020; Masoud, 2021), it is not obvious that digitally connected protests necessarily spearheaded structural, lasting changes, or that they became consolidated as political actors. Sustainable political action and significant social and policy changes demand conditions other than digital protest. Digital protest is one component of a sequence of actions in any process of political and social change—from raising awareness to policy debates, transformation, and implementation (Waisbord, 2018b).

Whatever hopes about the revolutionary potential of digital politics lingered, they crashed down by 2016—that *annus horribilis* for contemporary democracy. Notably, Brexit and the election of Trump to the U.S. presidency solidified the global ascent of far-right and populist politics. These movements have astutely used digital media to mobilize supporters and to spread disinformation. Both the Brexit and the Trump campaigns used sophisticated digital networks to promote reactionary causes, spread disinformation, and gain power. A rich literature, especially in the European context, has studied the ways far-right groups have used digital media to create dynamic and dense information ecosystems that serve multiple purposes, such as recruitment, indoctrination, information-sharing, and coordination (Hatakka, 2020; Wahlström & Törnberg, 2021). Just as platforms make it possible for far-right groups to come together in chat groups and alternative or mainstream social media, online organizing has been central to offline violence at local, national, and transnational levels.

January 6th is a prominent example of contemporary digital fascism—far-right ideology and actions, coordinated and communicated online, in order to advance by force the politics of white supremacy, hate, and antidemocracy. It demonstrates the ability of those groups to harness digital technologies with the complacency of Silicon Valley corporations (Silverman et al., 2021), which have allowed hate, violence, and disinformation to fester in their platforms and have taken half-hearted, incoherent, and pitiful measures to deal with the problem.

Questions about Digital Fascism

January 6th raises important questions for understanding far-right digital activism.

First, what if digital organizing, once thought to be a distinctive element of progressive and radical politics, may actually be essential to right-wing populism?

January 6th demonstrates that "connective actions" fit well with right-wing populism's communication and organization style, as scholars have shown in European cases (Gustafsson & Weinryb, 2020). This brand of populism is characterized by charismatic leadership, an individualist and libertarian ethos, and distrust of democratic institutions and political organizations (Waisbord, 2018a). Populist communication features direct, "unmediated" engagement between leaders and supporters that make it possible to bypass the "establishment" media and other democratic institutions. Digital media arguably suit populism even better than broadcasting media, populism's favorite communication platforms during the 20th century. Radio and television offered one-way, top-down communication with mass publics in specific moments, such as the apotheotic mass gatherings of rallies and marches. Instead, social media and other online platforms provide leaders with large-scale instruments to communicate *constantly* with the masses without media

90 UNDERSTANDING JANUARY 6, 2021

gatekeeping, offer followers means for bottom-up self-organizing, and foster experiences that maximize regular "personal" political engagement.

All these elements were present on January 6th. During the months leading up to and on that day, various social media platforms, especially Gab and Parler, provided fluid communication channels between Trump and his supporters, especially the most extreme and violent. In his tweets and other media appearances (such as during the September 29, 2020, presidential debate), Trump validated and instructed armed mobs to commit acts of violence. Just as they used street violence to intimidate citizens and elected officials in Michigan, Wisconsin, and several other states in the preceding months, these mobs acted as Trump's own Sturmabteilung (SA) as they overpowered the Capitol police in their assault. Proud Boys leader Enrique Tarrio established an encrypted chat for recruiting members for such actions, while members established crowdfunding campaigns to purchase protective gear and pay for their trip to Washington, D.C. (Bump, 2022b; Jackman et al., 2022). Multiple pleas to Trump to appeal to the mob to halt the violence rightly assumed that he was able to communicate directly and instantaneously. Widely recorded and live-streamed by participants, the assault on the Capitol offered the mob and other supporters the opportunity for personal engagement and "being there" at such a "historic" moment.

Second, the January 6th mob was an example of antidemocratic *counterpublics*. In the literature, "counterpublics" has a distinctive progressive and radical bent (Asen & Brouwer, 2001). It has been widely used in reference to anticapitalist, left-wing and progressive groups around the world that "counter" dominant regimes articulated in multiple dimensions: economic, social, political, racial, gender, and sexuality. Counterpublics demand a range of structural changes, from social equality to social justice.

Should counterpublics refer to antisystem groups of various ideological stripes? If far-right mobs subvert liberal democracy, do they count as counterpublics? What took place on January 6th was not the manifestation of a "conservative counter-sphere" (Major, 2012)—the aggregation of political and rhetorical spaces deliberately set up to be alternative to the perceived "liberal order" (including the media). Conservatism is not necessarily antidemocratic, nor does it fundamentally espouse violence as a political tactic. January 6th was different. It represents the open adoption of antidemocratic methods to impose a political will. It was deliberately antisystemic as it clearly aimed to overthrow a legitimately elected president and the constitutional order.

The January 6th mob was antisystemic, understanding by "system" the fundamentals of liberal democracy and the regime of human rights. The mob was distinctively antiestablishment, as demonstrated by their grievances, demands, and colorful rhetoric to refer to members of Congress of both political parties, the media, and intelligence and security agencies. Correct or not, they reflected the populist conviction that the system is rigged. Far-right resistance against the constitutional order was expressed in the mob's intention to kill public officials, harassing reporters and destroying media equipment, punching and stamping on police officers, and breaking into the Capitol.

Just as "alternative media" do not have a single meaning or ideological bent (Waisbord, 2022), counterpublics can adopt different ideological positions. It would be too narrow to understand what defines the dominant order as well as antisystemic resistance in simplistic manner. Radical conservatism is a violent reaction against the regime of liberal democracy, multiculturalism, and human rights. It is a countermovement to overthrow the present order. Just as connective action does not necessarily endorse certain kind of politics, counterpublics should not be seen only in terms of progressive or leftist radical politics.

Finally, how do forms of "connective actions" compare among different political and ideological groups? It could be argued that digital organizing is not linked similarly to mainstream, established politics. The literature originally underscored the autonomous nature of digital mobilization by progressive, pro-democracy groups, given that they were detached from (and opposed) organized politics or maintained tenuous linkages with party politics and civic society. They were viewed as representative of the potential of grassroots democracy and emancipatory politics against sclerotic, mainstream politics.

The January 6th mob was quite different. Again, while the full story on multiple aspects of what happened that day is not out yet, it is apparent that the mob was not a grassroots, autonomous movement. It was not an experiment in digitally enabled, people-centered democracy. Available information suggests that the assault on the Capitol was part of the coup orchestrated from the White House. The mob was the muscle that a fascist takeover of democracy demands. It was neither a riot nor the product of a spur-of-the-moment decision by people at Trump's rally in the Ellipse. It was not ragtag groups that decided to prolong their joyous stay in the National Mall as they sashayed to the Capitol. Rally participants do not usually carry military-level weapons, gear, ammunition, and explosives, nor are they ready for hand-to-hand combat. Their connection to President Trump and conspirators was not merely rhetoric; rather, they were part of a coordinated plan of action to throw out the electoral results and install Trump for a second presidential term.

Also, the far-right demimonde of January 6th was not isolated from the complex web of money, power, and digital networks of right-wing politics (Nelson, 2019). Digital organizing on January 6th needs to be examined in connection to the linkages of far-right groups and prominent Republican politicians, donors, and activists as part of a plot to overturn the results of the 2020 presidential election (Massoglia, 2021).

Another issue to examine is the consequences of the decision by Facebook, Twitter, and other internet corporations to deplatform far-right organizations (and Trump) in the aftermath of January 6th. That decision accelerated the mob's migration to "alternative" platforms and reinforced their conviction that Silicon Valley is determined to "cancel" them. Groups and individuals scattered across Telegram, Parler, Gettr, and other social media (Bump, 2022a). These dynamics raise questions about the future of far-right and right-wing digital organizing, especially considering that platform-hopping and regrouping have not yet resulted in high levels of engagement (Chayka, 2022). How does the exodus from mainstream platforms affect their capacity for connective actions? How do groups reorganize as they jump across platforms?

Conclusion

January 6th represents more than the feral, antidemocratic, "pitchfork politics" (Mounk, 2014) of white identity, mobilized in a failed insurrection against the U.S. government. It reveals the centrality of digital platforms for self-organizing, communication, and coordination among far-right groups. It shows remarkable affinities between digital politics and right-wing populism. It also reminds us that digital organizing and publics lack a single political blueprint, evolution, or objective. Just as digital platforms can be utilized for communication and organization in support of different goals, publics may come together in pursuit of antidemocratic goals or emancipatory politics.

References

Asen, R., & Brouwer, D. C. (Eds.). (2001). *Counterpublics and the state*. State University of New York Press.

Atlantic Council's DFRLab. (2021, Feb. 10). #StopTheSteal: Timeline of social media and extremist activities leading to 1/6 insurrection. Just Security. https://www.justsecurity.org/74622/stopthesteal-timeline-of-social-media-and-extremist-activities-leading-to-1-6-insurrection/

Bennett, W. L., & Segerberg, A. (2012). The logic of connective action: Digital media and the personalization of contentious politics. *Information, Communication & Society*, *15*(5), 739–768.

Bimber, B., Flanagin, A. J., & Stohl, C. (2005). Reconceptualizing collective action in the contemporary media environment. *Communication Theory*, *15*(4), 365–388.

Brooks, R. (2021). No one watches the Capitol Police closely. No wonder they failed. *Washington Post*, January 8, https://www.washingtonpost.com/outlook/capitol-police-failure-oversight/2021/01/08/d7ea1c5c-5136-11eb-bda4-615aaefd0555_story.html

Bump, P. (2022a, Apr. 23). The platform where the right-wing bubble is least likely to pop. *Washington Post*. https://www.washingtonpost.com/politics/2022/04/23/telegram-platform-right-wing/

Bump, P. (2022b, Mar. 15). Timeline: How two extremist groups planned for Jan. 6. *Washington Post* https://www.washingtonpost.com/politics/2022/03/15/timeline-how-two-extremist-groups-planned-jan-6/

Chandra, G., & Erlingsdóttir, I. (Eds.). (2020). *The Routledge handbook of the politics of the #MeToo movement*. Routledge.

Chayka, K. (2022, May 19). The online spaces that enable mass shooters. *New Yorker*.

Diamond, L., & Plattner, M. F. (Eds.). (2012). *Liberation technology: Social media and the struggle for democracy*. Johns Hopkins University Press.

DiMaggio, A. (2021). *Rising fascism in America: It can happen here*. Routledge.

Gustafsson, N., & Weinryb, N. (2020). The populist allure of social media activism: Individualized charismatic authority. *Organization*, *27*(3), 431–440.

Hatakka, N. (2020). Expose, debunk, ridicule, resist! Networked civic monitoring of populist radical right online action in Finland. *Information, Communication & Society*, *23*(9), 1311–1326.

Jackman, T., Weiner, R. & Hsu, S. (2022, July 8). Evidence of firearms in Jan. 6 crowd grows as arrests and trials mount. *Washington Post*. https://www.washingtonpost.com/dc-md-va/2022/07/08/jan6-defendants-guns/?utm_campaign=wp_afternoon_buzz&utm_medium=email&utm_source=newsletter&wpisrc=nl_buzz&carta-url=https%3A%2F%2Fs2.washingtonpost.com%2Fcar-ln-tr%2F3751c15%2F62c8917ccfe8a21601dd6013%2F59948bb49bbc0f2281e7e07a%2F9%2F62%2F62c8917ccfe8a21601dd6013&wp_cu=2dcf89e59c5346bf8325ec7262ae42a5%7C56E3871FD7C42953E0530100007F8D38,

Jackson, S. J., Bailey, M., & Welles, B. F. (2020). *#HashtagActivism: Networks of race and gender justice*. MIT Press.

MacFarquhar, N. (2021, Mar. 27). Moving on from "Stop the Steal," far right now vilifies vaccines, *New York Times*.

Major, M. (2012). Objective but not impartial: Human events, Barry Goldwater, and the development of the "liberal media" in the conservative counter-sphere. *New Political Science, 34*(4), 455–468.

Massoglia, A. (2021, Oct. 25). Details of the money behind Jan. 6 protests continue to emerge. Open Secrets. https://www.opensecrets.org/news/2021/10/details-of-the-money-behind-jan-6-protests-continue-to-emerge/

Masoud, T. (2021). The Arab Spring at 10: Kings or people? *Journal of Democracy, 32*(1), 139–154.

Mounk, Y. (2014). Pitchfork politics: The populist threat to liberal democracy. *Foreign Policy*, Sept./Oct. (5), 27–36.

Munn, L. (2021). More than a mob: Parler as preparatory media for the US Capitol storming. First Monday. https://firstmonday.org/ojs/index.php/fm/article/view/11574

Nelson, A. (2019). *Shadow network: Media, money, and the secret hub of the radical right.* Bloomsbury.

Rondeaux, C., Dalton, B. & Nguyen, C. (2022, Jan. 5). Parler and the road to the capitol attack investigating alt-tech ties to January 6. New America. https://www.newamerica.org/future-frontlines/reports/parler-and-the-road-to-the-capitol-attack

Silverman, C., Timberg, C., Kao, J., & Merrill, J. B. (2021, Jan. 4). Facebook hosted surge of misinformation and insurrection threats in months leading up to Jan. 6 attack, records show. *ProPublica/Washington Post.* https://www.propublica.org/article/facebook-hosted-surge-of-misinformation-and-insurrection-threats-in-months-leading-up-to-jan-6-attack-records-show

Szilagyi, H., Goodman, R., & Hendrix, J. (2022, May 12). Surveying evidence of how Trump's actions activated Jan. 6 rioters. Just Security. https://www.justsecurity.org/81468/surveying-evidence-of-how-trumps-actions-activated-jan-6-rioters/

Wahlström, M., & Törnberg, A. (2021). Social media mechanisms for right-wing political violence in the 21st century: Discursive opportunities, group dynamics, and co-ordination. *Terrorism and Political Violence, 33*(4), 766–787.

Waisbord, S. (2018a). Populism as media and communication phenomenon. In C. de la Torre (Ed.), *Routledge handbook of global populism* (pp. 221–234). Routledge.

Waisbord, S. (2018b). Revisiting mediated activism. *Sociology Compass, 12*(6), 1–9.

Waisbord, S. (2022). Alternative media/journalism and the communicative politics of contestation. *Digital Journalism, 10*(8), 1431–1439.

11

The Ordinary Insurrection

January 6 and the Mainstreaming of Political Violence

Alice E. Marwick

The dramatic January 6th hearings describe an embattled President Trump desperately trying to hold on to power as he watched television coverage of an unruly mob of antigovernment groups, militia members, white supremacists, and QAnon supporters clashing with police as they breached the Capitol perimeter. The role of Trump and other Republican politicians in planning, aiding, and abetting the riot is well-documented (Broadwater, 2022). Yet journalists, activists, scholars, and political pundits repeatedly describe the January 6th insurrection as the result of radicalization. Former ambassador Kenneth Brill (2022), writing in *The Hill*, described the insurrectionists as "a radicalized mob, fueled by a deliberate campaign of lies by the sitting president and some Members of Congress." Frank Figliuzi, a former FBI official, tweeted, "Radicalization includes suppression of truth," pointing to Fox News' decision not to air the January 6th committee hearings (Staten, 2022). Political scientist Andrew Kydd (2021, p. 3) wrote in the scholarly journal *Violence* that the attempted coup was the result of "radicalization of the conservative movement and the Republican party." Michael Edison of the Southern Poverty Law Center similarly wrote that the January 6th participants were the victims of "mass radicalization" (Fischer et al., 2022).

It is not immediately clear, however, what anyone means when they use this term. Radicalization is a complex phenomenon with no single scholarly definition. It can refer either to the adoption of extremist views or the enactment of political violence (Marwick et al., 2022). It presumes a set of "radical" views that are outside the ordinary, which, given the United States' well-documented history of white supremacy, is by no means the case with far-right ideologies in general, let alone the belief that the 2020 election was "stolen." In fact, a survey conducted by Robert Pape at the University of Chicago found that one in five Americans—47 million people—believed

Alice E. Marwick, *The Ordinary Insurrection* In: *Media and January 6th*. Edited by: Khadijah Costley White, Daniel Kreiss, Shannon C. McGregor, and Rebekah Tromble, Oxford University Press. © Oxford University Press 2024.
DOI: 10.1093/oso/9780197758526.003.0011

that "the 2020 election was stolen from Donald Trump and Joe Biden is an illegitimate president" (Pape & Chicago Project on Security and Threats, 2021, p. 12). A smaller but still significant number of people (21 million) believed that political violence was necessary to restore Trump's presidency (Dias & Healy, 2022). Among Republicans, surveys consistently find that about 70% believe the election results were illegitimate (Greenberg, 2022). Indeed, the Republican Party has repeatedly characterized the January 6th insurrection as "mainstream political discourse" (Weisman & Epstein, 2022). Reporters for the *Washington Post,* pointing to the massive success of election denialist rhetoric in the 2022 Republican primaries, wrote, "The collection of falsehoods that committee members have described as 'the big lie' is now a central driving force of the Republican Party" (Gardner & Arnsdorf, 2022).

Given the enduring popularity of this belief, January 6th is better described as the result of *mainstreaming* extreme and conspiratorial beliefs rather than radicalization. Mainstreaming, or "metapolitics," is a well-documented far-right strategy to inject white nationalism or the rejection of liberal democracy into mainstream political discourse (Maly, 2019; Stern, 2019). In Europe, "radical right" populists form their own parties espousing these ideas, such as the National Rally in France, the Forum for Democracy in the Netherlands, and the Swiss People's Party, all of which hold seats in the federal legislatures of their respective countries (Mudde, 2019). In the United States, however, third parties are generally unsuccessful, and so the far right has focused on bringing their ideas to prominence through the Republican Party, a process called "entryism" (Barkun, 2017; Miller-Idriss, 2020, pp. 119–120).

There are three ways to think about this mainstreaming. The first is the increased prominence of far-right ideas in public discourse, such as the Great Replacement Theory, which posits that Jews are attempting to "replace" white people with immigrants and other people of color for nefarious purposes (Ekman, 2022). The second is the (attempted) institutionalization of far-right beliefs through legislation, such as former president Trump's attempts to ban Muslim immigration and end birthright citizenship. The third is the increasing extremism of mainstream Republican political ideals and the leveraging of far-right ideas by establishment politicians to increase and maintain political power (Espinoza, 2021).

In this chapter, I distinguish *radicalization* from *mainstreaming,* arguing that January 6th is better framed as the result of mainstreaming far-right and conspiratorial beliefs into ordinary Republican and conservative politics rather than a radical break with the status quo. I trace how Trump operatives designed the Stop the Steal movement, primed fringe communities like QAnon to collect evidence supporting it, and then repeated that evidence to justify their attempts to hold on to the presidency. Similarly, Trump harnessed the considerable online participation of QAnon to support his efforts to stay in power, given that the Christian Nationalist presence at the January 6th insurrection was deeply intertwined with QAnon's concept of a "Great Awakening." The belief that the election was stolen and the hope that evildoers would be vanquished once Trump regained power created a sense of urgency that was exploited by the Trump administration to spur political violence. Overall, framing January 6th as the result of a complex set of interactions between mainstream Republican messaging and shadowy online spaces helps us better understand the roles of political elites and mainstream media in justifying violent activities and amplifying conspiracy theories.

Stop the Steal

The attacks on the Capitol on January 6, 2021, were unprecedented: never before had a group of mostly middle-class Americans broken into Congress in an attempt to overturn a democratic presidential election.[1] But they were unsurprising to anyone who follows conservative and far-right politics. The links between political violence, the accusation of a stolen election, and the characterization of the Democratic Party as a global cabal combined to create a powerful motive for action. The president, Republican politicians, hyperpartisan right-wing journalists, conservative pundits, and social media users repeated a coherent message about untrustworthy voting machines, widespread voter fraud, and corrupt local officials.

As media sociologist Francesca Tripodi (2022) chronicles in *The Propagandist's Playbook*, the "Stop the Steal" slogan was coined by Trump operative Roger Stone in 2016, but lay more or less dormant until October 2020, when it began trending on social media, spiking directly after the election. Research by Kate Starbird (2022) from the University of Washington found

---

[1] The presidential election of 1876, which led to the end of Reconstruction, was similarly contested but did not result in the same type of political violence and was ultimately decided by the Federal Electoral Commission.

that Trump and prominent conservatives repeatedly set expectations of a fraudulent election during 2020. On May 24, 2020, Trump tweeted:

> The United States cannot have all Mail In Ballots. It will be the greatest Rigged Election in history. People grab them from mailboxes, print thousands of forgeries and "force" people to sign. Also, forge names. Some absentee OK, when necessary. Trying to use Covid for this Scam!

Between May 2020 and January 2021 (when he was deplatformed), Trump tweeted about a "rigged" election 88 times. By setting this frame, Trump and other political elites primed conservative audiences on social media to search for and create false or misleading stories claiming that voter fraud was rampant and the election was illegitimate. These stories were amplified by conservative influencers and activists and reinforced by political elites, creating a shared sense of grievance and urgency.

Disinformation, or false or misleading information spread for profit, ideology, or power, can originate from a number of sources, including elites, so-called fake news and hyperpartisan websites, or on social media (Freelon & Wells, 2020). However, scholarly research on far-right and fringe social media sites, including 4chan, 8chan, Gab, Discord, and Telegram, demonstrates that disinformation is *participatory*, created by groups of people working together to interpret current events, share information, and push frames and stories that support their partisan beliefs (Marwick & Partin, 2022; Starbird, 2022). Often, these fringe groups are used as a sort of disinformative farm team by mainstream politicians and partisan news organizations, which amplify evidence gathered in obscure online spaces that supports their preferred narratives and ideological goals.

QAnon is a far-right conspiracy theory which positions Trump as a righteous savior working to take down an entrenched cabal of murderous Democratic pedophiles. QAnon supporters were key amplifiers of the Dominion conspiracy theory, which provided spurious "evidence" that the 2020 election was stolen. This theory held that employees of Dominion Voting Systems Corporation, a company that makes voting software and hardware used in the 2020 election, were in league with an evil, Democratic cabal and switched millions of votes from Trump to Biden. While theories connecting Dominion to the Clinton family and Jewish billionaire George Soros had floated around far-right social media since 2016, the theory took off in November 2020 after it was discussed in depth on the QAnon message board 8kun. QAnons drew false connections between Dominion, their competitor Smartmatic, the Clinton Foundation, Senator Dianne Feinstein, and Soros's Open Society Foundations. The theory spread quickly to Twitter, where it was amplified by dozens of QAnon-related accounts, including that of 8chan founder Ron Watkins (Collins, 2020). Watkins's claim was picked up by One America News Network, which aired a report on Dominion theories. This report was retweeted by President Trump on November 12. The Dominion theory was repeated two weeks after the election in a press conference at Republican Party headquarters held by Trump-supporting lawyers Rudy Giuliani and Sidney Powell. In this press conference, they tied Dominion not only to Soros but also to Venezuela and even leftist activists "Antifa," a favorite bugaboo of the right (Feuer, 2021). While this exemplifies the "trading up the chain" technique in which extremist views travel from the fringe to the mainstream, it's also clear that the impetus for collecting such information was the strategic deployment of the "Stop the Steal" narrative by Trump and his associates. This demonstrates how participatory disinformation is a complex process in which stories are amplified and guided by political elites and hyperpartisan news sources.

The Great Awakening

QAnon's January 6th mobilization provides us with another example of how mainstream politicians strategically use fringe and extremist groups for political gain (Argentino & Aniano, 2022). Participants in QAnon do not fit the stereotypes of the alt-right or the primarily young, internet-savvy men who typified the participants in far-right online communities during the 2016 election. In contrast, QAnon supporters are mostly white, Christian, and lower-middle-class to upper-middle-class men and women. A survey by political scientists at Denison found that 45% of Evangelicals believed in the QAnon conspiracy theory, and the American Enterprise Institute found that 27% of white Evangelicals maintained that the core tenets of QAnon were "mostly or completely accurate" (Djupe & Dennen, 2021; Jenkins, 2021). More specifically, QAnon is at its core a Christian Nationalist movement, which advocates that America is and should be a Christian nation and that the U.S. government should adhere to and support Christian values (Gorski & Perry, 2022; Whitehead & Perry, 2020).

There are many parallels between QAnon, Evangelical Christianity, and Christian Nationalism. The core tenets of QAnon map neatly to Evangelical concepts of "good" and "evil." QAnon maintains not that liberal Democrats are misguided but that they are evil and in league with Satanic forces. Both communities believe that Satan, demons, angels, and other supernatural figures are material figures that exist on earth and influence human events. Supporters think that a Revelations-style apocalypse called "the Great Awakening" or "Storm" is coming, in which Democratic elites will be held accountable for their crimes through mass arrests and executions. Many QAnons maintain that this event will bring about widespread peace and prosperity, in which Christian values will be upheld in American political culture, widespread sex trafficking of children will end, and knowledge held back by Satanic elites (such as improvements in healthcare) will spread throughout the populace. QAnon supporters widely believed that this would take place in January 2021, spurring their involvement in the January 6th attacks.

The Dominion conspiracy theory demonstrates how QAnon beliefs resonate with and are reinforced by mainstream conservative messaging, particularly during the Trump administration. Former president Trump frequently claimed that the mainstream media is strategically lying to its audience, that the "deep state" was working against him, that a "globalist" world order is undermining American values, and that something is deeply wrong with the current state of America. These are core QAnon messages. Trump repeatedly failed to condemn QAnon, and, claiming that he knew very little about the theory, instead stated that adherents "basically believe in good government" and "are very strongly against pedophilia," and he characterized them as "people that love our country" (Miller et al., 2021). Indeed, during his presidency, Trump retweeted QAnon-associated Twitter accounts such as "Major Patriot" and "MAGAPill" more than 300 times, including 8kun founder Ron Watkins five times (Kaplan, 2019). More recently, Republican politicians Marjorie Taylor Greene, Lauren Boebert, Josh Hawley, and others have "dog-whistled" to QAnon supporters by referencing child pornography and sex trafficking. Given their links to Evangelical communities and strong support for hard-right politics, QAnon constitutes a valuable constituency for far-right Republican legislators.

My fieldwork in QAnon spaces suggests that people participate in QAnon for a variety of reasons. It creates a form of peripheral political participation that makes people feel significant. People participate by interpreting the "secret messages" that Q left for others to find, or simply by consuming Q-adjacent content. Because Q purports to be a Trump insider with high-level security clearance, understanding Q's messages gives QAnons a sense of insider knowledge and global importance. The danger to children that QAnon emphasizes creates a sense of urgency for participants who may believe they must combat widespread sex trafficking, convince other people that QAnon is correct, or harass people who are "evil" or immoral (Jensen & Kane, 2021). (This explains why Pizzagate adherent Edgar Maddison Welch drove to Comet Ping Pong pizza in Washington, D.C. with a loaded assault rifle—he thought he could rescue children he believed were being held in the basement.) QAnon also provides a simple explanation for a complex set of social forces and reinforces the partisan and even religious beliefs of participants. QAnon is an example of a culture which encourages participation, camaraderie, and political involvement; nonetheless, it is antidemocratic and seeks to overthrow elected politicians in favor of Trump-aligned officials (Marwick & Partin, 2022). The large number of QAnon believers among the January 6th insurrectionists shows how such online participation can directly lead to political violence. And Trump's use of the movement for political gain demonstrates how even a patently absurd conspiracy theory can filter into the mainstream if it supports the goals of those in power.

Conclusion

The links between disinformation and political violence are increasingly clear. Disinformation provides a justification for political violence, whether it be mass casualty events fueled by hate, such as the white supremacist shooting in Buffalo, New York, in 2022, or the insurrection that is the subject of this volume. Because disinformation often hinges on stereotypes and conspiracy theories around marginalized identities, it resonates with appeals to whiteness and reinforces the idea that white identity is under threat. By positioning the Democratic Party as corrupt, criminal, or nefarious, Republican, conservative, and fringe communities set the stage for widespread acceptance of the 2020 election as stolen, prompting thousands of Americans to travel to Washington, D.C. to rectify this injustice. Framing disinformation as *solely* the provenance of the fringe, social media communities, or the "radical" ignores the complexity of the modern information ecosystem. Fringe ideas "trade up the chain" to the news media and political elites but are also guided by politicians and pundits who provide roadmaps for participatory disinformation. It is increasingly clear, and deeply troubling, that January 6th is not a break from the mainstream, but the new face of it.

References

Argentino, M.-A., & Aniano, S. (2022, Jan. 6). QAnon and beyond: Analysing QAnon trends a year after January 6th. Global Network on Extremism and Technology. https://gnet-research.org/2022/01/06/qanon-and-beyond-analysing-qanon-trends-a-year-after-january-6th/

Barkun, M. (2017). President Trump and the "fringe." *Terrorism and Political Violence, 29*(3), 437–443. https://doi.org/10.1080/09546553.2017.1313649

Brill, K. (2022, Jan. 5). Jan. 6 and the Americanization of radicalized violent extremism. *The Hill.* https://thehill.com/opinion/national-security/588306-jan-6-and-the-americanization-of-radicalized-violent-extremism/

Broadwater, L. (2022, June 9). "Trump was at the center": Jan. 6 hearing lays out case in vivid detail. *The New York Times.* https://www.nytimes.com/2022/06/09/us/politics/trump-jan-6-hearings.html

Collins, B. (2020, Nov. 13). QAnon's Dominion voter fraud conspiracy theory reaches the president. NBC News. https://www.nbcnews.com/tech/tech-news/q-fades-qanon-s-dominion-voter-fraud-conspiracy-theory-reaches-n1247780

Dias, E., & Healy, J. (2022, Jan. 23). For many who marched, Jan. 6 was only the beginning. *The New York Times.* https://www.nytimes.com/2022/01/23/us/jan-6-attendees.html

Djupe, P., & Dennen, J. (2021, Jan. 26). Christian nationalists and QAnon followers tend to be anti-Semitic. That was seen in the Capitol attack. *Washington Post.* https://www.washingtonpost.com/politics/2021/01/26/christian-nationalists-qanon-followers-tend-be-anti-semitic-that-was-visible-capitol-attack/

Ekman, M. (2022). The great replacement: Strategic mainstreaming of far-right conspiracy claims. *Convergence, 28*(4), 1127–1143. 13548565221091984. https://doi.org/10.1177/13548565221091983

Espinoza, M. (2021). Donald Trump's impact on the Republican Party. *Policy Studies, 42*(5–6), 563–579. https://doi.org/10.1080/01442872.2021.1950667

Feuer, A. (2021, Sept. 21). Trump campaign knew lawyers' voting machine claims were baseless, memo shows. *The New York Times.* https://www.nytimes.com/2021/09/21/us/politics/trump-dominion-voting.html

Fischer, J., Flack, E., & Wilson, S. (2022, Jan. 4). Jan. 6 didn't lower the political temperature—It heralded "mass radicalization," experts warn. WUSA9. https://www.wusa9.com/article/news/national/capitol-riots/far-from-lowering-the-political-temperature-january-6-has-ushered-in-mass-radicalization-experts-warn-proud-boys-oath-keepers-ashli-babbitt-tucker/65-d4d4a795-8f70-4be3-ae12-143e59adbe69

Freelon, D., & Wells, C. (2020). Disinformation as political communication. *Political Communication, 37*(2), 145–156. https://doi.org/10.1080/10584609.2020.1723755

Gardner, A., & Arnsdorf, I. (2022, June 14). More than 100 GOP primary winners back Trump's false fraud claims. *Washington Post.* https://www.washingtonpost.com/politics/2022/06/14/more-than-100-gop-primary-winners-back-trumps-false-fraud-claims/

Gorski, P. S., & Perry, S. L. (2022). *The flag and the cross: White Christian nationalism and the threat to American democracy.* Oxford University Press.

Greenberg, J. (2022, June 14). *Most Republicans still falsely believe Trump's stolen election claims.* Politifact, The Poynter Institute. https://www.politifact.com/article/2022/jun/14/most-republicans-falsely-believe-trumps-stolen-ele/

Jenkins, J. (2021, Feb. 11). Survey: More than a quarter of white evangelicals believe core QAnon conspiracy theory. Religion News Service. https://religionnews.com/2021/02/11/survey-more-than-a-quarter-of-white-evangelicals-believe-core-qanon-conspiracy-theory/

Jensen, M., & Kane, S. (2021). QAnon offenders in the United States. START: National Consortim for the Study of Terrorism and Responses to Terrorism. https://www.start.umd.edu/publication/qanon-offenders-united-states

Kaplan, A. (2019, Aug. 1). Trump has repeatedly amplified QAnon Twitter accounts. The FBI has linked the conspiracy theory to domestic terror. Media Matters for America. https://www.mediamatters.org/twitter/fbi-calls-qanon-domestic-terror-threat-trump-has-amplified-qanon-supporters-twitter-more-20

Kydd, A. H. (2021). Decline, radicalization and the attack on the US Capitol. *Violence: An International Journal, 2*(1), 3–23. https://doi.org/10.1177/26330024211010043

Maly, I. (2019). New Right metapolitics and the algorithmic activism of Schild & Vrienden. *Social Media + Society, 5*(2), 2056305119856700. https://doi.org/10.1177/2056305119856700

Marwick, A. E., Clancy, B., & Furl, K. (2022, May 10). Far right online radicalization: A review of the literature. Bulletin of Technology and Public Life. https://citap.pubpub.org/pub/jq7l6jny/release/1

Marwick, A. E., & Partin, W. C. (2022). Constructing alternative facts: Populist expertise and the QAnon conspiracy. *New Media & Society*, OnlineFirst. 14614448221090200. https://doi.org/10.1177/14614448221090201

Miller, Z., Colvin, J., & Seitz, A. (2021, Apr. 20). Trump praises QAnon conspiracists, appreciates support. AP NEWS. https://apnews.com/article/election-2020-ap-top-news-religion-racial-injustice-535e145ee67dd757660157be39d05d3f

Miller-Idriss, C. (2020). *Hate in the homeland*. Princeton University Press.

Mudde, C. (2019). *The far right today*. Polity Press.

Pape, R. A. & Chicago Project on Security and Threats. (2021). *Deep, destructive, and disturbing: What we know about the today's American Insurrectionist movement*. University of Chicago Press. https://d3qi0qp55mx5f5.cloudfront.net/cpost/i/docs/Pape_AmericanInsurrectionistMovement_2021-08-06.pdf?mtime=1628600204

Starbird, K. (2022, Feb. 17). Unraveling the Big Lie: Participatory disinformation and its threat to democracy. Paper presented at annual meeting of the American Association for the Advancement of Science.

Staten, A. (2022, June 7). Fox News not airing Jan. 6 hearing is "suppression of truth": Ex-FBI head. *Newsweek*. https://www.newsweek.com/fox-news-january-6-hearing-coverage-frank-figliuzzi-comments-1713468

Stern, A. M. (2019). *Proud Boys and the white ethnostate: How the alt-right is warping the American imagination*. Beacon Press.

Tripodi, F. (2022). *The propagandists' playbook: How conservative elites manipulate search and threaten democracy*. Yale University Press.

Weisman, J., & Epstein, R. J. (2022, Feb. 4). G.O.P. declares Jan. 6 attack "legitimate political discourse." *The New York Times*. https://www.nytimes.com/2022/02/04/us/politics/republicans-jan-6-cheney-censure.html

Whitehead, A. L., & Perry, S. L. (2020). *Taking America back for God: Christian nationalism in the United States*. Oxford University Press.

12

The Antidemocratic Feedback Loop

Right-Wing Media Responses to January 6

Becca Lewis

On January 6, 2021, for a brief hour or two, news sources across the country seemed to agree on something. From NBC, ABC, and CNN to Fox News, Newsmax, and One America News, television outlets denounced the storming of the U.S. Capitol and uniformly expressed shock and dismay at the violence that unfolded. It seemed for a fleeting moment like the nation's media sources may have reached a turning point. Perhaps the attack on the Capitol by a mob of Trump supporters was the event that would cause self-reflection among partisan news networks, media personalities, and social media celebrities alike. Perhaps some would even begin to reckon with their own role in facilitating the events of the day.

Of course, that did not happen. I spent the week following January 6 watching and taking notes on right-wing cable news and YouTube channels in the wake of the Capitol attacks. I watched dozens of hours of live television content and YouTube video uploads, and I read hundreds of articles and tweets. And what I found was that these outlets quickly began telling their own stories about the events, stories that shared little with other media responses. Through a range of tactics—specifically, drawing false equivalences, accusing coverage of bias, and claiming victimhood—these outlets performed a virtuosic act of rhetorical jujitsu that allowed them to avoid grappling with the role of the larger Trump movement in the attacks on the Capitol. In their version of events, the true threats to American democracy came from the left—that is, from the Black Lives Matter protests, the so-called mainstream media, and the Democratic Party.

Perhaps these reactions should not come as a surprise. In a deregulated, ratings-driven media landscape, news is guided by outrage, incivility, and a team mentality (Berry & Sobieraj, 2014; Jamieson & Cappella, 2008; Rosenwald, 2019). And yet, as the United States faced a global pandemic, a

Becca Lewis, *The Antidemocratic Feedback Loop* In: *Media and January 6th*. Edited by: Khadijah Costley White, ·
Daniel Kreiss, Shannon C. McGregor, and Rebekah Tromble, Oxford University Press. © Oxford University Press 2024.
DOI: 10.1093/oso/9780197758526.003.0012

president who threatened not to respect the outcome of an election, and ultimately an attack on the institutions of democracy themselves, it was easy to hope that there would be a tragedy big enough, an event horrible enough, to break through to a shared sense of reality. As it turns out, the opposite is true: in a right-wing media environment built explicitly on a rejection of democratic consensus, increasing threats to democracy from right-wing factions only lead to *heightened* accusations against others. In this way, the right-wing media's responses to the events of January 6 have become their own accelerating attack on democratic participation.

Drawing False Equivalences: From Capitol Stormers to Black Lives Matter

One of the first things I noticed about the right-wing coverage I watched was the widespread attempt to shift attention away from the Capitol stormers and onto Black Lives Matter. Of course, the social justice movement Black Lives Matter was not involved in the events of January 6 in any way. But for a range of right-wing outlets, the important thing was claiming that the Capitol storming was nowhere near as bad or as violent as the Black Lives Matter protests that had taken place the previous summer. Importantly, these claims were made by a group of media creators who are overwhelmingly white and who, historically, have stoked racial fears to an overwhelmingly white audience.

This was the case, for example, with the white, conservative political commentator and YouTuber Dave Rubin. Rubin hosts a political talk show called *The Rubin Report*, which is broadcast on YouTube and on the conservative network BlazeTV. His YouTube channel has over 1.7 million subscribers, and many of his videos have been viewed multiple millions of times. On January 6, Rubin (2021) posted a tweet attempting to call attention to Black Lives Matter by writing, "One man's burned down Target is another man's stormed Capitol," seemingly indicating that the looting of commercial properties in the summer of 2020 was equivalent to an attempted government takeover. Two days later, on a livestream viewed by over 400,000 people, Rubin and his guests continued this argument. One of them, right-wing commentator Karlyn Borysenko, argued, "[W]e watched for months as Black Lives Matter and Antifa rioted, lit fires up and down the streets, in all these major cities" (The Rubin Report, 2021). If the storming of the Capitol was violent, her words suggested, so too were the left-wing protests of the previous summer.

These narratives continued throughout 2021 and into the hearings of the U.S. House Select Committee on the January 6 Attack in June 2022, growing even bolder over time. For example, the ultraconservative television network Newsmax TV fixated on Black Lives Matter protests as a way of discrediting the inquiries. On June 9, 2022, the first evening of televised public hearings, Newsmax host Rob Schmitt stated, "[W]e saw a lot worse in the summer of 2020 . . . [protestors] that burned major cities in this country down." Continuing with the comparison, he asked, "Where's the hearing on that?" and answered, "Well, they don't have that hearing 'cause they don't care about your life, where you live. Mess with their office building? They go berserk." In other words, Newsmax's account of racial justice protests involved the burning down of major cities, and the storming of the Capitol had been reduced to messing with an office building.

By drawing these equivalences—both in the immediate aftermath of January 6 and in the hearings over a year later—right-wing media necessarily flattened the numerous differences between the events. They suggested that protests in the name of racial justice were comparable to those in the name of refusing a peaceful transfer of power; that the storming of the seat of U.S. government was akin to the looting of chain stores; and that property damage was as harmful as violence against humans. To make these comparisons seem reasonable, outlets also frequently made false claims about Black Lives Matter. (There were no cases of a Target being burned down in association with Black Lives Matter protests in the summer of 2020, nor were any cities burned down.)

Rhetorically, however, these claims were incredibly powerful: they both minimized the harms of the events of January 6, and they simultaneously raised the perceived threat of the racial justice protests that had preceded them. Thus, these narratives promoted the underlying idea that there was indeed a threat to democracy, but it consisted of left-wing activists (and especially Black-coded activists), not the Trump supporters who stormed the Capitol. The equivalences ultimately allowed right-wing media to redirect attention away from the Capitol stormers themselves.

Accusations of Bias: From Right-Wing Media to Mainstream Media

By drawing false equivalences between the Capitol storming and Black Lives Matter protests, right-wing media opened the door to a second popular argument: that the mainstream media coverage of January 6 was biased. Nearly every outlet I watched in the wake of January 6 made some form of this argument. Specifically, media figures claimed that Black Lives Matter protests had received more positive coverage than had the events of January 6. These claims of bias thus rested on the false equivalences between the two events.

This was explicitly the case in Newsmax TV's sister publication online, where, on January 7, writer Michael Dorstewitz (2021) published an article titled "Media Have Hypocritical Double Standard on Trump vs. Black Lives Matter Protests." In the article, he accused the *New York Times* of having "made excuses" for Black Lives Matter protestors who vandalized a federal courthouse in Portland, Oregon, the preceding summer. Similar accusations made their way around Twitter. The same day, for example, conservative columnist Rita Panahi (2021) tweeted, "Same media that defended or rationalised months of mayhem & violence is suddenly shocked by violence." These themes continued to dominate right-wing coverage of the Committee hearings in June 2022, which Newsmax alone called a "clown show" (Newsmax TV, 2022b), a "political smokescreen" and a "partisan spectacle" (Newsmax TV, 2022a).

Some of the figures blaming mainstream media even echoed white nationalist talking points. That is what I found when I watched January 6 coverage from Tim Pool, a highly successful YouTuber with over 2.5 million subscribers across his multiple channels. On the evening of the attack, Pool's frequent collaborator, the conspiracy theorist Luke Rudkowski, wore a shirt depicting the mainstream television news outlets prodding Democrats and Republicans into a civil war (see Figure 12.1) (Timcast IRL, 2021). At one point, they discussed the shirt, and Pool claimed the mainstream media was specifically using terms like "insurrection" to describe the event because they wanted everything to escalate into violence. These claims were unsettlingly like the white supremacist theory that a Jewish-run news media is pulling the strings behind the scenes to incite a "race war."

Just as blaming Black Lives Matter shifted responsibility away from Capitol stormers, blaming the mainstream media shifted responsibility away from right-wing broadcasters themselves. While none of the outlets I viewed was explicitly involved in the attack, some of them (particularly Newsmax and Tim Pool) had spent the previous several months spreading conspiracy theories that the election had been stolen from Donald Trump. By drawing false equivalences and then accusing others of bias, right-wing

Figure 12.1 Luke Rudkowski, appearing on Tim Pool's YouTube channel, wears a shirt depicting ABC, CNN, and CBS telling Republicans and Democrats, "C'mon do a Civil War!"

media outlets inoculated themselves from any potential introspection or outside blame.

Claiming Victimhood: From Democrats to Republicans

Given their false equivalences and their claims of bias, right-wing media helped redirect news narratives away from Capitol stormers and themselves and onto Black Lives Matter protestors and the mainstream media. Building on these narratives, right-wing media made preemptive claims that positioned themselves as the true victims of January 6. Specifically, they claimed that "the left" was bound to exploit the events of January 6 to persecute all conservatives. As in the other narratives, this helped redirect accountability away from the political party whose supporters stormed the Capitol, reframing Trump supporters and Republicans more broadly as the ultimate victims of January 6.

This is exactly the line of argument that YouTuber Ben Shapiro employed two days after the storming of the Capitol, in a segment called "Prepare for the Left's Revenge." As one of the most successful political YouTubers on the platform, Shapiro reaches 4.8 million subscribers, while his news outlet

The Daily Wire reaches another 2.84 million. In his segment, Shapiro (2021) claimed that Democrats were using the events as "a way to make a political gain" by lumping in "every good conservative" and every Trump voter with the Capitol mob. He likewise scolded Joe Biden and Kamala Harris for speaking about unity during their campaigns and then criticizing the stormers: "This should be a time of unity, right?" he asked. "This should be a time when we all come together . . . [but] every crisis is an opportunity when it comes to the left." Indeed, any attempts by Democrats to seek accountability for the events were quickly dubbed divisive, partisan attacks in a moment that required reconciliation (see Figure 12.2).

Other figures made even bolder claims about the threat of persecution faced by conservatives. For example, on January 8, conservative lawyer and publisher Will Chamberlain (2021) tweeted that "the conservative movement is about to face a level of collective discrimination by the institutions of our society not seen since Jim Crow." A few days later, on January 11, the popular conspiracy theorist Mike Cernovich (2021) wrote that "the U.S. is poised for a post-911 crackdown on civil liberties—which was a disaster then and will be a bigger disaster now," following up by likening this outcome to "authoritarianism" and akin to inciting a "civil war."

Right-wing claims of victimization by the left escalated following a series of decisions made by web platforms and publishing companies in the wake of the attack: first, on Thursday, January 7, 2021, the book publishing company Simon and Schuster decided to cancel its book deal with Republican senator Josh Hawley (which had been titled "The Tyranny of Big Tech"); the same day, Facebook banned Donald Trump's account "indefinitely"; the next day, January 8, Twitter permanently banned Trump's account from its services; on January 10, Amazon Web Services stopped hosting the alt-tech platform Parler. Given this series of events, right-wing media shifted their focus away from the Capitol storming entirely, instead raising the alarm about a supposed assault on free speech and censorship of conservative voices, which outlets variously compared to an Orwellian nightmare, a slide into "Communist China," and a "cultural coup."

Once again, this rhetoric grew even more heightened throughout the Committee hearings in June 2022. The real problems, Fox News hosts such as Sean Hannity, Laura Ingraham, and Tucker Carlson argued, were people illegally crossing the border, crime in urban areas, and high gas prices. Hannity called it a "multi-hour Democratic fundraiser" and Ingraham called it a "Kafka-esque show trial" (CNN, 2022). However, perhaps the boldest claims

Figure 12.2 Breitbart homepage as seen on January 6 (top) and January 8 (bottom). Note how the coverage shifted from "Capitol Chaos" to "Democrats Want Retribution, Not Reconciliation."

came from Carlson, who showed his audience that eight television news channels were broadcasting the hearings and told them, "[I]f at any time in your life you've ever made fun of totalitarian regimes that broadcast lies into the homes of the population that they can't turn off, take a look at that. That's happening right now." Tucker's statement showcased the remarkable rhetorical reversal that right-wing media outlets had achieved: the threat to democracy from the attackers had been largely erased, while the hearings meant to investigate those threats became a sign of totalitarianism.

The Antidemocratic Feedback Loop

Overall, as I consumed right-wing media on January 6 and beyond, the consistency and breadth of responses was striking. As early as the day of the Capitol storming itself, newscasters and commentators were deflecting blame away from the very people doing the storming—as well as the media outlets that had stoked their fears in the first place—and toward racial justice activists, other media outlets, and supporters of the Democratic Party. Just as important, they had reframed themselves as the true victims of January 6, against forces from the left that would allegedly try to persecute them. From the first week of responses to the storming to the hearings coverage over a year later, right-wing media coalesced around a shared set of narratives that placed the blame squarely on the shoulders of their opponents.

It's worth noting that none of these individual strategies or lines of argument was new or unique to January 6. Indeed, right-wing media personalities have been claiming that the mainstream media has a liberal bias since the 1950s (Hemmer, 2016), and they have a long history of adopting a shared sense of victimhood and co-opting the language of oppressed groups for their own purposes (Bebout, 2020). Media outlets across the ideological spectrum have likewise historically promoted stereotypes of Black criminality and violence (Dixon, 2011). Nor is the combative style here new: economic incentives and a radicalized Republican Party have created a media environment driven by outrage and vilification of opponents for over 30 years (Berry & Sobieraj, 2014; Jamieson & Cappella, 2008; Rosenwald, 2019).

Nonetheless, there are two aspects of January 6 coverage in right-wing media that I believe are particularly extraordinary. First, the reactions to January 6 were a case where false equivalences, accusations of bias, and claiming of victimhood were all embraced together, simultaneously, and in which each of these strategies helped bolster the other. The combination of these approaches suggests that, as antidemocratic actions among far-right groups have escalated in recent years, right-wing media has combined tactics of redirection and reversal. That is, as democratic crises have intensified, right-wing media figures have not seen cause for reflection but rather have built stronger metaphorical armor to shield themselves from accountability.

Second, these strategies, when used together, reveal an escalating feedback loop between antidemocratic actions and their media coverage. As far-right actions against the state escalate, right-wing media attacks on opponents also continue to escalate. To be able to equate the storming of the Capitol with Black Lives Matter protests, right-wing media must suggest that the latter protests were far more violent and destructive than they were. To claim victimhood against the left, they must equate their opponents to totalitarians suppressing dissent or civil rights protests. In short, antidemocratic escalation on the ground fuels further antidemocratic escalation in the media. And, as the right-wing media coverage of the 2020 election shows, antidemocratic conspiracy theorizing in the media helps create the justifications for antidemocratic action on the ground.

References

Bebout, L. (2020). Weaponizing victimhood: Discourses of oppression and the maintenance of supremacy on the right. In A. Nadler & A. Bauer (Eds.), *News on the right: Studying conservative news cultures* (pp. 64–83). Oxford University Press.

Berry, J. M., & Sobieraj, S. (2014). *The outrage industry: Political opinion media and the new incivility.* Oxford University Press.

Cernovich, M. [@Cernovich]. (2021, Jan. 11). *The U.S. is poised for a post-911 crackdown on civil liberties—Which was a disaster then and will be a bigger disaster now. You cannot enforce authoritarianism against 40% of the country. To do so is to incite a "civil war," which won't be what people think.* [Tweet]. Twitter. https://twitter.com/Cernovich/status/1348462379693080578

Chamberlain, W. [@willchamberlain]. (2021, Jan. 8). *The conservative movement is about to face a level of collective discrimination by the institutions of our society not seen since Jim Crow* [Tweet]. Twitter. https://twitter.com/willchamberlain/status/1347639551683145740

CNN. (2022, June 10). Watch how pro-Trump personalities covered the prime-time January 6 hearing. https://www.youtube.com/watch?v=FvTMeiCPOv4

Dixon, T. L. (2011). Teaching you to love fear: Television news and racial stereotypes in a punishing democracy. In S. J. Hartnett (Ed.), *Challenging the prison-industrial complex: Activism, arts, and educational alternatives* (pp. 106–123). University of Illinois Press.

Dorstewitz, M. (2021, Jan. 7). Analysis: Media have hypocritical double standard on Trump vs Black Lives Matter protests. Newsmax. https://www.newsmax.com/newsfront/media-black-lives-matter-antifa-protests/2021/01/07/id/1004650/

Hemmer, N. (2016). *Messengers of the right: Conservative media and the transformation of American politics*. University of Pennsylvania Press.

Jamieson, K. H., & Cappella, J. N. (2008). *Echo chamber: Rush Limbaugh and the conservative media establishment*. Oxford University Press.

Newsmax TV. (2022a, June 9). The January 6th Committee is a political smokescreen | Sen. Roger Marshall | "American Agenda." YouTube. https://www.youtube.com/watch?v=DI09mIR0Iik

Newsmax TV. (2022b, June 9). This witch hunt is all about going after Trump supporters and voters | Jim Banks. YouTube. https://www.youtube.com/watch?v=w9I27.YFpbSU

Panahi, R. [@RitaPanahi]. (2021, Jan. 7). *Violence begets violence. Same media that defended or rationalised months of mayhem & violence is suddenly shocked by violence.* [Tweet]. Twitter. https://twitter.com/RitaPanahi/status/1347314364815126529

Rosenwald, B. (2019). *Talk radio's America: How an industry took over a political party that took over the United States*. Harvard University Press.

Rubin, D. [@RubinReport]. (2021, Jan. 6). *One man's burned down Target is another man's stormed Capitol.* [Tweet]. Twitter. https://twitter.com/RubinReport/status/134692167913866 8551

The Rubin Report. (2021, Jan. 8). Storming the Capitol: Michael Malice, Karlyn Borysenko, Elijah Schaffer | ROUNDTABLE | Rubin Report. YouTube. https://www.youtube.com/watch?v=M2qmsW0haE8

Shapiro, B. (2021, Jan. 8). Prepare for the left's revenge. Ep. 1169. YouTube. https://www.youtube.com/watch?v=T8MuUwm1HhU

Timcast IRL. (2021, Jan. 6). Timcast IRL—Trump SUSPENDED, woman died, CNN declares insurrection in DC w/ Jack Murphy. YouTube. https://www.youtube.com/watch?v=-zBFYhmkyoQ

PART II

WHAT SHOULD RESEARCH LOOK LIKE AFTER JANUARY 6, 2021? HOW CAN WE PREVENT ANOTHER JANUARY 6, 2021?

Chapters in Part II take up twin questions of what research should look like after January 6th and how we (as researchers) can prevent another attempted coup from happening. These chapters collectively grapple with how research needs to change, including the development of new conceptualizations of media dynamics and right-wing media and starting from clearer normative commitments to democracy, as well as advocating for those things we do not control, such as better access to platform data. Building off the scholarship from Part I, the contributors gathered here are in general agreement about the political threats to American democracy, how platforms interact with political dynamics to shape them and provide new opportunities for extremist discourse and organizing, and the underlying questions of power that are at stake between vying political and social groups—a theme especially resonant with the chapters in Part I.

Echoing the growing calls across the world in recent years, Megan A. Brown opens this section by laying bare the many limitations of the platform data that researchers have available to understand events such as January 6th, including more broadly humanitarian and political crises. While these scholars pose a number of innovative conceptualizations for research after January 6th, Brown notes that empirically our understandings will always be limited by platform data access. Among the questions that Brown notes cannot be answered are how the insurrectionists organized online, the role of algorithms in promoting extremist content, and the failure (or success) of content moderation after the election. Data access is limited by its ephemerality, the control that profit-driven platforms exercise over it (including what

116 THE MEDIA AND JANUARY 6TH

is completely hidden from view given commercial imperatives), and the limited ways researchers can work with it (as well as the many different types of costs of doing so).

While all scholars in this volume would embrace calls for greater data access, a number of contributors focus on the conceptual, methodological, and normative charge of research after January 6th. For example, building from their work at the Center for Communication and Civic Renewal at the University of Wisconsin–Madison, Sadie Dempsey and Jianing Li shift our conceptual attention. They demonstrate that processes at the local level (such as the dynamics of county Republican Parties) help account for the origination and dissemination of national narratives about election fraud. And national narratives influenced these local processes in a feedback loop. As these scholars argue, these reinforcing feedback loops are essential to the power of disinformation in terms of how and where it potentially takes root and when strategic actors take up election fraud claims (i.e., in counties that have competitive elections and favorable partisanship). Given this, they argue that mixed-method approaches combining quantitative and qualitative inquiry are necessary. Qualitative analysis helps scholars identify narratives designed to undermine the legitimacy of elections that are not as overt as "Stop the Steal" and helps researchers develop theory that guides subsequent analysis. Quantitative analysis, meanwhile, enables hypothesis testing and claims about the generalizability of phenomena. In the end, Dempsey and Li argue that this mixed-method, multilevel approach reveals the complexity of the dynamics that created the context for January 6th to occur.

With a similar emphasis on the systems and contexts that gave rise to January 6th and that should guide analysis going forward, Whitney Phillips and Regina Lawrence argue that the toxic soil of January 6th includes media environments that amplify antidemocratic extremism, such as algorithmic recommendations that connect people to right-wing extremist content, "bullshit" that is economically incentivized and proves fertile ground for social sharing, and identity-based, exclusionary narratives that find easy solidarity given engagement algorithms. Normatively, Phillips and Lawrence argue that we need to not only address what happened on January 6th but also focus on the importance of the mundane machinery of democracy—such as elections boards—and work to analyze and reform the media systems that support and economically incentivize disinformation. Also advancing a twin conceptual and normative argument, Yunkang Yang argues that right-wing media outlets are actually "political organizations," which is reflected not only in their content and use of media in the service of politics (see White, this volume) but also in the "semi-clientelist" relationship some of these outlets enjoy with billionaire financiers, who use them to pursue political objectives, including interventions within the Republican Party's coalition. Through this lens, Yang reveals how in the days after the attempted coup, sites such as the One America News Network, Breitbart, and the Daily Caller actively fundraised for Republicans who contested the legal election results. These and other findings lead Yang to argue that, normatively, scholars need to assess whether these political outlets are compatible with democracy.

Anthony Nadler also offers a conceptual, methodological, and normative argument for research after January 6th. In a complementary analysis to Lewis (this volume), Nadler analyzes conservative media claims that Democrats were going to use January 6th to their advantage and blame all conservatives for the violence while liberal elites looked down on them. Nadler argues that these are all elements of conservative news cultures, the study of which requires analysis of media and meanings, social and political identities, and emotion and attachment as they take shape within media systems at historical moments in time and amid different technological infrastructures. Similar to others in Part II looking to the normative ends of research, Nadler urges us to clearly embrace the mission of critical scholarship, centering our values as scholars as a means of achieving rigorous analysis. After January 6th, Nadler calls for more research on the ecosystem of large-audience, influential outlets such as conservative local news, podcasts, and Fox News, the ways that conservative news cultures shape conservative and Republican Party politics, conservative ideals for what the polity should be like, and the identity work that helps to shore up racial orders but also makes variegated identity appeals, including to nonwhite racial and ethnic groups across cross-cutting identities.

As for what is to be done to prevent another January 6th, scholars here offer different answers. Cynthia Burack urges us to critically examine our own biases and identity-based group commitments as a means toward recognizing our own affective polarization (i.e., negative feelings toward opposing partisan and social groups) and identify the sources of it. At the same time, Burack argues that politically left-identifying academics should think about how to promote the salience of shared "American" identities. This includes recovering an American patriotism on the left, as well as recognizing the common bonds of shared sacrifice across the political aisle. Taking a different approach, Daniel Kreiss argues that the interdisciplinary

118 THE MEDIA AND JANUARY 6TH

field of researchers concerned with threats to democracy needs to move from its empirical and normative concern over polarization to talking about status threats. This requires centering an understanding of both social structure (the relative position of varying groups in societies) and perceptions of those positions as well as threats to them. As scholars in this volume document (Thompson, Young), in the case of January 6th, Trump and his Republican allies told a clear story that the dominant coalition represented by the party—whites and white Christian nationalists—was under significant threat from those formerly marginalized in America's racial and social hierarchy.

It is only by acknowledging that the January 6th attack was political violence rooted in political interests that we can work to prevent another one. Indeed, reflecting this, a number of scholars in Part II focus on norms and the role of the scholar in public life. For example, taking up the case of conservative legal scholar John Eastman, who abetted Trump's efforts to illegally overturn the election and seize power, Dave Karpf argues that we must defend important norms by repeatedly and vociferously shaming and shunning those who lied to the public about the election. Otherwise, Karpf warns, there will be no norms against lying to the public or attempting to subvert the peaceful transfer of power—and that will surely mean another attempt on U.S. democracy. Meanwhile, Lewis Friedland reminds us that not all states are the same; they vary widely in their racial demographics, media ecosystems, and political contexts. Yet states are central to keeping authoritarians from the highest office in the country, and there is an urgent need to check the growing illiberalism of Republican state parties looking to undermine competitive elections. If political communication scholars are to matter in the struggle to hold onto democracy, they should focus on "usable, practical questions" centering democracy that are accessible and useful to citizens and political activists. Political communication scholars should abandon false equivalence, and clearly recognize that achieving necessary democratic reforms requires the Democratic Party to assume and hold political power. Finally, Friedland argues that researchers need to see themselves as "scholar-citizens" with a bevy of skills that can be put in the service of defending and promoting democracy and finding pathways to power for those who would protect it.

Meredith Clark argues for the much-needed transformation of an adjacent, democracy-serving institution: journalism. Clark argues for what she calls "reparative journalism," which is oriented toward the creation of a more equitable society, and shows us how coverage of an event such as January 6th would look different through this lens. Reparative journalism would center analysis and coverage of the racial dynamics of January 6th, see them as part of a broader historical campaign of white symbolic and physical violence designed to maintain political power (see also Tripodi, this volume), and ground understandings of them in the context of America's racial politics. Like scholarly calls for the transformation of research in these chapters, reparative journalism would also have an explicit normative lens of centering work towards multiracial, multiethnic democracy. Indeed, reparative journalism would explicitly *embrace* the browning of America as an opportunity for social and civic repair.

13

Online Data and the Insurrection

Megan A. Brown

Marked by a pandemic, protests, and a momentous presidential election, the events of 2020 and early 2021 played out largely online. As the COVID-19 pandemic took hold and in-person social and political events were canceled, social media platforms saw huge increases in posting volumes. And even large-scale protests, such as those against police violence, held in the wake of the murder of George Floyd, were accompanied by large surges in online activity. While social media spaces offered a place for community in isolation, a place for grieving loss and organizing in protest during a difficult year, they also enabled the spread of misinformation and conspiracy theories at an unprecedented scale. Early in the pandemic, conspiracy theories about the origin of the coronavirus, harms from vaccines, and government involvement in COVID's spread proliferated across social platforms. And as the presidential election approached, conspiracy theories and misinformation about a pandemic-altered vote propagated further, culminating in the January 6th insurrection, when violent protestors stormed the U.S. Capitol building in an attempt to overturn the results of the election.

In a year of momentous events, a variety of questions remain about the role of online platforms in political life. But perhaps none loom larger than the questions regarding the role of these platforms in fomenting the January 6th insurrection. When and how did insurrectionists use social media platforms to organize? How did platform use affect individuals' perceptions of election legitimacy? Was this driven by the platforms' own recommendation algorithms? How were content moderation policies regarding election misinformation enforced, and what was their effect?

Unfortunately, many of these questions cannot be answered. There are many long-standing challenges in digital data research broadly speaking, often related to social platforms and the way they grant (or restrict) researchers' access to platform data (Bruns, 2019; Freelon, 2018; Lazer et al., 2020; Tromble, 2021; Tucker & Persily, 2020). Platforms limit researcher access to data in

Megan A. Brown, *Online Data and the Insurrection* In: *Media and January 6th*. Edited by: Khadijah Costley White, Daniel Kreiss, Shannon C. McGregor, and Rebekah Tromble, Oxford University Press. © Oxford University Press 2024.
DOI: 10.1093/oso/9780197758526.003.0013

three ways: (1) restricting the data they choose to make publicly available, (2) restricting which researchers they grant access to, and (3) requiring advanced tools and technical skills for researchers to properly access and analyze the data. However, the insurrection poses additional challenges to social platforms' data sharing operations. Thus, when platforms (or platform users) removed election fraud-related content following the insurrection, the data for that content was no longer available to researchers, journalists, and other stakeholders. The ephemerality of this data[1] creates challenges for both data collection and research replicability. These challenges, both data ephemerality and platform limitations on researchers, affect what questions we can answer about the insurrection and the role online platforms played.

Broader Data Access Challenges

The first challenge researchers face when working with online platform data is related to data access. There are several factors limiting researchers' access to data, including platforms making data available via public application programming interfaces (APIs),[2] platforms deciding which researchers get access to the APIs, and researchers' resources for collecting and maintaining large data sets of online data.

Across mainstream platforms such as Twitter, Facebook, and YouTube, researchers are limited to studying data available via the platform's APIs. In some cases, like Facebook and Instagram, researchers have had extremely limited access to platform data in the wake of the Cambridge Analytica scandal (Bruns, 2019; Tromble, 2021). During the 2020 election and after the insurrection, researchers could access Facebook or Instagram data only through Crowdtangle, which is limited to public pages or groups with high numbers of followers, or the Social Science One URL Shares Dataset, which notoriously contained erroneous data for multiple years (Alba, 2021). On the other hand, platforms like Twitter allow researchers increased access to data beyond the standard API access, including access to full archival data.

---

[1] Data can be removed by the platform itself for violating platform policies. However, it can also be removed because the original author of the content removed it. For particular platforms such as SnapChat or platform features such as Instagram Stories, ephemerality is an inherent feature of the post: It is only accessible for 24 hours after it is posted.

[2] APIs allow two different programs to "speak" to each other. For researchers, APIs are used to collect online data from social media sites using scripts in programming languages such as R or Python.

ONLINE DATA AND THE INSURRECTION   123

However, while mainstream platforms such as Facebook, Twitter, YouTube, Instagram, and Reddit have public-facing data APIs or data archives, alternative platforms—such as Gab, Gettr, and Rumble—offer no public APIs or data access. This presents unique challenges for studying the insurrection in particular. While many election fraud conspiracies spread on mainstream platforms, they also flourished on alternative platforms such as Gab, Rumble, and Parler.[3] These platforms remain largely inscrutable to researchers since data from them is not readily available to researchers within the terms of service.

Beyond simply providing a public API, platforms can also limit who outside the company can access the API. In the most liberal of cases, researchers must get an account with the platform to get access to data. In practice, many platforms require researchers to provide a use case, defining the parameters of the research project and what types of data analysis will be conducted on any data collected from the API. In one of the most restrictive examples, external researchers must partner with researchers internal to the platforms to get access to data and may require legal reviews of articles before they can be publicized or filed for peer review. On the other hand, researchers can collect data adversarially outside the explicit permission and sanctions of the platform, typically via web scraping (Freelon, 2018). However, this can come at a substantial cost. While this type of data collection allows for the most distance between a researcher and the platform they are researching, the costs for collecting data using adversarial methods can be high.[4] In addition to risks of platform sanctions and legal actions, adversarial data can be much more expensive to collect. While APIs are designed to be stable and consistent over long periods of time, the interfaces that researchers may scrape data from are subject to change as platforms perform regular updates. This can cost researchers valuable time and money, requiring that they update their data infrastructure much more frequently than if they relied on API access.

---

[3] In addition to these platforms, following the major deplatformings after the insurrection, new antimoderation platforms have proliferated, including Gettr, a Twitter clone, and Truth Social, a Twitter-like social media platform operated by Trump's new media company. The proliferation of these alternative platforms presents additional challenges for researchers in understanding how individuals consume different content across platforms and how this content spreads across platforms.

[4] For example, in October 2020, Facebook attempted to shut down New York University's Ad Observatory, a project that collects Facebook ad data from users who consent to sharing their data with the Observatory, for violating their terms of service regarding bulk data collection (Horwitz, 2020). The researchers running the Ad Observatory later lost their Facebook accounts and access to other Facebook data platforms, including CrowdTangle and the Ads Library.

Finally, access to data is predicated on a certain amount of resources and technical expertise for researchers, meaning only the most resourced researchers and research centers can undertake the types of large-scale data collections often required to conduct platform research (Lazer et al., 2020). Bills for collecting and storing the data on cloud services such as Google Cloud Platform or Amazon Web Services can be thousands of dollars per month. In addition, once researchers have the financial resources to collect and store the data, they must also have the technical expertise to set up data pipelines and architecture for collecting, storing, and analyzing the data. While programming training is becoming increasingly common in social science doctoral programs, many researchers still do not receive training in DevOps or Information Technology operations. Unfortunately, because of the wide variety of platform data sharing practices, if researchers aim to study more than one platform, they have to repeat infrastructure set up many times, resulting in more time and financial resources spent to collect and store data. Researchers without these kinds of funds and knowledge may be unable to collect and analyze the data required to answer research questions about the role of online platforms in the insurrection.

The Challenge of Ephemerality

One of the main challenges when working with online data related to the insurrection is that online data is ephemeral. The data exists only as long as the post remains on the platform, so when posts are removed by users or the platforms themselves, researchers can no longer access the data. While the content moderation policies that platforms implemented in the wake of widespread election fraud conspiracy theories are a welcome development, hopefully improving the quality of the online information ecosystem, the ephemerality of the data makes it impossible for researchers to answer questions about the roles of online platforms in fomenting the insurrection. While famous accounts such as Donald Trump's Twitter, Facebook, and YouTube accounts were frequently collected and archived by researchers, journalists, and citizen scientists, other types of data are archived only if researchers were collecting the data in advance.

We already know of many such data sets due to the announcements of platforms themselves. Shortly following the insurrection, Twitter announced the removal of 70,000 QAnon-related accounts and updated their civic integrity policies (Twitter Safety, 2021). Similarly, YouTube announced that they would begin moderating content that raised doubt regarding the results of the election (YouTube Team, 2020), and Facebook announced they would remove content containing "Stop the Steal" rhetoric ahead of the inauguration of President Biden (Rosen & Bickert, 2021). Removing this data without its archiving for research severely limits what researchers can understand about online platforms and the insurrection. Researchers cannot understand user behavior on the platforms because they do not have access to the content that users were posting in the lead-up to the insurrection. Recall earlier questions of substantive importance: When and how did insurrectionists use social media platforms to organize? How did platform use affect individuals' perceptions of election legitimacy? Since the data is gone from the platform, researchers are unable to generate key insights into these research questions.

While previous studies have assessed the representativeness of available APIs in political communication (Gonzalez-Bailon et al., 2014; Tromble et al., 2017), the insurrection presents unique challenges for researchers using digital trace data. Deleted posts or accounts are a feature of missingness in any digital trace research; however, election fraud and insurrection-related posts are much more likely to be removed, either by the platforms because of content moderation policies or by the users themselves. If they managed to collect the data prior to platforms or users deleting the data, researchers are often required to maintain compliance with the platforms' terms of service, meaning they are required to delete data from their own data sets when that content has been deleted on the platform. Methodologies do exist to study moderated data sets; however, these data sets have been shown to be limited because they are removed from their original contexts (Acker & Donovan, 2019).

Platforms' policies also often limit the extent to which researchers can share data with other researchers, prohibiting sharing the content of posts and their associated metadata outside of one's own research team. When other researchers aim to replicate or expand these studies, they are hampered by the ephemerality of this data because it is impossible to recollect. Furthermore, due to the lack of transparency by social media companies regarding their moderation decisions, there are limited ways for researchers to know to what extent the data they have collected is representative of user behavior. Each of these limitations applies to research on any topic. However, they are especially pronounced for researchers trying to study the insurrection, since even more content than usual was removed by the platforms. In other words, substantial amounts of the data needed to study vital questions vanished in the months following the election, and thus our understanding of the influence of these platforms in the insurrection is limited at best.

Recommendations

Models for sharing these types of moderated data sets—that is, data sets containing metadata for content taken down by platforms—exist already. For example, Twitter regularly releases data sets related to information operations on their platforms, making the metadata (with some limitations for user privacy) available to the broader public. In addition, researchers can apply for enhanced access to data sets with more identifying information if that is necessary for their research projects. However, Twitter's data sharing model does not exist on other platforms. Similar data sets exist for Facebook but are limited to a select group of researchers or partners. YouTube and alternative platforms such as Gab and Parler make no such data available. While limited for studying the January 6th insurrection since much of that data has been deleted or removed from platforms entirely, these types of data sharing paradigms can serve as useful models for Twitter and other platforms to share data about political crises playing out online. The data need not be limited to the narrow case of influence operations. In the future, platforms could remove content, preventing further spread and consumption, while making the content available for researchers to study and increase public understanding of the content.

Despite their increased importance, online platforms are still difficult to study, particularly with respect to events where relevant content is removed from the platform. Platform policies on research also generate challenges for researchers who aim to understand the role of online platforms in the January 6th insurrection. Platforms should not be in the position to control what researchers can study about the platforms, whether through direct policies or threats to limit data access. In the immediate term, researchers, where possible and ethical, should collect data necessary to study threats to democracy, regardless of platform policy against doing so. When collecting public data, this potentially means using multiple accounts to overcome rate limits or scraping public data when not available via an API. For private data, researchers should receive full consent from individuals who donate their data and make sure those individuals' privacy is protected throughout the collection, analysis, and publication of findings from that data. In the long term, new data sharing practices between platforms and researchers allowing researchers to fully study online behavior related to political events should be implemented. Finally, both researchers and platforms should build tools that make accessing and analyzing platform data more equitable, increasing the scope of fields and diversity of researchers that are working to understand the role of online platforms in the insurrection.

References

Acker, A., & Donovan, J. (2019, July 20). Data craft: A theory/methods package for critical internet studies. *Information, Communication & Society*, *22*(11), 1590–1609. https://doi.org/10.1080/1369118X.2019.1645194

Alba, D. (2021, Sept. 10). Facebook sent flawed data to misinformation researchers. *The New York Times*. https://www.nytimes.com/live/2020/2020-election-misinformation-distortions#facebook-sent-flawed-data-to-misinformation-researchers

Bruns, A. (2019, July 11). After the "APIcalypse": Social media platforms and their fight against critical scholarly research. *Information, Communication & Society*, *22*(11), 1544–1566. https://doi.org/10.1080/1369118X.2019.1637447

Freelon, D. (2018). Computational research in the post-API age. *Political Communication*, *35*(4), 665–668. https://doi.org/10.1080/10584609.2018.1477506

Gonzalez-Bailon, S., Wang, N., Rivero, A., Borge-Holthoefer, J., & Moreno, Y. (2014). Assessing the bias in samples of large online networks. *Social Networks*, *38*, 16–27. https://doi.org/10.1016/j.socnet.2014.01.004

Horwitz, J. (2020, Oct. 23). Facebook seeks shutdown of NYU research project into political ad targeting. *Wall Street Journal*. https://www.wsj.com/articles/facebook-seeks-shutdown-of-nyu-research-project-into-political-ad-targeting-11603488533

Lazer, D. M. J., Pentland, A., Watts, D. J., Aral, S., Athey, S., Contractor, N., Freelon, D., Gonzalez-Bailon, S., King, G., Margetts, H., Nelson, A., Salganik, M. J., Strohmaier, M., Vespignani, A., & Wagner, C. (2020). Computational social science: Obstacles and opportunities. *Science*, *369*(6507), 1060–1062. https://doi.org/10.1126/science.aaz8170

Rosen, G., & Bickert, M. (2021, Jan. 11). Our preparations ahead of inauguration day. Facebook. https://about.fb.com/news/2021/01/preparing-for-inauguration-day/

Tromble, R. (2021). Where have all the data gone? A critical reflection on academic digital research in the post-API age. *Social Media + Society*, *7*(1). https://doi.org/10.1177/2056305121988929

Tromble, R., Storz, A., & Stockmann, D. (2017). We don't know what we don't know: When and how the use of Twitter's public APIs biases scientific inference. SSRN. http://dx.doi.org/10.2139/ssrn.3079927

Tucker, J. A., & Persily, N. (2020). Conclusion: The challenges and opportunities for social media research. In Tucker, J. A., & N. Persily, (Eds.) *Social media and democracy: The state of the field, prospects for reform* (pp. 313–331). Cambridge University Press. https://doi.org/10.1017/9781108890960

Twitter Safety. (2021, Jan. 12). An update following the riots in Washington, DC. https://blog.twitter.com/en_us/topics/company/2021/protecting—the-conversation-following-the-riots-in-washington—

YouTube Team. (2020, Dec. 9). Supporting the 2020 U.S. election. https://blog.youtube/news-and-events/supporting-the-2020-us-election/

14

What Can "We" Do?

Reflections on Politics after January 6

Cynthia Burack

On January 6, 2021, I was on the National Mall in Washington, D.C. For over 20 years, I've written about the Christian conservative movement, especially its politics and rhetoric on sexual rights. In the course of investigating the movement, I've often attended conservative events, including some on the Mall. I also live mere blocks from the Capitol. So on January 6, I went to see for myself what kind of fruit President Donald Trump's rhetorical and institutional campaign against democracy might bear. As I kept a pandemic distance from the unmasked crowd, I observed men in military-style gear, some of whom no doubt invaded the Capitol later that afternoon. And I saw convivial crowds of people who looked as happy as those who descended on D.C. for the first march and rally I ever attended there: the 1979 March for Gay and Lesbian Rights. Because I had to rush home for a Zoom meeting, I missed what was yet to come that day: the first assault on the Capitol since the War of 1812.

Scholars who have addressed the political dynamics that brought us January 6 have diagnosed right-wing politics and movements by way of "America first" nationalism, populism, racism, xenophobia, and right-wing authoritarianism. These aren't identical phenomena but are, rather, intersecting and overlapping ideological currents, logics, impulses, and ideologies (Berlet & Lyons, 2000; de Cleen & Galanopoulos, 2016). Available modes of interpretation emphasize racism, cultural backlash, demographic change, and the appeal of authoritarianism (Applebaum, 2020; Norris & Inglehart, 2019). Political scientists now routinely identify Trump, his Make America Great Again movement, and the Republican Party that enabled his rise as elements in a process of democratic decay and backsliding in U.S. politics. Similar dynamics of democratic backsliding and rising illiberalism are afoot in other countries. These threats didn't begin with Trump, and it's likely

Cynthia Burack, *What Can "We" Do?* In: *Media and January 6th.* Edited by: Khadijah Costley White, Daniel Kreiss, Shannon C. McGregor, and Rebekah Tromble, Oxford University Press. © Oxford University Press 2024.
DOI: 10.1093/oso/9780197758526.003.0014

they won't subside back to the fringes of American life and politics as his popularity wanes or he's replaced by another, possibly "Trumpier" leader. Thus, we may diagnose Trump as a symptom as well as a particularly malign accelerant rather than the cause of populist right-wing authoritarianism in the United States.

For the purposes of this short chapter, I will stipulate that the assault on the Capitol building on January 6 was the most visible sign of an attempted insurrection; that its goal was to keep Trump in power by force and against the will of the majority of U.S. voters; that, although many of Trump's followers participated in the attack opportunistically, the attack itself was planned and coordinated by right-wing groups with the assistance of national Republican figures; that the groundwork for such an event was laid not only by these right-wing groups but also by members of the administration, Republican elected officials, and prominent conservative opinion leaders; that despite all evidence to the contrary, millions of Americans were persuaded by a campaign of right-wing propaganda that the 2020 election was "rigged" against Trump; that the failure and refusal of Republican elected officials to criticize Trump and his enablers have intensified the threat he and they pose to American democracy; and that, unwilling as too many Republican elites are to repudiate it, a firehose of disinformation continues to threaten the future of democratic institutions. Many of these factors were facilitated and supercharged by the proliferation of online platforms (Brown, this volume) and digital organizing (Waisbord, this volume).

I stipulate all these points not just because they're accurate but because in this essay I want to express a different set of concerns. Among other questions, contributors to this volume were challenged to consider how we can prevent another January 6, 2021. In my response, I choose to emphasize the *we* in this question because what efforts we engage in to prevent another January 6 are likely to vary depending on who "we" are and where we're situated, both in terms of the roles we inhabit and where we and those with whom we identify are located on a left–right political continuum. I analyze right-wing beliefs, discourse, and media as an academic who identifies with the political left. I also grew up working class, the first member of my extended family to enroll in college, and this background animates my interest in Americans who distrust progressive politics.

Thus, when I ask myself what I and others like me can do to prevent another such assault on liberal democracy, I argue that we shouldn't interpret the exhortation *only* as another invitation to "call out" and condemn the political right. Rather, I believe we can take this urgent appeal as an opportunity to ask what those of us who see Trump and his movement as a threat to civil liberties, rule of law, and other crucial features of liberal democracy can do to protect fragile political institutions and improve political discourse. In that spirit, I offer two proposals and brief final reflections.

Two Modest Proposals

What can *we* do? No doubt there are many things we might do to push back against democratic backsliding in the United States. Here, I suggest only two interventions that concerned citizens and scholars on the political left can make in a context of threats to democracy. First, we can recognize the likely signs, in ourselves and those with whom we share political affinities, of "affective polarization" and the deformations of politics and public discourse such polarization can occasion. Second, we can examine our orientation toward our own U.S. citizenship—in particular, considering a "liberal" or "progressive patriotism" that can signal a commitment to shoring up flawed and vulnerable liberal democratic institutions.

The Problem of Affective Polarization

My first suggestion is that we work to recognize and minimize the effects of affective polarization, "a natural offshoot of [a] sense of partisan group identity: 'the tendency . . . to view opposing partisans negatively and copartisans positively'" (Iyengar et al., 2019, p. 130; Tappin & McCay, 2019). In plain language, affective polarization means "colder feelings, more negative trait attributions, and greater social distance" between opposing political camps in American life (Huddy & Yair, 2021, p. 183). Such a tendency, grounded in attachments to social identity groups, is perennial; as psychologist Jonathan Haidt notes, "we're born to be righteous, but we have to learn what, exactly, people like us should be righteous about" (2013, p. 31). Even so, political scientists agree that recent "changes in the contemporary political and media environment have exacerbated the divide" between the two sides in American politics (Iyengar & Westwood, 2015, p. 691).

One manifestation of affective polarization is what the scholar and Democratic strategist Ruy Teixeira (2021) calls the "Fox News fallacy." By this, Teixeira means "the idea that if Fox News . . . criticizes the Democrats for X then there must be absolutely nothing to X and the job of Democrats is to assert that loudly and often." At first glance, it might appear that Teixeira is referring to policy differences between Democrats and Republicans, the traditional context of polarization. But he observes that issue and policy divergence can become secondary to a repudiation of anything associated with the other side in a constant reenactment of highly bifurcated, culture-war enmity. Such enmity can prevent us from perceiving problems that should be addressed democratically, either because they have been identified by the other side or because they primarily affect Americans who don't identify with "our" side.

One suggestion by scholars of affective polarization is that we make efforts "to shift the salience of respondents' partisan identities." What this means in practice is acknowledging that "partisan animus"—dislike, distaste, contempt, or hatred of those on the other side of U.S. politics—"subsides" "when we bring forward what unites Democrats and Republicans, rather than emphasizing what divides and differentiates them" (Iyengar et al., 2019, p. 140). Even as we criticize elements of the political beliefs and commitments of those with whom we disagree, treating them as fellow citizens can lower the temperature of politics and humanize those on both sides (Levendusky, 2017). The prescription to "shift the salience of . . . identities" leads me to my second suggestion: that we shore up our own commitment to liberal democracy by rethinking our tendency to distance ourselves from membership in a community defined by U.S. history and institutions.

A Patriotism for the Left

Like their forebears in the tumultuous 1960s, well-educated young Americans today identify overwhelmingly with the political left, and many want no part of a patriotism that they associate with right-wing politics. I teach at a flagship public research university and, especially in recent years, my students have affirmed that they have no interest in any version or conceptualization of patriotism, even one that might, as the progressive scholar Todd Gitlin suggests, enable "the work of civic engagement—the living out of the democratic commitment to govern ourselves" (2003, p. 125). Indeed, I think my students are typical of many of their peers when they express a desire to "burn it [the U.S. government and/or U.S. institutions] down," presumably to annihilate all the errors of our collective past and inaugurate a process of atonement.

While those on the political left have long repudiated patriotism as tantamount to approval of, for example, racism, xenophobia, misogyny, militarism, and climate change denial, Americans on the political right have traditionally embraced patriotism. However, Christian conservatives increasingly disparage and disidentify with the United States because of Americans' support for abortion and LGBTQ rights (Burack, 2022, pp. 40–43). Likewise, elements of the far right mainstreamed by Trump have become contemptuous of American liberal democracy and openly advocate for illiberalism and authoritarianism (Bump, 2022; Main, 2018, pp. 195–209). I'm not at all surprised to learn of a pro-Trump activist whose online handle is "Burnitdown" because destroying the United States in order to remake it as a utopia is an order of business for many on the right as well as the left (McCrummen, 2022). When my students encounter such anomalies of political alignment, they're surprised to realize that they may now be misapprehending Trump followers—that they may, in fact, have more in common with those they despise than they would have imagined. Realizing such a continuity between some communities of the right and left can catalyze productive rethinking on the ethics and pragmatics of patriotism in an imperiled liberal democracy.

The view that liberals and progressives should embrace a kind of patriotism in response to political extremism has been offered by scholars such as Timothy Snyder (2017), whose "lessons from the twentieth century" include #2, "defend institutions" (pp. 22–25) and #19, "be a patriot" (pp. 111–114). Practical political actors, including civil rights advocates and political strategists, also recommend patriotism as a matter of values and practical reason. For example, in May 2022, I received a subscriber email from Norman Lear, the white founder of the liberal organization People for the American Way. The subject line of the email was "Patriotism in These Times." In it, Lear professes to be a patriot, which he defines as "loving our country even when it is hard to do—like when . . . 10 people are murdered at a grocery store by a young man whose heart and mind are poisoned by racist ideology." Acknowledging the distance between his values and the values of many on the political right, Lear exhorts Americans on the left *to push and fight and speak out and do everything we can to move our country in a better direction* "*as patriots, and lovers of liberty, equality, and the American Way*" (emphasis in the original).

Theodore R. Johnson (2022) is a Black military veteran, former director of the Fellows program at the Brennan Center for Justice, and a contributing columnist for *The Washington Post*. Johnson concurs with Lear on the centrality of struggle to U.S. history: "[T]he story of America is in large part an anthology of domestic fights, often along racial and ethnic lines, about citizenship, democracy, rights, property, and access to opportunity." Despite those struggles, Johnson writes of himself and other service members embracing the United States as "*our country*": "something we each believed in as well as a thing on which we disagreed." Reflecting on the sacrifices of military veterans of diverse races and classes throughout U.S. history and all that remains to be done for the United States to "reconcile its errors," Johnson concludes that "Americans gave their lives to give the nation the most precious gift possible: more time" (emphasis in the original).

Under extreme circumstances, we may not be inclined to do as Johnson suggests and "work with those we disagree with" for the "survival of America," but under extreme circumstances our choices are constrained. Johnson and Lear suggest one way forward under these dire conditions.

What's In It for Us?

Neither Trump supporters, Never Trump conservatives, nor conservatives who may drift away from Trumpism in the future will magically disappear from the landscape of U.S. politics. Hence, progressives, liberals, center-right conservatives, and others who oppose authoritarianism on moral or democratic grounds must consider a variety of strategies by which to advocate for our values in the context of a liberal democracy in which neither side may realize its maximal demands. One strategy is to remind ourselves that political identities are neither fixed nor completely coherent. For example, ethnographies of groups excavate many more divergences from group doctrine than are apparent from comprehensive depictions of groups as, for example, anti-LGBTQ (Moon, 2004). Over time, many individuals can reconcile themselves to realities they have contested (see, e.g., dramatic shifts in support for interracial and same-sex marriage), leave social groups, and disavow all or part of belief systems they once espoused (Saslow, 2018).

As the hearings of the House Select Committee to Investigate the January 6th Attack on the United States Capitol unfolded, one strategy of the Committee was evident: hold leaders responsible for criminality and unconstitutional behavior while inviting followers, whom Committee members characterized as having been systematically deceived about the 2020 presidential election, to return to normal, constitutional citizenship. None of the strategies I've outlined guarantees that "we" will always win our political battles. But unless we intend to take up arms to force those who disagree with us to yield, it's hard to imagine how we will do so in their absence. My disagreements with Never Trump Republicans such as Representative Liz Cheney (Wyoming) and Representative Adam Kinzinger (Illinois) are, in Yascha Mounk's (2018) terms, the stuff of "ordinary times." But threats to democracy have catapulted us into "extraordinary times, when the basic contours of politics and society are being renegotiated" (pp. 18–19). At stake is the existence of a political realm in which disagreement is possible; I hope we rise to that challenge.

References

Applebaum, A. (2020). *Twilight of democracy: The seductive lure of authoritarianism.* Doubleday.

Berlet, C., & Lyons, M. N. (2000). *Right-wing populism in America: Too close for comfort.* Guilford Press.

Bump, P. (2022, May 23). That the American right hopes to emulate Hungary is telling. *The Washington Post.*

Burack, C. (2022). *How Trump and the Christian right saved LGBTI human rights: A religious freedom mystery.* State University of New York Press.

de Cleen, B., & Galanopoulos, A. (2016, Oct. 25). Populism, nationalism, and transnationalism. *Open Democracy.* https://www.opendemocracy.net/can-europe-make-it/antonis-galanopoulos-benjamin-de-cleen/you-can-use-populism-to-send-migrants-back

Gitlin, T. (2003). Varieties of patriotic experience. In G. Packer (Ed.), *The fight is for democracy: Winning the war of ideas in America and the world* (pp. 105–138). Perennial.

Haidt, J. (2013). *The righteous mind: Why good people are divided by politics and religion.* Vintage.

Huddy, L., & Yair, O. (2021). Reducing affective polarization: Warm group relations or policy compromise. *Political Psychology, 42*(2), 291–309. https://doi.org/10.1111/pops.12699

Iyengar, S., Lelkes, Y., Levendusky, M., Malhotra, N., & Westwood, S. J. (2019). The origins and consequences of affective polarization in the United States. *Annual Review of Political Science, 22,* 129–146. https://doi.org/10.1146/annurev-polisci-051117-073034

Iyengar, S., & Westwood, S. J. (2015). Fear and loathing across party lines: New evidence on group polarization. *American Journal of Political Science, 59*(3), 690–707. https://doi.org/10.1111/ajps.12152

Johnson, T. R. (2022, May 29). Memorial Day—For all Americans. The Bulwark. https://www.thebulwark.com/memorial-day-for-all-americans/

Levendusky, M. S. (2017). Americans, not partisans: Can priming American national identity reduce affective polarization? *Journal of Politics, 80*, 59–70. https://doi.org/10.1086/693987

Main, T. J. (2018). *The rise of the alt-right*. Brookings Institution Press.

McCrummen, S. (2022, June 11). The town crier. *The Washington Post*. https://www.washingtonpost.com/nation/2022/06/12/election-suspicion-georgia-greene-trump/

Moon, D. (2004). *God, sex, and politics: Homosexuality and everyday theologies*. University of Chicago Press.

Mounk, Y. (2018). *The people vs. democracy: Why our freedom is in danger and how to save it*. Harvard University Press.

Norris, P., & Inglehart, R. (2019). *Cultural backlash: Trump, Brexit, and authoritarian populism*. Cambridge University Press.

Saslow, E. (2018). *Rising out of hatred: The awakening of a former white nationalist*. Anchor.

Snyder, T. (2017). *On tyranny: Twenty lessons from the twentieth century*. Tim Duggan Books.

Tappin, B. M., & McCay, R. T. (2019). Moral polarization and out-group hostility in the US political context. *Journal of Social and Political Psychology, 7*(1), 213–245. https://doi.org/10.5964/jspp.v7i1.1090

Teixeira, R. (2021, Aug. 5). The Fox news fallacy. *The Liberal Patriot*.

15

Political Communication Research at a Time of Democratic Crises

Daniel Kreiss

January 6, 2021 is not mentioned in the theme statements of the American Political Science Association's annual meetings in 2021 or 2022. It is not mentioned in the Association's Political Communication division's preconference themes in 2021 or 2022 either. Neither is the word "democracy." These are the nation's premier political science association's gatherings less than two years after an attempted coup at the U.S. Capitol building (see Althaus et al., this volume).

Of course, these are massive conferences. There are many speakers and panels that will address democracy, and threats to it such as January 6th, in some way.

However, the failure to clearly *center* January 6, 2021 and threats to democracy in our field's public statements and research imagination is glaring. If as social scientists we do not clearly, publicly, and consistently state the mortal danger posed by January 6, 2021 and the erosion of American democracy more broadly, research democratic threats with urgency and clarity, and tirelessly work to create a future for multiracial and multiethnic democracy— why are we even gathering?

I believe that the lack of urgency in many of our professional bodies and conversations reflects long-standing normative and conceptual approaches in the field. For too long, scholars in many quarters of the discipline have relied on a set of value-neutral conceptual and methodological approaches that all too easily elide, and even obscure, the nature of threats to democracy in the United States and abroad.

As such, the subject of this chapter is what we should do differently going forward as researchers in the interdisciplinary fields of disinformation studies and political communication if we want to clearly address threats to global democracies.

Daniel Kreiss, *Political Communication Research at a Time of Democratic Crises* In: *Media and January 6th*.
Edited by: Khadijah Costley White, Daniel Kreiss, Shannon C. McGregor, and Rebekah Tromble, Oxford University Press.
© Oxford University Press 2024. DOI: 10.1093/oso/9780197758526.003.0015

First, We Need to Move from Talking about Polarization to Talking about Status Threats

There are many varieties of polarization—enough to be the subject of their own books (and they are). In general, the term refers to the distance between people or groups on any number of measures, including ideology, affect (or feelings toward one another), sociality, and morality. (For a review of the literature on social media and polarization, see Kubin & von Sikorski, 2021.) In comparative literature, polarization is often held up as a primary cause of democratic backsliding (Haggard & Kaufmann, 2021). This helps explain how polarization has become an international research phenomenon over the past decade—so much so that it has become the de facto democratic normative concern of the field (e.g., Tyler & Iyengar, 2022).

This is the wrong view (see Kreiss & McGregor, 2023). Polarization is a symptom of underlying democratic or political inequalities, not the cause (Stewart et al., 2021). Polarization is often just more visible, easier to study, and politically neutral to talk about than political, racial, economic, and social inequalities. It is more ready to hand for scholars as a concept. But in relying on narratives of polarization, scholars embrace a fundamental value-neutralness that obscures what should be our real concerns.

As the political theorist Juliet Hooker (2009, p. 10) has argued, there is a "racialized politics of solidarity" that works against struggles for racial equality. Whites view racism as aberrant and are generally ignorant of injustice. For whites, Black struggles against racism and for justice are polarizing, undermining democratic solidarity. As Hooker argues, the reality is that for whites, solidarity is drawn on the terms of political inequality. If we want "reciprocal relations of trust and obligation . . . an obligation to live with others on terms of fairness, reciprocity, and mutual respect" (p. 4), then first we must have justice. This requires "abandoning the fundamental presupposition of liberal political thought that the state is color-blind and racism is a temporary deviation from the norm" (p. 15).

For a racialized politics of solidarity blind to inequality, look no further than how the right has embraced the language of being antipolarization in its attacks on critical race theory and the 1619 Project. Republican rhetoric across the country often reflects back polarization scholarship in decrying the "divisiveness" that supposedly stems from the teaching of America's racial history. Republicans also condemned efforts to address the reality of January 6, 2021, as "divisive" and "partisan."

From the civil rights movement to Black Lives Matter, the movement for LGBTQIA+ equality to efforts to achieve economic justice, activists who have threatened existing, and unequal, racial and social orders have been attacked for undermining social solidarity.

A better conceptual approach for researchers than "polarization," and one that proposes a causal mechanism theoretically and empirically backed by the research literature, would be to study status threats (Craig & Richeson, 2014; Major et al., 2018; Mutz, 2018; Parker, 2021). The analysis of status threats better places the events of January 6th in the context of a Republican president, his party, and their primary coalition of whites attempting to subvert the legitimate and peaceful transfer of power. The idea of status threats also helps us place January 6th in historical context: it was not polarization that caused the Civil War; polarization was the result of efforts by slaves and Black abolitionists to end slavery (Sinha, 2016). Movements that challenge the dominant social and political status of groups *always* cause polarization; dominant interests in societies seek to protect their dominant status (White, 2018).

Status is both a perceptual and a social structural phenomenon (Gest, 2016; Kydd, 2021; Lamont et al., 2016). During the 2020 election, Trump and other antidemocratic Republican actors pounded out a continual drumbeat of stories about a loss of status for white, white Christian, white rural, and white American men. As they did so, they raised the salience of these groups' statuses under the overarching identity of Republican partisanship, often through identity appeals (Kreiss et al., 2020) and victimhood claims (Barton-Hronešová, 2020)—especially ones that tied together religious and racial identities and conspiratorial narratives (Armaly et al., 2022; Pirro & Taggart, 2023).

As a general matter, a perceptual phenomenon may or may not map onto empirical reality. But in the case of January 6th, the idea of status threat does capture central social and political shifts (but see Thompson, this volume about the lack of any *necessary* valence of those shifts). The growing white (and would-be white) Christian nationalist backlash to a diversifying country—against the backdrop of economic precarity (Baccini & Weymouth, 2021)—where formerly excluded groups demand equality is proportionate to the seriousness of the challenge. This explains the well-documented call among the insurrectionists: "We want our country back." (See, e.g., extensive reporting on and from the event, such as CNN, 2021.)

POLITICAL COMMUNICATION RESEARCH   139

This reality, coupled with the understanding of how status threats are communicated, perceived, and map onto social structures, should be a foremost concern for scholars.

Second, Center Power and Interest in Studies of Disinformation

In the months after January 6, 2021, a dominant narrative of "disinformation" about the election again took root to explain how thousands stormed the U.S. Capitol (e.g., Napoli, 2021), just as it had after the 2016 election. In this account, people were driven to attack the Capitol based on false beliefs they held about the election, especially those propagated on social media platforms. These accounts, however, often leave out analysis of the interests that create and propagate disinformation. And they rarely ask why people might be motivated or why it might be in their interest to believe or cynically cite falsehoods. January 6, 2021, was first and foremost a political problem, the result of a struggle over power and interests—not *primarily* a media environment problem. That does not mean that media are not important. To the contrary, strategic political actors capitalize on and work within media environments to advance their political interests, which are grounded in power, status, and social structures (e.g., Ng et al., 2021).

We have made a lot of strides as a field in understanding the nature, spread, and effects of disinformation. What we have not made equal progress on, however, is our analyses of how disinformation is often a tool in the service of power. Too often researchers privilege individual psychology (such as making assumptions that people are victims of mis- and disinformation), narrowly analyze the distribution of disinformation as if it is simply all around us, and focus on individual pieces of content and messages.

If instead we centered questions of power and interest, we would see that disinformation is often a tool (and an elite one at that) for gaining and securing power for one's group (Soto-Vasquez, 2021). Political elites use disinformation in accordance with larger social, cultural, political, and economic structures, such as conveying threats to status, provoking racial and ethnic hatreds, and creating and exploiting fear (Reddi et al., 2021). We would see that disinformation is often part of concerted campaigns and unfold over long time horizons. And we would see more clearly how strategic disinformation appeals map onto political interests, such as gaining and maintaining power for particular social groups—especially powerful ones (see Muhammad & Nirwandy, 2021; Ziblatt, 2017).

The attempted coup on January 6th looks different in the light of considerations about power and interest—a conceptual perspective that accords much better with the extensive facts gathered by the congressional January 6th committee. In this case, election disinformation was first and foremost a political, elite-driven, top-down phenomenon designed to undermine accountability at the ballot box by both creating and reinforcing perceptions of an illegitimate election (over many, many months, if not years). Republican elites across the country created and deployed election disinformation for *years* (Hicks et al., 2015; Tripodi, this volume), including questioning the security of the vote in racialized terms (i.e., voter identification laws targeting Black and brown people). This provided the context and a set of ready-to-hand narratives for Republican party leaders and candidates in 2020 to help them contest the peaceful transfer of power. This tactic was quite visible even in the wake of the violent assault on the Capitol when Republicans continued to embrace stolen election claims (Strawbridge & Lau, 2022) as well as in postelection, GOP-led opportunistic efforts to restrict the voting rights of racial minorities in municipalities across the country.

For too long, research in the field concerned with disinformation has centered on social media, not the role of elites and institutions such as the Republican Party and Fox News in deploying it as a political tactic (see Kreiss, 2021; Nadler, this volume; Yang, this volume). Even more, public discourse often proposes that those who participated in January 6th were the dupes of disinformation. This might be true for some people who were there, of course (see Graham & Yair, 2023), but it is first and foremost an empirical question. Taking people's potential motivations and interests seriously as reasoning agents, including how they actively engaged with elite "identity leaders" in pursuit of collective goals (Haslam et al., 2022), rather than ignoring or dismissing them or assuming they were manipulated, should be at the forefront of any post–January 6th research agenda (e.g., Gilmore et al., 2021).

The more compelling hypothesis, derived from extensive reporting by outlets such as the *New York Times* and the findings of the congressional January 6th committee, is that many, many people were there for political reasons, such as to secure power and defend their social and political position—including to defend white status at the top of the racial hierarchy. And even if some were deluded by conspiracy, scholars must ask how it is that they were deluded in ways that happen to accord with their particular political and racial interests. To take one example, a QAnon conspiracy theorist and January 6th participant explained his motivations for being at the Capitol in a register that mixes political and racial interest *and* the conspiracy of a stolen election:

> What about Black Lives Matter burning these cities down, and they don't get nothing. We go in, we try to, you know, we can't have a president for four years. He won. Why can't we just have him as the president for four years? (FBI, 2021)

It takes *work* for researchers to actively overlook the sea of white faces, numerous Confederate flags, and symbols of white Christian nationalism on display on January 6th and the presence of white paramilitary groups such as the Proud Boys and the Oath Keepers. This has meant that scholars often provide explanations that fail to diagnose the underlying causes behind January 6th, such as power and political interest. Narratives of election fraud might have provided a proximate reason for some and a legitimating excuse for others, but a primary cause of January 6th is that (dominant) white and white Christian nationalist power is under very real threat. As a prominent report on white Christian nationalism and January 6th concluded based on overwhelming evidence:

> One of the most ubiquitous symbols on January 6 was the Christian cross. . . . Crosses were everywhere that day in D.C., on flags and flagpoles, on signs and clothes, around necks, and erected above the crowd. The Proud Boys also erected a massive cross using ropes in a viral video of the Michigan Capitol (a sister rally, not in D.C.). A cross with "Jesus Saves" written on one plank was featured in some news stories, and it was also paraded next to Alex Jones as he paused on the march to the Capitol, climbed atop a fountain—like a stage—and ranted on a megaphone. The lead image on a New York Times article showed a white cross, maybe three feet tall, atop a flagpole with a "Trump: Keep America Great 2020" flag thrust high above the crowd in front of the Capitol as people chanted "Fight for Trump." (BJC, 2022)

Third, We Need More Explicit Efforts to Synthesize the Insights of Media Scholars and Political Institutionalists in Our Analyses of Democratic Crises

The body of work on democratic crisis or backsliding often only deals with media in a cursory fashion, and often not at all with platforms and social media. Meanwhile, work that centers political institutions in questions of democracy, and even many studies of phenomena such as polarization and political identity in the literature within political science and sociology, often fails to systematically analyze communication and media (see Bail, 2021). Political scientists identify polarization and status threats, but without an understanding of information and communication there is no clear mechanism for how people come to perceive themselves as members of social groups, different from other groups, or perceive that their place in society is under threat (Harton et al., 2022; Solopova et al., 2021).

The literature on political institutions and comparative accounts of democratic backsliding often have very thin understandings of the complexity of contemporary hybrid media systems. Many studies of democratic health often collapse media into categories of "free" or "independent" versus "not free" or "state-backed." In these models, commercial or independent public media are generally seen as independent checks on political authority, and the protection of free expression is used to assess democratic health. Rarely does this literature consider that nonstate, commercial media can weaken democracy, or that free expression can be weaponized in the service of authoritarianism. Media scholars tell us instead that contemporary media may serve antidemocratic ruling or oppositional parties—while still being independent and commercial—such as Fox News, far-right media (Lewis, this volume; Yang, this volume), and "conservative news cultures" (Nadler, this volume). And media scholars tell us how independent, commercial platforms may facilitate the rise of global conspiracy movements such as QAnon that are aligned with and serve as surrogates for right-wing political interests (e.g., Lukito et al., 2023; Marwick, this volume).

At the same time, as detailed above, as a field political communication and media studies would benefit greatly from clearer analysis of what comparativists and institutionalists focus on and the potential role of media in political systems. This includes declines in tolerance, growing views of the opposition as illegitimate, erosion of public faith in democracy, loss of gatekeeping in party nominations, the decreased accountability of political elites, declines in norms among political and social elites (see also Karpf, this volume), and the undermining of the administrative state, rule of law, and institutions. We also should not be limited by what is most visible or accessible to us, including through platform data, at the expense of the data that can reveal the behind-the-scenes coordination that made January 6th an attempted coup.

Fourth, Make the Move from Analysis of Individuals to Analysis of Institutions and Groups

Finally, and more speculatively, I think there is a view that wants to put an "individualizing" instead of a political frame on January 6th. Individualizing and criminalizing January 6th by narrowly hunting down the perpetrators of violence, overly focusing on Trump, or detailing the individuals involved and their motivations takes us away from understanding January 6th as funda-mentally, irrevocably *political* in the sense of being concerned with the distri-bution of power among groups in America. As Mahmood Mamdani (2020, p. 329) has argued, "violence" is

> an act of constructing the political community. . . . Violence is a means of defining who is a member and who is not—where the boundaries of the community lie. As such, political violence tells us that something is amiss in the political community: someone who wants membership is being denied; someone who is a member wants to expel others.

If we take Mamdani's point, we cannot see January 6th as an aberration. It is part of an ongoing, historical project to construct and protect the status of a particular kind of political community: a white Christian–dominant United States. As Mamdani argues, dominant groups need to be seen as much in terms of being survivors of the political systems that created them as nondominant groups, but with collective responsibilities to imagine inclu-sive citizenship, secure and protect access to politics, and compel the state to redress those historical legacies of inequality to afford full democratic par-ticipation. Only by acknowledging that January 6th was political violence, with political objectives, rooted in political history, can we start the work of creating inclusive, equitable, multiracial, and multiethnic democracy and solidarity—where difference is articulated in terms of adversaries, not enemies (Mamdani, 2020).

References

Armaly, M. T., Buckley, D. T., & Enders, A. M. (2022). Christian nationalism and political violence: Victimhood, racial identity, conspiracy, and support for the Capitol attacks. *Political Behavior, 44*(2), 937–960.

Baccini, L., & Weymouth, S. (2021). Gone for good: Deindustrialization, white voter backlash, and US presidential voting. *American Political Science Review, 115*(2), 550–567.

Bail, C. (2021). *Breaking the Social Media Prism*. Princeton University Press.

Barton-Hronešová, J. (2020). *The struggle for redress*. Springer International Publishing.

BJC. (2022, Feb. 9). Christian nationalism and the January 6, 2021 insurrection. https://bjconline.org/wp-content/uploads/2022/02/Christian_Nationalism_and_the_Jan6_Insurrection-2-9-22.pdf

CNN. (2021, Jan. 24). Special report: The faces of the Trump insurrection. https://transcripts.cnn.com/show/csr/date/2021-01-24/segment/01

Craig, M. A., & Richeson, J. A. (2014). On the precipice of a "majority-minority" America: Perceived status threat from the racial demographic shift affects white Americans' political ideology. *Psychological Science, 25*(6), 1189–1197.

FBI. (2021, Jan. 8). Interview of Douglas Austin Jensen. *United States of America v. Douglas Austin Jensen.* https://www.documentcloud.org/documents/21582970-douglas-jensen-jan-6-defendant-case-no-121-cr-00006-fbi-interview-jan-8-2021

Gest, J. (2016). *The new minority: White working class politics in an age of immigration and inequality*. Oxford University Press.

Gilmore, J. N., Hamer, M., Erazo, V., & Hayes, P. (2021). "It's 1776, baby!" Broadcasting revolutionary performance during the US Capitol riots. *AoIR Selected Papers of Internet Research.*

Graham, M. H., & Yair, O. (2022). *Expressive responding and Trump's big lie*. https://m-graham.com/papers/GrahamYair_BigLie.pdf

Haggard, S., & Kaufman, R. (2021). *Backsliding: Democratic regress in the contemporary world*. Cambridge University Press.

Harton, H. C., Gunderson, M., & Bourgeois, M. J. (2022). "I'll be there with you": Social influence and cultural emergence at the Capitol on January 6. *Group Dynamics: Theory, Research, and Practice, 26*(3), 220.

Haslam, S. A., Reicher, S. D., Selvanathan, H. P., Gaffney, A. M., Steffens, N. K., Packer, D., & Platow, M. J. (2023). Examining the role of Donald Trump and his supporters in the 2021 assault on the US Capitol: A dual-agency model of identity leadership and engaged followership. *The Leadership Quarterly, 34*(2), 101622.

Hicks, W. D., McKee, S. C., Sellers, M. D., & Smith, D. A. (2015). A principle or a strategy? Voter identification laws and partisan competition in the American states. *Political Research Quarterly, 68*(1), 18–33.

Hooker, J. (2009). *Race and the politics of solidarity*. Oxford University Press.

Kreiss, D. (2021). Social media and democracy: The state of the field, prospects for reform. N. Persily & J. A. Tucker (Eds.) *The International Journal of Press/Politics* (pp. 505–512).

Kreiss, D., Lawrence, R. G., & McGregor, S. C. (2020). Political identity ownership: Symbolic contests to represent members of the public. *Social Media+ Society, 6*(2), 2056305120926495.

Kreiss, D., & McGregor, S. C. (2023). A review and provocation: On polarization and platforms. *New Media & Society,* 14614448231161880.

Kubin, E., & von Sikorski, C. (2021). The role of (social) media in political polarization: A systematic review. *Annals of the International Communication Association, 45*(3), 188–206.

Kydd, A. H. (2021). Decline, radicalization and the attack on the US Capitol. *Violence: An International Journal, 2*(1), 3–23.

Lamont, M., Silva, G. M., Welburn, J., Guetzkow, J., Mizrachi, N., Herzog, H., & Reis, E. (2016). *Getting Respect: Responding to stigma and discrimination in the United States, Brazil, and Israel*. Princeton University Press.

Lukito, J., Gursky, J., Foley, J., Yang, Y., Joseff, K., & Borah, P. (2023). "No reason [.][I] t/should/happen here": Analyzing Flynn's retroactive doublespeak during a QAnon event. *Political Communication*, 1–20.

Major, B., Blodorn, A., & Major Blascovich, G. (2018). The threat of increasing diversity: Why many white Americans support Trump in the 2016 presidential election. *Group Processes & Intergroup Relations, 21*(6), 931–940.

Mamdani, M. (2020). *Neither settler nor native: The making and unmaking of permanent minorities*. Harvard University Press.

Muhammad, R., & Nirwandy, N. (2021). A study on Donald Trump Twitter remark: A case study on the attack of Capitol Hill. *Journal of Media and Information Warfare, 14*(2), 75–104.

Mutz, D. C. (2018). Status threat, not economic hardship, explains the 2016 presidential vote. *Proceedings of the National Academy of Sciences, 115*(19), E4330–E4339.

Napoli, P. (2021, Jan. 14.) The DC riot is the Sandy Hook of the disinformation crisis. *Wired*. https://www.wired.com/story/opinion-the-dc-riot-is-the-sandy-hook-of-the-disinformation-crisis/

Ng, L. H. X., Cruickshank, I., & Carley, K. M. (2021). Coordinating narratives and the Capitol riots on Parler. *arXiv preprint arXiv:2109.00945*. https://arxiv.org/abs/2109.00945

Parker, C. S. (2021). Status threat: Moving the right further to the right? *Daedalus, 150*(2), 56–75.

Pirro, A. L., & Taggart, P. (2023). Populists in power and conspiracy theories. *Party Politics, 29*(3), 413–423. 13540688221077071.

Reddi, M., Kuo, R., & Kreiss, D. (2021). Identity propaganda: Racial narratives and disinformation. *New Media & Society, 25*(8), 2201–2218. 14614448211029293.

Sinha, M. (2016). *The slave's cause: A history of abolition*. Yale University Press.

Solopova, V., Scheffler, T., & Popa-Wyatt, M. (2021). A Telegram corpus for hate speech, offensive language, and online harm. *Journal of Open Humanities Data, 7*.

Soto-Vasquez, A. D. (2021). Coup with a Q: Misinformation, the US Capitol insurrection, and perspectives from the field of communication. *The Whitehead Journal of Diplomacy and International Relations, 22*, 73.

Stewart, A. J., Plotkin, J. B., & McCarty, N. (2021). Inequality, identity, and partisanship: How redistribution can stem the tide of mass polarization. *Proceedings of the National Academy of Sciences, 118*(50), e2102140118.

Strawbridge, M. G., & Lau, R. R. (2022). House Republican decision making following the Capitol riot. *PS: Political Science & Politics, 55*(3), 484–489.

Tyler, M., & Iyengar, S. (2022). Learning to dislike your opponents: Political socialization in the era of polarization. *American Political Science Review, 117*(1), 1–8, 347–354.

White, K. C. (2018). *The branding of right-wing activism: The news media and the Tea Party*. Oxford University Press.

Ziblatt, D. (2017). *Conservative political parties and the birth of modern democracy in Europe*. Cambridge University Press.

16

It's Not Just the Fruit, It's the Factory Farm

Assessing the Past, Present, and Future of January 6th

Whitney Phillips and Regina Lawrence

Even before rioters crossed the Capitol barricades, the "March to Save America" rally held in Washington, D.C., on January 6, 2021, was primed for conflict. That day, Congress was to certify the 2020 election results. Citing baseless claims of voter fraud, a number of Republican members of Congress had publicly committed to contesting several states' election results, ensuring that the typically mundane, otherwise ceremonial vote would be engulfed in controversy and conspiracy theories. Citing the same false claims of electoral fraud, a hodgepodge of pro-Trump groups, including militia and extremist groups, had coalesced to organize the rally, hoping lawmakers inside the Capitol would overturn the election. The long roster of Big Lie spreaders— most notably Donald Trump himself—scheduled to speak would only add fuel to the fire. Bad news, and perhaps even some degree of violence, was inevitable.

What was surprising—and shocking, and terrifying—was the sheer intensity of the riot that unfolded, captured in a frenzy of real-time visuals: of the rioters storming the Capitol steps; of the mayhem inside the gallery; of roaming bands of insurrectionists laughing and standing at the dais, sitting at Nancy Pelosi's desk, victoriously waving a Confederate flag; of guns drawn at the chamber door as the mob roared closer and closer; of members of Congress in gas masks ducking for cover. Social media posts from inside and outside the Capitol told us even more: that the crowd was chanting to hang Mike Pence, that shots had been fired inside the Capitol, that the House chaplain was leading members in prayer.

Images from that day have circulated and been replayed so frequently that many of us can no longer be sure what we actually saw in the moment and what we only experienced later, as journalists and politicians combed

Whitney Phillips and Regina Lawrence, *It's Not Just the Fruit, It's the Factory Farm* In: *Media and January 6th*.
Edited by: Khadijah Costley White, Daniel Kreiss, Shannon C. McGregor, and Rebekah Tromble, Oxford University Press.
© Oxford University Press 2024. DOI: 10.1093/oso/9780197758526.003.0016

through the remnants, bringing new outrages to light. For many, "January 6th" has become a visceral, jumbled torrent of very time-specific imagery.

Since that day, investigative work undertaken by reporters, researchers, and the House Select Committee probing the attack on the U.S. Capitol has helped establish a more coherent timeline for the torrent. Through this work, we have learned an enormous amount about the concerted, coordinated effort to overturn the election in the lead-up to the riot, including how Republican electors in seven states won by Joe Biden signed fraudulent certifications claiming that Trump was the true winner. We learned that many close advisors told Trump that he had lost the election; there was no evidence of widespread voter fraud. Former attorney general William Barr went so far as to characterize election fraud claims frankly as "bullshit." We have also learned about the links connecting various domestic violent extremist groups, including the Proud Boys and Oath Keepers, whose members traveled to Washington on January 6th because they believed Trump had summoned them there.

The painstaking efforts by journalists, researchers, and investigators to reconstruct exactly what happened on January 6th are impressive and laudable. They are essential to establishing the criminal and constitutional liability of those involved, up to and including the former president, who must be held accountable for the violent storming of the Capitol. These efforts are also crucial to helping the public make sense of that chaotic day.

Yet the attack on democracy didn't end on January 6th. It continued well after the Capitol was cleared. It continues now.

If we are to fully understand what happened on January 6th itself, produce the most eye-opening and historically salient research about it, and help prevent another attack, we need to think about January 6th as one particularly conspicuous moment in a long-standing and *ongoing* assault on democracy.

Tilling the (Big Lie) Fields

To do so, it may be helpful to think of the continued assault on democracy as an antidemocratic agribusiness in which industrial information polluters have continued to pump out toxicity long after that season's harvest has rumbled off to market.

On an actual farm, a harvest reflects, by definition, yesterday's effort, with the crops' sell-by date emphasizing its shift to past tense. But the farm

148   RESEARCH AFTER JANUARY 6, 2021

remains a present-tense operation, with future-tense implications: So long as the soil and environmental conditions that cultivated that crop remain, so long as the farm equipment works in the same ways by operators of the same skill with the same market incentives, those same crops can and will continue to grow.

Similarly, while the chaos of the January 6th riot has long been cleared by the Capitol police, the soil and environmental conditions that existed before the attack remain. This includes wide, deep, and growing networks of domestic extremists eager to harness the current political moment to boost recruitment. (As one extremist group leader recently mused, "There's a pretty big percentage of people who think like us" [Dickson, 2021].) It also includes a political landscape that helps normalize white nationalist beliefs and extremist violence (Belew, 2022; Smith, 2022), even among a swath of Americans who are not active members of such groups (ADL, 2022). To this end, dark money funders are fertilizing belief in antidemocratic conspiracy theories (Pogue, 2022), seeds already sown by a long American history of far-right antigovernment sentiment, conspiratorial thinking, and white supremacy (Anderson, 2016; Diamond, 1995; Morone, 1998).

Moreover, the farm equipment integral to the January 6 attack—a hospitable digital media environment that allows far-right messages to root down and spread across many fields—also remains. From recommendation algorithms to cable companies bundling right-wing channels into customer subscriptions, this machinery transmits and amplifies conspiratorial narratives about liberals, the Biden administration, and anyone accused of threatening the beliefs, speech, and votes of "real" Americans (that is to say, MAGA conservatives). This machinery ensures the crops aren't just brought to the marketplace of ideas, but that they're displayed in a prime spot. Before January 6th, the machines of doubt were humming along, ensuring that the "Stop the Steal" crop was distributed quickly and efficiently. After January 6th, there was an initial slowdown thanks to a wave of social media takedowns—most notably Twitter banning Trump. But the root of the Big Lie was never excised, and those takedowns were quickly roped into conservative discourses about censorship, feeding into the same industrial farming techniques that preceded January 6th.

On an actual farm, soil conditions and farm equipment are two distinct categories. In the context of industrialized disinformation farming, soil and equipment are more symbiotically connected: as the soil is fertilized, tilled, and cultivated by the equipment, the equipment is necessitated, strengthened, and weaponized by the soil. Put less delicately: the antidemocracy machinery is powered by bullshit, and bullshit is fortified by antidemocratic machinery.

In this context, the contemporary Republican Party is both machinery and soil: active cultivator of antidemocratic action and fertile ground for antidemocratic belief. The result is to bring even worse fruit to even more markets as institutional efforts to propagate the Big Lie of a stolen 2020 election are complemented by the party's efforts to commit election fraud of its own. As one Trump-endorsed candidate recently put it, "The election system is rigged, and who best to steal it but our clerks" (Przybyla, 2022), a sentiment reflected in a series of news stories that broke as we worked on this essay. These included the revelation that several Republican gubernatorial candidates were removed from the ballot due to fraudulent signatures on their nominating petitions, and that another Republican candidate, Ryan Kelly, was arrested by the FBI for his role in the Capitol attack (Paybarah, 2022).

The relationship between machinery and soil is also evident in the spread of narratives about how the "real" American *us* is under threat from the liberal un-American *them*. Some of these beliefs are tethered to specific accusations of voter fraud, the bedrock of the "Stop the Steal" movement following the 2020 election. Others are more diffuse, like the idea—publicly embraced by many Republican politicians (Blake, 2021; Luscombe, 2022)— that Democrats are trying to dilute "real" American votes by easing immigration restrictions or simply making it easier for citizens in heavily Democratic areas to vote. These kinds of messages pump more and more toxicity into the soil. And as they do, more farm equipment is added to support production, ensuring that existing audiences of these messages get more of what they want *and* that the messages filter out to new audiences. Demand fuels supply, and supply feeds demand.

Considered from this perspective, even the most critical legal investigations, like the work of the House Select Committee, and scholarship focused on the specifics of who did what on January 6th and immediately beforehand send the misleading message that identifying, removing, and quarantining the toxic fruits of last year's harvest is enough to save democracy. It is not. Factory disinformation farming is humming along as well as it ever did, maybe even more efficiently, as the energy heading into the 2022 midterms and 2024 presidential election is supercharging the symbiosis between machinery and soil.

By underselling the present-tense threat, systemic changes to soil and equipment become much less likely. Most basically, citizens won't demand changes, disincentivizing their elected representatives from pushing a potentially losing issue too hard. Focusing on what happened rather than what is still happening also underestimates and essentially concedes to the marketing arm of factory disinformation farming. Through dense wraparound messaging spanning social media, radio, and cable news, millions of Americans have been persuaded that the toxic fruit of January 6th is actually health food, and that anyone who says otherwise is part of the plot to steal America away from "real" patriots. This includes the January 6th Select Committee, whose work has been reframed by political and corporate disinformation farmers as yet another effort to shut down conservative speech and install leftist tyranny. (Echoing many of his colleagues, Republican senator Marco Rubio huffed that the Committee was a "complete partisan scam" [Quinn, 2022].)

Where We Go from Here

So what can researchers do? Most basically, they can emphasize the present- and future-tense nature of antidemocratic agribusiness. This means explaining the political mechanisms through which power is being consolidated, including why local election boards matter, why local elections matter, and why civic participation is a key defense against democratic decay. It also means assessing and developing usable messaging around disinformation farming and the market conditions that support it, in the process connecting the dots between the soil, the farming equipment, and the crop.

Research that carefully and empirically documents the networks and activities central to disinformation farming, particularly the role media play, is critical. Building on key research already conducted, we need more thorough documentation and cataloging of *modes and patterns* of online information sharing and content creation in digital networks to better understand how the soil of extremism is being cultivated (e.g., Chadwick & Stanyer, 2022; Di Resta et al., 2022; Krafft & Donovan 2020). And, expanding on existing work, we need a deeper and fuller understanding of the corporate media entities that are so central both to cultivating antidemocratic soil and bringing toxic crops to market on a daily basis (e.g., Confessore, 2022; Nadler, 2020; Peck, 2019).

Above all, mainstream political communication research needs to contend with the fact that the active, deliberate disruption of public spheres (Bennett & Pfetsch, 2018) through factory disinformation farming is not a sideline activity to supposedly "normal" processes of political communication, including agenda setting, framing, campaign advertising, and the like. Antidemocratic agribusiness and its active, industrial production of toxic crops is now an endemic element of contemporary political communication (Bennett & Livingston, 2018; Freelon & Wells, 2020) and must be approached as such: as an ongoing, highly profitable, and increasingly mainstream enterprise. As Bennett and Pfetsch (2018, p. 250) suggest, the field of political communication needs a working vocabulary of concepts that do not "assume the existence of coherent democratic public spheres and media systems" that effectively regulate the antidemocratic agribusiness.

Moreover, policymakers, journalists, civic organizations, mutual aid networks, and other information providers and opinion leaders must address these deeper roots and do so in a way that is clear and accessible to the public. Work that remains ensconced in the analytic equivalent of a grain silo won't be very helpful to anyone. We need to produce a different sort of crop, one that has a greater chance of enriching the body politic. We need to show what will happen if we fail to disrupt our informational systems rather than focusing only on the crises we have managed to avert.

References

Anderson, C. (2016). *White rage: The unspoken truth of our racial divide*. Bloomsbury Books.

Anti-Defamation League. (2022, January 4). A Year after the insurrection, 2020 election lies continue to animate the right. *The Anti-Defamation League*. https://www.adl.org/resources/blog/year-after-insurrection-2020-election-lies-continue-animate-right.

Belew, K. (2022, May 17). The long game of white-power activists isn't just about violence. *The New York Times*. https://www.nytimes.com/2022/05/17/opinion/buffalo-shooting-replacement-theory.html

Bennett, W. L., & Livingston, S. (2018). The disinformation order: Disruptive communication and the decline of democratic institutions. *European Journal of Communication, 33*(2), 122–139. https://doi.org/10.1177/0267323118760317

Bennett, W. L., & Pfetsch, B. (2018). Rethinking political communication in a time of disrupted public spheres. *Journal of Communication, 68*, 243–253. https://doi.org/10.1093/joc/jqx017

Blake, A. (2021, June 14). The GOP's increasingly blunt argument: It needs voting restrictions to win. *The Washington Post*. https://www.washingtonpost.com/politics/2021/06/14/gops-increasingly-blunt-argument-it-needs-voting-restrictions-win/

Chadwick, A., & Stanyer, J. (2022). Deception as a bridging concept in the study of disinformation, misinformation, and misperceptions: Toward a holistic framework. *Communication Theory, 32*(1), 1–24. https://doi.org/10.1093/ct/qtab019

Confessore, N. (2022, Apr. 30). How Tucker Carlson stoked white fear to conquer cable. *The New York Times*. https://www.nytimes.com/2022/04/30/us/tucker-carlson-gop-republican-party.html

Diamond, S. (1995). *Roads to dominion: Right-wing movements and political power in the United States*. Guilford Press.

Dickson, E. J. (2021, June 15). The rise and fall of the Proud Boys. *Rolling Stone*. https://www.rollingstone.com/culture/culture-features/proud-boys-far-right-group-1183966/

DiResta, R., Grossman, S., & Siegel, A. (2022). In-house vs. outsourced trolls: How digital mercenaries shape state influence strategies. *Political Communication*, *39*(2), 222–253. doi:10.1080/10584609.2021.1994065

Freelon, D., & Wells, C. (2020). Disinformation as political communication. *Political Communication*, *37*(2), 145–156. https://doi.org/10.1080/10584609.2020.1723755

Krafft, P. M., & Donovan, J. (2020). Disinformation by design: The use of evidence collages and platform filtering in a media manipulation campaign. *Political Communication*, *37*, 194–214. https://www.tandfonline.com/doi/full/10.1080/10584609.2019.1686094

Luscombe, R. (2022, May 16). Scrutiny of Republicans who embrace "great replacement theory" after Buffalo massacre. *The Guardian*. https://www.theguardian.com/us-news/2022/may/16/buffalo-massacre-great-replacement-theory-republicans

Morone, J. (1998). *The democratic wish: Popular participation and the limits of American government*. Yale University Press.

Nadler, A. (2020, Oct. 2). The great anti-left show. *Los Angeles Review of Books*. https://lareviewofbooks.org/article/the-great-anti-left-show/

Paybarah, A. (2022, June 9). Ryan Kelley, a candidate for Michigan governor who was at the Capitol on Jan. 6, is arrested by the F.B.I. *The New York Times*. https://www.nytimes.com/2022/06/09/us/politics/ryan-kelley-michigan-governor-arrest-jan-6.html

Peck, R. (2019). *Fox populism: Branding conservatism as working class*. Cambridge University Press.

Pogue, J. (2022, Apr. 20). Inside the new right, where Peter Thiel is placing his biggest bets. *Vanity Fair*. https://www.vanityfair.com/news/2022/04/inside-the-new-right-where-peter-thiel-is-placing-his-biggest-bets

Przybyla, H. (2022, June 1). "It's going to be an army": Tapes reveal GOP plan to contest elections. *Politico*. https://www.politico.com/news/2022/06/01/gop-contest-elections-tapes-00035758

Quinn, M. (2022, Feb. 7). Rubio says January 6 Committee is a "complete partisan scam." CBS News. https://www.cbsnews.com/news/marco-rubio-january-6-committee-partisan-face-the-nation/.

Smith, D. (2022, May 22). "Replacement theory" still Republican orthodoxy despite Buffalo shooting. *The Guardian*. https://www.theguardian.com/us-news/2022/may/22/great-replacement-theory-republicans

17

Not Just Higher Truths

Critical Inquiry into Conservative Media after January 6th

Anthony Nadler

On January 7, 2022, conservative pundit Ben Shapiro opened his podcast by recognizing the one-year anniversary of the attacks on the U.S. Capitol. He offered his viewers a condensed version of what had become the dominant memory of January 6th in popular conservative media. Shapiro (2022) acknowledged that the attacks were "wrong" and "not good." Yet, instead of pointing viewers to the crimes committed that day, he focused on what he saw as a more pressing concern. According to Shapiro, immediately following the attacks it had become "wildly apparent that for the Democrats and for the media" January 6th was "gold." Democrats and the media, Shapiro said, were trying to ensnare all their political enemies in a wide net of blame, "so that if you voted for Trump or if you voted against Biden, or if you'd ever consider voting for Trump, or if you would ever consider voting for any other Republican, you were complicit in the actions of January 6th." Shapiro predicted that efforts to condemn all conservatives to collective guilt for January 6th would lead to greater censorship and other measures to deprive conservatives of legitimacy in political life.

It is tempting to approach Shapiro's narrative of January 6th as "disinformation." For many scholars, journalists, and foundation funders, disinformation has become the preferred framework for understanding right-wing communication strategies and their threats to democracy. Many factors make disinformation an appealing frame: its promise of political neutrality, its claim to be more objective and less condescending than the lens of propaganda analysis, and the sheen of novelty the term has acquired through the repeated suggestions it has special relevance to a platform society. Yet Shapiro's narrative illustrates shortcomings of this approach. What's most troublesome for Shapiro's critics is not that he makes claims about discrete

Anthony Nadler, *Not Just Higher Truths* In: *Media and January 6th*. Edited by: Khadijah Costley White, Daniel Kreiss, Shannon C. McGregor, and Rebekah Tromble, Oxford University Press. © Oxford University Press 2024.
DOI: 10.1093/oso/9780197758526.003.0017

facts that are provably inaccurate. Rather, Shapiro misses and distorts a larger truth about January 6th. He passes over the crimes of that day, ignores the symbols of hate wantonly signaled by many participants, and dismisses January 6th's significance as a violent assault on U.S. democracy. Nothing much to see there, he signals to his viewers.

For Shapiro, the story about January 6th that's really worth telling is the same conceit every major conservative host has been relentlessly telling their audiences for many years: Liberal elites and Democrats hate you, and they'll do anything they can to rob you of your dignity and your political rights. (For analysis of the centrality of this motif in conservative media, see Nadler, 2020, 2022.) That's the higher truth—the deep story—Shapiro wants his audience to understand about January 6th and its aftermath. (For more on "deep stories" in conservative media, see Hochschild, 2018; Nadler & Bauer, 2019; Polletta & Callahan, 2017.) Weaving this deep antiliberal story into the daily narratives of conservative news is a matter of myriad subtle (and not so subtle) judgments: which stories to prioritize, which facts to select and highlight, what kinds of context to add to breaking news. Typically, deep stories cannot be verified or disproven through any consensus-based standard nor countered through fact-checking. Nor can "deep stories" be condemned as a category the way disinformation can; emotionally powerful stories about identity are a normal, and likely inescapable, part of democracy. (On the centrality of identity stories for democratic politics, see Kreiss et al., 2020; Gutmann, 2009). Conservative media figures are hardly alone in mobilizing support through them.

The violence of January 6th further raises the urgent need for sophisticated analyses of the media landscape that fostered conditions that helped make January 6th possible and has prevented truth and reconciliation in its wake. Most important, we need this analysis to better understand the terrain on which struggles over political meanings, emotions, and loyalties are taking place today. In the years leading up to January 6, 2021, disinformation research exploded in prominence and quantity in response, in part, to surging and volatile right-wing mobilizations. Yet broader scholarship on conservative news media advanced at a much slower pace. Disinformation studies— based on a clean demarcation of truth and falsehood—does not offer a paradigm conducive for critical and cultural analysis of *conservative news cultures*.[1] In the wake of the January 6th attacks, media researchers—and I'm

---

[1] A. J. Bauer and I propose the term "conservative news cultures" as an interdisciplinary object not only limited to conservative news texts but one that also encompasses the production, encoding, reception, and circulation of conservative news media (Bauer & Nadler, 2019).

speaking particularly to those of us inspired by the cultural studies and critical theory traditions—must work toward developing more compelling, more historically and sociologically informed, and more rigorously scrutinized accounts of right-wing media cultures and communication strategies. We must be able to place them in local, national, and international contexts.

Many pressing questions about the future of the American right after January 6th can't be answered with any confidence now. What will become of its paramilitary wing in the coming years? Will the right press further in eroding basic rights to democratic participation? Might the right be able to expand its coalition—perhaps by serving as a conduit for amorphous discontent and political frustrations? As media scholars, our challenge is not to predict answers to these questions. But we can illuminate crucial aspects of the context in which these battles will take place. We can offer detailed insights on (1) how right-wing mobilizations are taking shape through mediated processes that engage in contests over meanings, the borders of social and political identities, and emotional attachment to those identities; (2) how these processes are connected to sociotechnical landscapes and historical conditions; and (3) drawing on the normative and utopian side of critical scholarship, what possibilities are open for challenging antidemocratic advances and building stronger coalitions in support of egalitarian politics.

Since 2016, conservative news cultures have become more prominent objects of study for media historians and sociologists as well as media and journalism scholars. Despite this wave of scholarship offering fresh ideas and insights, I think we're still seeing a less systematic and sustained approach to analyzing right-wing news and information cultures than we need, nor are we seeing the full potential for cross-disciplinary engagement in this area realized. (For a map of trends in research on conservative media across disciplines, see Nadler & Bauer, 2019.) Scholarship on conservative media only occasionally engages deeply with prior research, and we rarely see scholars scrutinizing and building upon each other's hypotheses. Further, key aspects of conservative news cultures continue to receive scant scholarly attention.

For the rest of this brief chapter, I will outline five areas where I'd like to see critical scholarship on conservative media grow, producing thicker and richer empirical and theoretical analysis. With responding to January 6th in mind, my focus here is specifically on research relating to U.S. conservative news cultures, though we also desperately need more research that is international, cross-national comparative, and transnational in scope.

More Research on the Popular Right

For understandable reasons, critical media scholars examining the right have been especially drawn to studies of "the extreme right," "the alt right," the manosphere, and other online communities positioning themselves as the right's digital vanguards. We need to continue investigating these sites, but we also urgently need more scholarship that investigates the *popular right*. By "popular right," I'm thinking of activity around outlets like Fox News, *The Dan Bongino Show*, conservative talk radio programs, and local news stations owned by Sinclair Broadcasting. Popular right outlets not only are characterized by relatively large and heterogeneous audiences, but specifically these outlets claim to represent the organic voice of "ordinary" conservatives or of the social groups conservatives are courting. Popular conservative outlets position themselves differently than vanguardists. Even when they flatter their audiences with the promise of a special ability to see through political mystifications, popular outlets put an emphasis on the ordinariness of their audiences and the rootedness of their perceptions in shared common sense. (For an analysis that highlights the importance of Fox News's claims to represent ordinariness, see Peck, 2019.)

Studying the popular right entails not only looking closely at the narrative worlds constructed by conservative news outlets but also examining how they engage in struggles over popular memory and sensibilities. We need to see what meanings right-wing outlets are promoting and how they are trying (successfully or not) to make their interpretations of debates and events the dominant ones—at least among targeted populations. To do this requires exploring what might make these interpretations appealing and what strategies proponents are using to try to outflank competing political narratives.

Consider, for instance, the battle over popular memory of January 6th. Commentators like Shapiro want to *code* the meaning discussions of January 6th (outside of conservative circles) as revenge politics or Democratic attempts at political distraction. To grapple with such an attempt to capture political common sense means trying to figure out what might make this an emotionally compelling narrative to some people and social groups and the circumstances that give rise to that appeal. If we dismiss narratives like this as superficial, a mere gloss of discourse masking the real ideological conflict below, we gravely underestimate the importance of the hegemonic struggle over meanings.

More Analysis of Conservative Media and Their Role in Transformations on the Right

In the wake of the 2016 U.S. presidential election, leading scholars of American conservatism strove to counter perceptions that Trump represented a great rupture on the American right (e.g., McGirr, 2021; Robin, 2018). Rick Perlstein (2017), for instance, suggested critics needed to turn to American conservatism's long, but relatively overlooked, history of "political surrealists and intellectual embarrassments, its con artists and tribunes of white rage." These are points well taken. Still, we should be careful not to overcorrect. Scholars need to be able to offer detailed accounts not only of continuities but also of transformations in ideology, mobilizing passions, coalitional makeup, and more. We won't be able to understand the right's dynamism without this dual vision.

A special challenge facing conservative news scholars is that we're working with a patchy historical backdrop. To be able to identify transformations in conservative news cultures, we need to make comparisons with the past. This entails engaging with both broad social and cultural histories and specific histories of conservative media; the latter are still underdeveloped. Fortunately, scholars like Nicole Hemmer (2016), Heather Hendershot (2011, 2016), and A. J. Bauer (2017) have given us excellent and in-depth analyses of conservative media that took shape in the United States in the postwar period. We also have several detailed analyses of religious right media networks from the 1980s onward (Hendershot, 2010; Kintz, 1997; Ward, 2015). Nonetheless, researchers would be hard-pressed, for instance, to find scholarship detailing the innovations of *The Drudge Report* or Andrew Breitbart's explosive career or the rise of the conservative blogosphere in the mid-2000s. Each of these has been extremely influential in shaping the digital conservative sphere today. For incisive accounts of transformations in right-wing media, we need to cultivate knowledge that will allow us to discern changes and continuities clearly.

Deeper Analyses of Conservative Media and Racial and Cultural Resentments

Racism, xenophobia, and misogyny on the right have been central to much of the cultural scholarship on conservative media. Nonetheless, we need more research that offers detailed accounts of just how conservative discourses and news cultures mobilize emotional attachments to support racial hierarchy and other forms of subordination. Many analysts start from the premise that conservatism speaks to social groups already primed for cultural resentment by a backlash reflex against perceived threats to a privileged status, like white racial identity (Norris & Inglehart, 2019; Robin, 2018). While we can recognize a broad tendency for social groups to protect privileges under many conditions, critical scholars should be wary of approaching backlash as if it is unmediated and an innate aspect of psychology. The backlash model cannot offer answers to critical questions about why some privileged subgroups are more prone to backlash and right-wing mobilization than others. Looking at white Americans, for instance, we know that particular white subgroups—for instance, rural whites, older whites, and those with less formal education—have each been significantly more likely to be drawn toward the right in recent years. (For a detailed analysis of demographic shifts in the Democratic Party in the United States—particularly in regard to education—and comparisons with shifts in the demographic of support for left and social democratic parties in Europe, see Piketty, 2020.) Rather than assuming something inherently reactionary in the life experiences or cultural values of these subgroups, we need more detailed analyses of the cultural work and social processes that forge articulations between particular social groups and conservative identities or outgroup antagonisms.

More Analysis of Conservative News Cultures among Diverse Communities

Relatedly, we need a greater understanding of how conservative news cultures circulate among different communities and speak to different social identities. Conservative media audiences, news content, and circulation networks are not homogeneous. Scholars need to further investigate conservative media among Black communities, Hispanic communities, and others not typically associated with the right-wing base in the United States; we also need scholarship that looks at how conservative media targets specific and distinct communities associated with that base, such as rural whites and business elites. Researchers like Lillianna Mason (2018) have shown the importance of links between partisan identity and social identities based on race, geography, education, religion, and more. Scholarship on conservative media should not reify a notion that the people drawn to conservative media are simply individuals who happen to find its messages and fantasies appealing. Human agency is certainly part of the story, but, of course, we do not form our choices in conditions of our own making. We need rich sociological observations and insight into how conservative media bid for people's loyalty as they are situated in specific social locations.

Compelling Normative Arguments While Not Just Seeing "Higher Truths"

I think critical media scholarship is strongest when we are forthright about the normative arguments and dimensions in our work. This is not to say our analysis consists of nothing but normative claims. Yet I think it's fair to say that a quest for a more emancipatory and egalitarian social order lies at the heart of most currents that make up critical scholarly traditions. There's no need to hide the fact that some inspired by these traditions study conservative media seeking a better understanding of forces mobilizing against the kinds of social changes we'd like to see. This, of course, doesn't mean we're interested in understanding only what's "wrong" with conservative media. Critical studies of the right—from Frankfurt School studies of fascism (Lowenthal & Guterman, 1949) to Stuart Hall's (1979, 1988) innovative analysis of Thatcherism to Reece Peck's (2019) landmark study of Fox News— show that the right can speak to aspirations not solely bound to a will toward domination. Conservative discourses may speak to popular yearnings that have liberatory potentials, though of course those of us on the left think such yearning needs to be channeled in different directions. If critical scholarship on the right is going to be at its sharpest and most compelling, we need not only to engage seriously with conservative news cultures as objects of analysis but also to apply scrutiny to conservative ideas.

Most critical scholars hope their research ultimately contributes some pragmatic value to political struggle, be that helping prevent another January 6th or pointing toward opportunities for broader egalitarian ambitions. Yet this pragmatic value may be of different kinds, and those differences pose what can be a productive tension. On one hand, we're called to offer narratives that clarify the ethical and moral stakes of what we study. We draw connections between particular events or objects and grander narratives with

160 RESEARCH AFTER JANUARY 6, 2021

a normative edge. These might be about digital capitalism, white supremacy, or other links to broader social theory. Like Shapiro, critical media scholars, too, speak to "higher truths." (For an engaging discussion of tensions around intellectuals and the responsibility of speaking to "higher truths," from the Dreyfus Affair throughout the 20th century, see Judt & Snyder, 2012, pp. 287–294.)

On the other hand, while critical media scholarship is drawn toward normative social theory, there's also a pull from a different direction. This one orients us toward an astutely perceptive and descriptive form of analysis; we must try to discern aspects of the objects we're studying that are surprising and resistant to our already existing explanatory frameworks and assumptions. When we're studying the right, we need to bring a curiosity that allows us to see its dynamics, to perceive the preferred meanings and interpretations arising from its discourses, and to examine aspects of its appeal easily missed if we're too confident that we have its impulses and its raison d'être all figured out. The pragmatic value here is not the moral clarity of a scholarly narrative but the strategic usefulness of mapping complex social and cultural processes intertwined in battles for hegemony. So the aim of critical scholarship includes not only a ruthless criticism of existing institutions and injustices, nor only visions for what emancipatory and egalitarian social arrangements would look like. We also need maps to navigate how to get from point A to B.

* * *

We need to see the attacks of January 6th as part of a long history of political violence in the United States. At the same time, we can see January 6th as warning of newly emerging threats and a potential reshuffling of the balance of forces on the right. We can hope that street violence and paramilitary activity have a minimal influence in U.S. politics in the years ahead. But we are guaranteed to be living in a period of flux and instability as key political institutions—including news media—undergo challenges to their previously held authority and experience unpredictable transformations. This is an exciting, difficult, and weighty time for media and journalism scholarship and criticism. In almost any realistic scenario, battles for popular loyalties and consent are going to have more impact shaping our politics than the direct use of force. We will continue to need new insights to grasp how these battles are mediated. More incisive study of conservative news cultures and informational networks will offer a crucial component of that understanding. I'm hopeful that a momentum will continue to build for studying those aspects of our media landscape and we'll see ever more nimble, heterogeneous, and vibrant scholarly conversations grow in this area.

References

Bauer, A. J. (2017). *Before "fair and balanced": Conservative media activism and the rise of the new right* [Unpublished doctoral dissertation]. New York University.

Bauer, A. J., & Nadler, A. (2019). Taking conservative news seriously. In A. M. Nadler & A. J. Bauer (Eds.), *News on the right: Studying conservative news cultures* (pp. 1–16). Oxford University Press.

Shapiro, B. (Host) (2022, Jan. 7). *It's the Democrats' January 6 spectacular!!! P. 1407* [Video podcast episode]. *The Ben Shapiro Show*. https://www.youtube.com/watch?v=Wp7h l2x2dDY

Gutmann, A. (2009). *Identity in democracy*. Princeton University Press.

Hall, S. (1979). The great moving right show. *Marxism Today*, *23*(1), 14–20.

Hall, S. (1988). The toad in the garden: Thatcherism among the theorists. In C. Nelson & L. Grossberg (Eds.), *Marxism and the interpretation of culture* (pp. 35–57). Springer.

Hemmer, N. (2016). *Messengers of the right: Conservative media and the transformation of American politics*. University of Pennsylvania Press.

Hendershot, H. (2010). *Shaking the world for Jesus: Media and conservative evangelical culture*. University of Chicago Press.

Hendershot, H. (2011). *What's fair on the air? Cold War right-wing broadcasting and the public interest*. University of Chicago Press.

Hendershot, H. (2016). *Open to debate: How William F. Buckley put liberal America on the Firing Line*. HarperCollins.

Hochschild, A. R. (2018). *Strangers in their own land: Anger and mourning on the American right*. The New Press.

Judt, T., & Snyder, T. (2012). *Thinking the twentieth century*. Penguin.

Kintz, L. (1997). *Between Jesus and the market: The emotions that matter in right-wing America*. Duke University Press.

Kreiss, D., Lawrence, R. G., & McGregor, S. C. (2020). Political identity ownership: Symbolic contests to represent members of the public. *Social Media + Society*, *6*(2). https://doi.org/10.1177/2056305120926495

Lowenthal, L., & Guterman, N. (1949). *Prophets of deceit: A study of the techniques of the American agitator*. Harper.

Mason, L. (2018). *Uncivil agreement: How politics became our identity*. University of Chicago Press.

McGirr, L. (2021, Jan. 13). Trump is the Republican Party's past and its future. *The New York Times*. https://www.nytimes.com/2021/01/13/opinion/gop-trump.html

Nadler, A. (2020, Oct.). The great anti-left show. *Los Angeles Review of Books*. https://lare viewofbooks.org/article/the-great-anti-left-show/

Nadler, A. (2022). Political identity and the therapeutic work of U.S. conservative media. *International Journal of Communication*, *16*, 1–13.

Nadler, A., & Bauer, A. J. (2019). Conservative news studies. In A. Nadler & A. J. Bauer (Eds.), *News on the right: Studying conservative news cultures* (p. 232). Oxford University Press.

Norris, P., & Inglehart, R. (2019). *Cultural backlash: Trump, Brexit, and authoritarian populism.* Cambridge University Press.

Peck, R. (2019). *Fox populism: Branding conservatism as working class.* Cambridge University Press.

Perlstein, R. (2017, Apr. 11). I thought I understood the American right. Trump proved me wrong. *The New York Times.* https://www.nytimes.com/2017/04/11/magazine/i-thought-i-understood-the-american-right-trump-proved-me-wrong.html

Piketty, T. (2020). *Capital and ideology.* Harvard University Press.

Polletta, F., & Callahan, J. (2017). Deep stories, nostalgia narratives, and fake news: Storytelling in the Trump era. *American Journal of Cultural Sociology, 5*(3), 392–408. https://doi.org/10.1057/s41290-017-0037-7

Robin, C. (2018). *The reactionary mind: Conservatism from Edmund Burke to Donald Trump.* Oxford University Press.

Ward, M. (2015). *The electronic church in the digital age: Cultural impacts of evangelical mass media.* ABC-CLIO.

18

Rethinking Right-Wing Media in the Wake of an Attempted Coup

Yunkang Yang

On January 7, the day after the Capitol insurrection, One America News (OAN) displayed a front-page story on its website titled "OAN Call to Action: How to Donate to Lawmakers Who Stayed True to President Trump." If you click the headline, you are then directed to a page that lists the links to the fundraising sites of five Republicans: Josh Hawley, Ted Cruz, Matt Gaetz, Louie Gohmert, and Marjorie Taylor Greene. All had just voted to overturn the 2020 election results.

It was not just OAN supporting Republicans who objected to the election results. Both Breitbart and the Daily Caller pleaded with their subscribers to fund Josh Hawley's and Kelly Loeffler's 2020 election campaigns.[1] Federal Election Commission filings show that the Daily Caller and the Daily Wire leased their mailing lists to the National Republican Congressional Committee for a payment of $126,768 and $442,663, respectively. The Committee funded 36 Republican candidates who voted to overthrow the 2020 election, including Louie Gohmert, Marjorie Taylor Greene, and Madison Cawthorn.

Academic scholarship has long treated right-wing media outlets as partisan news organizations per se, placing their reporting practices at the center of academic inquiry and examining the conservative slant of their coverage. This partisan media paradigm gave rise to an industry of studies that juxtaposed right-wing media such as Fox News with left-wing news organizations such as MSNBC, as if they are two sides of the same coin (Aday, 2010; Feldman et al., 2012; Groeling, 2008; Hyun & Moon, 2016; Levendusky, 2013b). Using ever more creative field experiments, survey instruments, and computational methods, many of these studies have demonstrated

---

[1] Kelly Loeffler rescinded her objection to the Electoral College results after January 6.

Yunkang Yang, *Rethinking Right-Wing Media in the Wake of an Attempted Coup* In: *Media and January 6th*.
Edited by: Khadijah Costley White, Daniel Kreiss, Shannon C. McGregor, and Rebekah Tromble, Oxford University Press.
© Oxford University Press 2024. DOI: 10.1093/oso/9780197758526.003.0018

the harmful effects of right-wing media's bias, including polarization, misperception, and distrust (Broockman & Kalla, 2022; Garrett et al., 2019; Guess et al., 2020; Prior, 2013). Since the 2016 election, scholars have adopted the relatively loosely defined term "hyperpartisan media" to describe right-wing media such as Breitbart (Pennycook & Rand, 2019; Tucker et al., 2018). All of this work suggests that the key problem with right-wing media is partisan bias—excessive and extreme bias, certainly, but the core focus remains on news coverage.

Yet, as the examples above illustrate, right-wing media such as OAN, Breitbart, the Daily Caller, and Daily Wire have gone well beyond the bounds of traditional journalistic enterprises, with reporting at their core, becoming instead a type of political organization, coordinating with Republican elites to fundraise and mobilize for specific—often antidemocratic—political aims and candidates.

This suggests the need for a fundamental shift in research on right-wing media, one that better aligns our scholarship with empirical political realities. The January 6 attempted coup at the Capitol should be a wake-up call that reified concepts such as partisan bias and polarization have distracted us from far more serious problems. As media scholars, we need to rethink and retire some of the existing narratives about right-wing media. Only by doing so can we truly begin to take seriously the threats right-wing media pose to American democracy.

Beyond Partisan Media

For more than two decades, "partisan media" has served as the lingua franca for communication scholars, political scientists, and economists examining right-wing media. In the United States, partisan media are understood as opinionated media that "present the facts in such a way to support a particular conclusion" (Levendusky, 2013a, p. 7). They are "framed, spun and slanted so that particular agendas are advanced" (Jamieson et al., 2007, p. 26). According to this view, although partisan media provide biased news coverage and commentary—for example, they cover stories that favor their side (selection bias) and put an ideological spin on news (framing bias)— they are still analyzed fundamentally as traditional, fact-based news organizations. Because right-wing media are seen as partisan news organizations capable of presenting the facts in an ideologically coherent way, scholars have tasked them with an important role in American democracy—namely to inform and contribute to public debate by supplying alternative ideas unconstrained by the "fair and balanced" norm of objective journalism (Jamieson et al., 2007).

The view that right-wing media are biased but still fact-based news enterprises has been promoted by many right-wing media themselves (Nadler et al., 2020). For example, more than 10 major right-wing media outlets, including Breitbart, the Daily Caller, and *Western Journal*, profess a commitment to facts on their websites. In an interview, Breitbart's editor-in-chief Alex Marlow told the *New York Times*, "[Our] bias now comes in story selection. We're not going to cover the Russia scandal as much as we're covering the cartels coming over the border" (Hylton, 2017).

However, there is ample evidence that many right-wing media did more than just selectively cover stories that favor Republicans or reframe news with a conservative spin. Fox News, for example, spread numerous lies about Democratic politicians such as Barack Obama, Hillary Clinton, and Joe Biden (AP, 2021; Benkler et al., 2018; Hananoki, 2011); in 2017, it even made up a story about the death of the Democratic National Committee staffer Seth Rich to distract the public from the ongoing Mueller investigation (Yang, 2020). Disinformation, defined as "intentional falsehoods spread as news stories or simulated documentary formats to advance political goals" (Bennett & Livingston, 2018, p. 124), is not journalism with a partisan spin. It is not about selecting stories from a shared universe of news events or helping audiences interpret news in an ideologically coherent fashion. Rather, it is about creating a different, parallel political reality to advance strategic political objectives, such as influencing voters, discrediting opponents, disrupting political processes, inflaming social divides, or creating confusion and distrust (Bennett & Livingston, 2020). It is a form of distorted and democratically dysfunctional communication (Chadwick et al., 2018; Friedland et al., 2006) that "challenges the basic norms and values on which institutional legitimacy and political stability depend" (Bennett & Livingston, 2020, p. 1).

In a new large-scale study of four million stories published by more than 30 right-wing media outlets between 2017 and 2020, I show that disinformation is not just occasional or episodic, but a consistent key feature of the online right-wing media sphere in the United States. Disinformation topics were among the most prominent topics of the most popular right-wing media content every year, and almost every major right-wing media outlet, ranging from Fox News to Breitbart, from the Daily Caller to Newsmax, participated

166 RESEARCH AFTER JANUARY 6, 2021

in spreading disinformation stories, such as the Trump Tower wiretapping story in 2017,[2] the Nunes Memo in 2018,[3] the Ukraine-Biden conspiracy theory in 2019,[4] and the hydroxychloroquine story in 2020.[5] Given the prominence of disinformation in right-wing media content, it is important for the scholarly community to move beyond the language of partisan bias, which all too often implies that right-wing media is structurally and functionally akin to left-wing media and overlooks more serious problems that go beyond the "slant" of reporting—such as disinformation and attacks on the rule of law, the press, and racial minorities (Bennett & Livingston 2020; Reddi et al., 2021).

Beyond Commercialism

In the book *Network Propaganda*, Yochai Benkler, Robert Faris, and Hal Roberts (2018) argue that the right-wing media sphere should be considered primarily a sphere of network propaganda. Defining "propaganda" as "communication designed to manipulate a target population by affecting its beliefs, attitudes, or preferences in order to obtain behavior compliant with the political goals of the propagandist" (p. 29), Benkler and his colleagues drew attention to right-wing media's deliberate attempts to mislead and manipulate the public. Their book is an important step away from the partisan media paradigm.

However, according to Benkler (2020), right-wing media's propaganda is largely a profit-driven behavior that seeks to exploit a new market segment:

> Changes in political culture created a large new market segment for media that emphasized white, Christian identity as a political identity; and that a series of regulatory and technological changes opened up enough new channels that the old strategy of programming for a population-wide media viewer, and hoping for a share of the total audience, was displaced

---

[2] The Trump Tower wiretapping story falsely claimed that Barack Obama secretly wiretapped Trump's phone at Trump Tower during the 2016 campaign.

[3] The Nunes Memo story suggested that the FBI sought a Foreign Intelligence Surveillance Act warrant to spy on Trump's former advisor Carter Page as part of a politically motivated conspiracy.

[4] The Ukraine-Biden conspiracy theory alleged that Joe Biden engaged in corrupt activities to protect his son's interest in the Ukraine energy company Burisma.

[5] The hydroxychloroquine story falsely claimed that the antimalaria drug can effectively treat COVID-19.

RETHINKING RIGHT-WING MEDIA 167

by a strategy that provided a substantial part of the market with uniquely-tailored content. (Benkler, 2020, p. 52)

This political economy approach that puts market demand at the center of the explanation is characteristic of a specific line of work that focuses on right-wing media's commercial aspect. Adept at building a successful corporate brand based on populist and tabloid aesthetics (Peck, 2019), Fox News, for example, was dubbed the "second generation" of right-wing media, distinct from the first generation such as the *National Review* and *Human Events*, which had a much smaller following. To highlight their commercial success, the media historian Nicole Hemmer (2016, p. 264) called right-wing media such as Fox "entertainers first, conservatives second."

However, Fox News's commercial success may well be the exception rather than the norm of today's right-wing media sector.[6] In a saturated market that is both dominated by industry giants such as Fox and flooded with small-budget clickbait sites (Munger, 2018), turning profits has become increasingly difficult. Many right-wing media organizations have relied on donors' support to stay afloat. Hit by a boycott campaign that tanked Breitbart's ad revenue by 90% in 2017, Steve Bannon, then CEO of Breitbart, lamented that "all the right-wing media—the top ten companies by the end of the year, except for Fox, will be donor-base." "There is no economic model," Bannon added. "You will have a donor come in and write a check" (Ellefson, 2019).

Among the top 10 right-wing media sites ranked by aggregate online traffic between 2018 and 2021 (Therighting, 2021), nine[7] have received financial support from ultra-rich conservative financiers such as Charles Koch and the Mercer family. These rich individuals and families usually had already amassed tremendous wealth in the oil or financial industry before funding right-wing media. Their priority was not making more profits but advancing their ideological agendas. Foster Freiss, the funder of the Daily Caller, said he was not worried about the Daily Caller not turning a profit: "They are breaking great stories and changing the discussion" (Fang, 2012).

In some cases, the reliance on billionaires' financial support has translated into a semi-clientelist relationship in which the financiers influence—and

---

[6] There are a handful of right-wing media personalities who have amassed extreme wealth from their personal talk radio show programs, which tend to have much lower organizational overhead than "news" organizations such as Breitbart.

[7] They are Washington Times, *Washington Examiner, The Blaze, National Review*, Breitbart, *Western Journal*, Daily Wire, Daily Caller, and Newsmax.

168 RESEARCH AFTER JANUARY 6, 2021

sometimes dictate—the editorial process. For example, Breitbart's financier Rebekah Mercer—who was also a major backer of Donald Trump's 2016 campaign—was highly involved in its day-to-day business: she suggested areas of coverage, read every story, and even called editors to correct grammatical errors and typos during the 2016 election cycle (Mayer, 2017). To get Trump elected in 2016, Breitbart published numerous hit pieces on Trump GOP opponent Marco Rubio, sometimes at the direct order of Trump's political ally Stephen Miller (Vazquez & Sidner, 2019). Once Trump was elected in 2016, Breitbart's goal seemed to shift toward pushing Trump to implement Mercer's and her hired hand Steve Bannon's preferred policies. For example, in 2017 Breitbart launched a sustained campaign to oust Trump's National Security advisor H. R. McMaster even after Trump openly defended McMaster (Yang, 2020).

The overemphasis on Fox News's commercial success within the scholarly community could lead us to believe that right-wing media outlets are discrete, independent business enterprises whose main goal is to maximize profits through programming. This is simply not true. Many right-wing media organizations are embedded in a sprawling network of think tanks, campaign organizations, political candidates, and professional provocateurs who are usually funded by the same group of right-wing donors (Meagher, 2012). Many right-wing media fundraise on behalf of political candidates during elections; they also promote Astroturf organizations—groups created by powerful elites but designed to give the appearance of grassroot organizations—on air, coordinate with right-wing think tanks, and help run Republican PACs and super PACs. Hence, we should consider right-wing media an important layer of what might be called the campaign infrastructure (Kreiss, 2012) for the right-wing donor class, capable of participating in a wide range of political activities.

Beyond Activism

It is important to note that contemporary right-wing media outlets are building on long-standing structures and practices in the conservative media sector. Concerned that they had too little access to power within traditional institutional politics, conservatives operating in the media sector have long embraced an activist role. Believing that the mainstream press had ignored alternative points of view, in the 1940s and 1950s conservative media figures such as Clarence Manion, Henry Regnery, and William F. Buckley Jr. created a number of programs and publications, including the *Manion Forum*, *Human Events*, and the *National Review*. Besides editorializing, these conservative activists engaged in various political organizing activities to advocate for their causes, helping to organize protests and rallies, promoting grassroots organizations, and functioning as intermediaries between political candidates and voters (Hemmer, 2016).

Building on this model, contemporary conservative media continued to embrace an activist role in the 2010s. Fox News, for example, played a pivotal role in orchestrating the Tea Party movement. Some Fox News hosts attended Tea Party rallies, some actively promoted the Tea Party on air, and some even allowed Tea Party activists to solicit donations on Fox programs. Indeed, the boundary between conservative media and the Tea Party movement became so porous that Skocpol and Williamson (2016) argue the latter could not exist without the former. Similarly, in her book *The Branding of Right-Wing Activism*, White (2018) argues that the news media played such an important role in constructing the Tea Party brand that they functioned as both an organizer of and an active participant in the movement.

And yet the January 6 insurrection raises a serious question about whether the "activist" framework is itself adequate to characterize the political activities transpiring outside of institutional channels. Does fomenting an insurrection at the Capitol to overthrow a democratic election constitute "activism"? Is this kind of "activism" compatible with democracy?

The political theorist Iris Young (2001) reminds us that activism should have a universalist characteristic. Unlike an interest group whose goal is to win the most for their group members, an activist, Young argues, is not motivated by personal gain or by the gain of her group members. Instead, the activist's aim is to bring about broad social change and push for greater social justice from which all groups can benefit.

Even if we relegate activism to the status of interest advocacy and understand democratic politics through the lens of perpetual group conflicts, there are still important limits. In an agonistic democracy, different social groups fight passionately for their interests and worldviews. But they should share a common allegiance to democratic principles and procedures that regulate how group confrontation plays out (Mouffe, 2014). As Mouffe writes, the crucial issue—and the prime task—of democratic politics is to establish the kind of us-versus-them distinction that is compatible with the recognition of pluralism and is anchored on democratic norms and objectives.

However, many right-wing media organizations are promoting radical agendas that seek to exclude entire social groups from the democratic process. From the "Big Lie" to "replacement theory," they have embraced and are helping mobilize direct threats to liberal democracy. Calling such activities "right-wing activism" fails to capture the deeper antidemocratic issues that animate and define the right-wing media sector. It clouds our ability to see the real threats that many right-wing media such as Fox News pose to American democracy.

References

Aday, S. (2010). Chasing the bad news: An analysis of 2005 Iraq and Afghanistan war coverage on NBC and Fox News channel. *Journal of Communication*, *60*(1), 144–164.

AP. (2021, Nov. 13). Fox News edits video of Biden to make it seem he was being racially insensitive. *The Guardian*.

Benkler, Y. (2020). A political economy of the origins of asymmetric propaganda in American media. In L. Bennett & S. Livingston (Eds.), *The disinformation age: Politics, technology, and disruptive communication in the United States* (pp. 43–66). Cambridge University Press.

Benkler, Y., Faris, R., & Roberts, H. (2018). *Network propaganda: Manipulation, disinformation, and radicalization in American politics*. Oxford University Press.

Bennett, W. L., & Livingston, S. (2018). The disinformation order: Disruptive communication and the decline of democratic institutions. *European Journal of Communication*, *33*(2), 122–139.

Bennett, W. L., & Livingston, S. (2020). A brief history of the disinformation age. In L. Bennett & S. Livingston (Eds.), *The disinformation age: Politics, technology, and disruptive communication in the United States* (pp. 43–66). Cambridge University Press.

Broockman, D., & Kalla, J. (2022). The manifold effects of partisan media on viewers' beliefs and attitudes: A field experiment with Fox News viewers. OSF Preprints. https://osf.io/jrw26/

Chadwick, A., Vaccari, C., & O'Loughlin, B. (2018). Do tabloids poison the well of social media? Explaining democratically dysfunctional news sharing. *New Media & Society*, *20*(11), 4255–4274.

Ellefson, L. (2019, Aug. 7). Breitbart's audience has dropped 72% since Trump took office—as other right-wing sites have gained. *The Wrap*.

Fang, L. (2012). *The machine: A field guide to the resurgent right*. New Press.

Feldman, L., Maibach, E. W., Roser-Renouf, C., & Leiserowitz, A. (2012). Climate on cable: The nature and impact of global warming coverage on Fox News, CNN, and MSNBC. *International Journal of Press/Politics*, *17*(1), 3–31.

Friedland, L., Hover, T., & Rojas, H. (2006). The networked public sphere. *The Public*, *13*(4), 5–26.

Garrett, R. K., Long, J. A., & Jeong, M. S. (2019). From partisan media to misperception: Affective polarization as mediator. *Journal of Communication*, *69*(5), 490–512.

Groeling, T. (2008). Who's the fairest of them all? An empirical test for partisan bias on ABC, CBS, NBC, and Fox News. *Presidential Studies Quarterly, 38*(4), 631–657.

Guess, A. M., Barberá, P., Munzert, S., & Yang, J. (2021). The consequences of online partisan media. *Proceedings of the National Academy of Sciences, 118*(14), 1–8.

Hananoki, E. (2011, Mar. 29). Cruise ship confession: Top Fox News executive admits lying on-air about Obama. Media Matters. https://www.mediamatters.org/fox-news/cruise-ship-confession-top-fox-news-executive-admits-lying-air-about-obama

Hemmer, N. (2016). *Messengers of the right*. University of Pennsylvania Press.

Hylton, W. (2017, Aug. 16). Down the Breitbart hole. *The New York Times*.

Hyun, K. D., & Moon, S. J. (2016). Agenda setting in the partisan TV news context: Attribute agenda setting and polarized evaluation of presidential candidates among viewers of NBC, CNN, and Fox News. *Journalism & Mass Communication Quarterly, 93*(3), 509–529.

Jamieson, K. H., Hardy, B. W., & Romer, D. (2007). The effectiveness of the press in serving the needs of American democracy. In K. H. Jamieson (Ed.), *Institutions of American democracy: A republic divided* (pp. 21–51). Oxford University Press.

Kreiss, D. (2012). *Taking our country back: The crafting of networked politics from Howard Dean to Barack Obama*. Oxford University Press.

Levendusky, M. (2013a). *How partisan media polarize America*. University of Chicago Press.

Levendusky, M. S. (2013b). Why do partisan media polarize viewers? *American Journal of Political Science, 57*(3), 611–623.

Mayer, J. (2017). *Dark money: The hidden history of the billionaires behind the rise of the radical right*. Anchor.

Meagher, R. (2012). The "vast right-wing conspiracy": Media and conservative networks. *New Political Science, 34*(4), 469–484.

Mouffe, C. (2014). Democratic politics and conflict: An agonistic approach. In M. Lakitsch (Ed.) *Political power reconsidered: State power and civic activism between legitimacy and violence* (pp. 17–29). Lit Verlag.

Munger, K. (2020). All the news that's fit to click: The economics of clickbait media. *Political Communication, 37*(3), 376–397.

Nadler, A., Bauer, A. J., & Konieczna, M. (2020). *Conservative newswork: A report on the values and practices of online journalists on the right*. Tow Center for Digital Journalism. Columbia Journalism School.

Peck, R. (2019). *Fox populism: Branding conservatism as working class*. Cambridge University Press.

Pennycook, G., & Rand, D. G. (2019). Fighting misinformation on social media using crowdsourced judgments of news source quality. *Proceedings of the National Academy of Sciences, 116*(7), 2521–2526.

Prior, M. (2013). Media and political polarization. *Annual Review of Political Science, 16*, 101–127.

Reddi, M., Kuo, R., & Kreiss, D. (2021). Identity propaganda: Racial narratives and disinformation. *New Media & Society, 25*(8), 2201–2218.

Skocpol, T., & Williamson, V. (2016). *The Tea Party and the remaking of Republican conservatism*. Oxford University Press.

Therighting. (2021). Rankings of traffic to the top right-wing websites based on unique monthly visitors. https://www.therighting.com/metrics

Tucker, J. A., Guess, A., Barberá, P., Vaccari, C., Siegel, A., Sanovich, S., Stukal, D., & Nyhan, B. (2018). *Social media, political polarization, and political disinformation: A review of the scientific literature*. Hewlett Foundation.

Vazquez, M., & Sidner, S. (2019, Nov. 19). Emails show Stephen Miller targeted Rubio, had editorial sway at Breitbart. CNN. https://www.cnn.com/2019/11/19/politics/stephen-miller-marco-rubio-breitbart-southern-poverty-law-center/index.html

White, K. C. (2018). *The branding of right-wing activism: The news media and the Tea Party*. Oxford University Press.

Yang, Y. (2020). *The political logic of the radical right media sphere in the United States* [Unpublished doctoral Dissertation]. University of Washington.

Young, I. M. (2001). Activist challenges to deliberative democracy. *Political Theory, 29*(5), 670–690.

19

The Local Roots of January 6th

A Mixed-Methods, Multilevel Approach to Political Communication

Sadie Dempsey and Jianing Li

January 6th is largely conceptualized as a moment manufactured by President Donald Trump and national far right political elites or movements such as QAnon (BBC, 2022; Feuer et al., 2022; Hodges, 2022; Rubin et al., 2021). Historical accounts trace how these elite actors used election fraud claims to build on past movements like the Tea Party with the goal of upholding white supremacy (Tripodi, this volume; White, this volume). This makes it tempting to study January 6th purely as a national, elite-driven phenomenon. In our own work, we argue that this approach obscures the roles that local political institutions, local political elites, and everyday citizens played in perpetuating election fraud claims and fanning the flames of the "Stop the Steal" movement.

In this methodological essay, we illustrate how researchers can utilize a mixed-methods, multilevel perspective to shift their analytical vantage point to capture the micro- and meso-level processes at play in this political moment. We build on work from our group, the Center for Communication and Civic Renewal at University of Wisconsin–Madison, on communication ecologies and contentious politics (Dempsey et al., 2020; Friedland et al., 2022; Wells et al., 2017). We studied the role that county Republican parties played in perpetuating election fraud claims on Facebook, and our methodological approach revealed that local Republican parties were strategic actors. We traced how they systematically shaped the quantity and quality of their posts across different counties to maximize their effectiveness and mobilize support for "Stop the Steal." Without these methods, we would have missed all the action happening at the local level that is key to understanding the broader dynamics that made January 6th possible.

Sadie Dempsey and Jianing Li, *The Local Roots of January 6th* In: *Media and January 6th*. Edited by: Khadijah Costley White, Daniel Kreiss, Shannon C. McGregor, and Rebekah Tromble, Oxford University Press. © Oxford University Press 2024. DOI: 10.1093/oso/9780197758526.003.0019

In this chapter, we highlight four ways that a mixed-method, multilevel perspective benefited our own analysis and illustrate how it can be useful elsewhere. First, mixing methods can generate better measurements. Without engaging in a careful qualitative analysis, we would have neglected the subtler narratives that eroded trust in the 2020 election results. Second, taking into account multiple levels (e.g., state, county) can provide more analytical specificity, particularly in determining how local and state sociopolitical contexts shape outcomes. Without this multilevel perspective, we would have missed how *local* contextual factors like voting patterns shaped election fraud claims. Importantly, mixed-methods and multilevel perspectives can work together to offer new insights. Third, a multilevel approach can be combined with qualitative analysis to study content flows and processes that bridge the micro, meso, and macro levels. Without it, we would have overlooked the local-national feedback loop, whereby local election fraud claims bolstered the national "Stop the Steal" movement. Fourth, combining a mixed-method and multilevel perspective provides opportunities to generate, test, and contextualize theories. Without combining these approaches, we would have missed how county Republican parties highlighted fraud claims locally *or* from other states in strategic ways that cater to features of their locality. Finally, we demonstrate how the lessons we've learned from using this approach can be useful in other contexts.

It is important to note that we aren't advocating that this is the best or only way to study January 6th or any other research object. Instead, we are suggesting that these are useful tools in a researcher's analytical toolkit that can aid in looking at a familiar phenomenon from a different perspective. We invite other researchers to explore these tools in their own work and see what surprising new findings or insights they might uncover.

Mixing Methods for Better Measurement

Combining qualitative and quantitative methods has numerous advantages in the age of big data, one of which is more accurate measurements (Grigoropoulou & Small, 2022). In our own work, we wanted to identify all posts that undermined the 2020 election results. Keywords or hashtags like #StopTheSteal or #RiggedElection can be incredibly useful (Abilov et al., 2021), but this approach captures only the most overt claims of election fraud. To capture the full spectrum of fraud claims, we used a human-driven, mixed-methods, iterative process to create a fraud dictionary that identified the full spectrum of language markers used to talk about election fraud. To do so, we qualitatively analyzed random samples of Facebook posts from each of our states and identified terms, word combinations, and narratives that undermined the results of the 2020 election. To ensure validity, we applied the dictionary to a separate set of random samples from each state and audited the samples for accuracy and noise.

This process captured a wide range of election fraud narratives. Some were overt claims about ballots dumped by nefarious poll workers, Democrats conspiring with Dominion Voting Systems, or Representative Ilhan Omar getting "caught" engaging in ballot harvesting by Project Veritas. But the real advantage of our approach was that we captured more subtle narratives that slowly chipped away at the election's legitimacy, such as reports of "funny numbers" from the key states of Michigan and Wisconsin, "irregularities" in election results, and "mysterious" boxes of ballots that appeared at the last minute. These posts often didn't include overt language about fraud or a stolen election, but they were key in perpetuating the belief that the 2020 election results should not be trusted. These keywords, when combined with qualifying keywords such as "ballot," "vote," or "mail-in," enabled us to detect more complex and subtle patterns and co-occurrences that can be easily lost in dictionaries relying on hashtags or single-word references.

Theoretically, we believe this is critical because even these more subtle expressions of doubt can help produce fertile ground for election fraud beliefs. Without using qualitative analysis to develop this dictionary, we would have missed out on the full breadth of fraud-related claims being made and underestimated the amount of fraud posts in our sample. Other researchers may benefit from using qualitative analysis to develop more accurate measures of popular discourse, which can ultimately produce more reliable results in quantitative analysis.

Multilevel Perspectives for Improved Analytical Specificity in Explaining When, Where, or Why

In analyzing our data, we go beyond asking "How much does election disinformation spread?" and specify our inquiry by asking "What communities are strategically targeted by and most vulnerable to disinformation campaigns?" Adopting a multilevel approach exposed that local Republican parties' posts on election fraud target communities based on local sociopolitical features in order to maximize their electoral advantage.

The prevailing approach of multilevel analysis combines survey responses with community data (measured by zip code, county, or media market) to study the micro-meso relationship between individuals and their locality. Despite the insights this approach generates, the micro-meso relationship is only one type of multilevel relationship in the complex layers of structures, forces, and actors on the transnational, national, regional, state, county, city, neighborhood, or familial level (Friedland et al., 2022). More important, we still know little about how multiple layers *intersect and interact*. The broader takeaway of our work on January 6th is that disinformation cannot be explained by macro-, meso-, or micro-level factors *alone*.

We aimed to capture the multilevel dynamic by taking account of both state-level politics and more granular county-level sociopolitical features. This approach revealed how Facebook posts about election fraud were deployed in strategic ways. Posts about election fraud were most prevalent in states where Trump lost in 2020 and were particularly concentrated in counties with growing Trump support. From other work in this volume, we know that these election fraud claims tapped into the white Christian identities that unify much of the political right to induce feelings of threat (Thompson, this volume; Young, this volume). We argue that this patterned posting was an effort to mobilize outrage among supporters in places where a recount could flip the state for Trump. This state-county interaction suggests that although the digital presence of local political parties is dwarfed by national partisan elites, the platform-empowered, antidemocratic attacks from county Republican parties have been strategic, targeting locations that would yield the most politically advantageous results.

This example illustrates the methodological advantages of taking account of multilevel dynamics: without paying careful attention to local contextual factors, we would have missed the strategic agency that local actors use alongside the nationalized actors that dominate the literature. While we focus on geographic variation, there are many other multilevel dynamics that disinformation researchers could explore. For example, how does disinformation spread across national, regional, and local media? How do conspiratorial beliefs vary across or within cultural, racial, or ethnic communities and families?

Multilevel Qualitative Analysis for Studying Content Flows in Hybrid Information Environments

Although the term "multilevel analysis" is mostly used in quantitative research, our research highlights the benefits of studying multilevel dynamics of disinformation using qualitative or mixed methods. Reflecting the nationalization of American politics (Hopkins, 2018), the popular discourse on January 6th, antidemocratic movements, and the disinformation crisis are often nationalized. However, by paying attention to local context during our qualitative analysis, we were able to detect election fraud narratives that were hyperlocal. Doing so enabled us to study *the local-national feedback loop*, whereby local and national instances of disinformation mutually reinforce one another to bolster election fraud claims.

To illustrate this, we'll use the example of the "lost" flash drive in Milwaukee, Wisconsin. The statewide conservative news outlet Wisconsin Right Now published a story alleging that Milwaukee's chief election official misplaced a flash drive containing absentee votes, which disproportionately went to Biden (Piwowarczyk, 2020). This story rapidly circulated across Facebook, spread to other social media platforms like Twitter and Parler, and was picked up by major national conservative outlets like The Gateway Pundit (Hardee & Chen, 2020; Hoft, 2020). The local story became so widespread that it was fact-checked by *USA Today* as "100% wrong" (Litke, 2020). In reality, the chief election official accidentally left a flash drive in a voting machine and, immediately upon realizing her mistake, contacted a colleague who was still on location. The flash drive was never unattended, and this entire ordeal took less than 10 minutes.[1] This was an example of human error, not a highly coordinated conspiracy.

This exemplifies how local stories play an important role in spreading disinformation. National-level claims of election fraud certainly influenced local discourse surrounding the Milwaukee flash drive incident, but these local claims also fed back up into the national discourse. This story was used by national political elites and conservative media as a concrete example of how this election went so wrong and how local election officials played a role in this larger conspiracy.

---

[1] Executive Director Claire Woodall-Vogg, letter to Administrator Meagan Wolfe, Wisconsin Election Commission, Nov. 9, 2020, https://s3.documentcloud.org/documents/20404086/wolfe-letter-regarding-flash-drivedocx-2.pdf.

178 RESEARCH AFTER JANUARY 6, 2021

There are countless other instances like this that emerged in our analysis, among them, the false claim that Arizona's Maricopa County audit found 17,000 duplicate votes (Kim, 2021), the false claim that a "glitch" in Antrim County, Michigan, "switched" 6,000 votes from Trump to Biden (Putterman, 2020), and the false claim that more than 20,000 dead people voted in Pennsylvania (Alba, 2020). Instances like these are powerful because they allow people at the national level to cite specific instances of "fraud," but also because they enable people locally to see "evidence" of fraud in their own backyard. By paying particular attention to the local dimensions of disinformation, we were able to examine how these hyperlocal disinformation narratives are part of a local-national feedback loop that bolstered election fraud claims. We encourage other researchers to use a multilevel, mixed-methods approach to examine these dynamics in other disinformation campaigns—from the national spread of conspiracy theories about "crisis actors" in the wake of mass shootings to the transnational spread of conspiracy theories related to COVID-19 vaccines and social justice protests (Corley, 2021; Perrone & Loucaides, 2021; Wilson, 2018).

Mixed-Methods, Multilevel Analysis for Generating, Testing, and Contextualizing Theory

Combining mixed-methods and multilevel perspectives offers opportunities to generate, test, and contextualize theories. A multilevel approach enables researchers to detect local-, state-, and national-level dynamics, while mixed methods allow researchers to leverage multiple methodological approaches "in complementary strengths and nonoverlapping weaknesses" to inform theory development (Johnson & Onwuegbuzie, 2004, 18). In our project, we implemented a sequential, integrative design (Small, 2011), meaning we moved between qualitative and quantitative analysis over time, using the same data set. This approach allowed us to generate working theories about variations in accusations of election fraud across different levels qualitatively and test those hypotheses quantitatively.

Our qualitative analysis revealed that county parties often referenced events or actors from other states to bolster their own fraud claims. While this occurred in all of our cases, stark differences emerged. In Georgia and Michigan, posts about election fraud were overwhelmingly focused on local events. By contrast, in Ohio and North Carolina (the only states in our sample where Trump won in 2020), fraud-related events in other states dominated newsfeeds. This suggested that local county parties strategically deployed election fraud claims to mobilize followers in ways that were most likely to benefit Trump. In states where Trump lost and the election results were contested, they mobilized followers locally to put pressure on election officials and state government. In states where Trump won and there wasn't much to accomplish locally, they riled up supporters to focus their energy outward, toward other states or the national "Stop the Steal" movement.

To test this hypothesis quantitatively, we developed a set of state-specific dictionaries that included locations (e.g., Milwaukee, Wisconsin; Berks County, Pennsylvania) and key actors from each state (e.g., Michigan secretary of state Jocelyn Benson, Georgia secretary of state Brad Raffensperger). We applied these dictionaries to each state, identifying whether fraud posts were focused locally or on other states, using a multilevel perspective. What we found confirmed our working theory. In states where Trump lost, fraud posts were overwhelmingly focused on in-state fraud claims and targeted counties with growing Trump support. In states where Trump won, fraud posts tended to focus on fraud claims in other states. Our multilevel analytical perspective, combined with our iterative approach of using qualitative analysis to generate hypotheses and quantitative analysis to test these hypotheses allowed us to uncover new dimensions of the political strategy used by local county parties to perpetuate 2020 election fraud claims and mobilize supporters.

Mixed-Methods, Multilevel Analysis beyond January 6th

There are many opportunities to leverage a multilevel, mixed-methods approach in the study of political communication. We believe this approach could be especially useful in studying other disinformation campaigns, like the recent explosion of discourse surrounding critical race theory (CRT) at the national *and* local levels, which obscures the origins of this theoretical perspective and elicits fear over how race is taught in schools. As reported by Popular Information, websites publishing anti-CRT disinformation have taken on the appearance of "local news" sites (Gabbatt, 2021). These websites are coordinated by a large media network, Media Metric, that operates more than a thousand "local news" sites across the United States (Legum et al., 2021). These websites often publish stories with identical headlines and content but add a "local" touch, situating the story in their respective communities by swapping out the name of the city or county. Versions of these reports were repetitively populated hundreds of times on the same site, with only a few days between each version. This phenomenon even occurs among more legitimate local news sources, exemplified by the "must-runs" at Sinclair affiliates (Ember, 2017). While the most fertile grounds for anti-CRT stories published by these websites are states where lawmakers have pushed or passed bills targeting how race is taught in schools (e.g., Florida, Texas, Ohio), stories are also picked up by national far-right websites and anti-CRT groups as talking points for the national movement against addressing systemic racism (Legum et al., 2021).

This is one of many cases where local sources, often regarded as more trustworthy and less partisan than their national counterparts (Gottfried & Liedke, 2021), are strategically utilized to spread disinformation as a part of a nationwide campaign. By paying attention to how local, state, and national dynamics intersect and interact, researchers will be better equipped to study how disinformation is amplified, coordinated, and recycled in public opinion.

Conclusion

Throughout this chapter, we have encouraged researchers to shift their analytical vantage point, using a mixed-methods, multilevel perspective to examine a familiar phenomenon from a new perspective. In our own work on January 6th, this approach allowed us to refine our measurements, gain analytical specificity, uncover new mechanisms such as the local-national feedback loop, and generate and test new hypotheses. Drawing on a breadth of methodological tools allowed us to be creative and curious in ways that were reflexive and generative.

The utility of this methodological approach extends well beyond the academy. Rather than seeing events like January 6th as the result of nationalized (or internationalized) forces much bigger than ourselves, we can begin to see how local context, subnational institutions, and ordinary people all play an integral role in these political moments. That recognition is powerful. In paying close attention to people's lived experiences, uncovering new processes, and improving analytical specificity, our approach makes it possible to imagine the different types of interventions that can preserve the health of our democracy. This means that local policymakers, activists, media practitioners, and educators all have a role to play in repairing civil society by investing in trusted journalism, using evidence-based tactics to correct misperceptions in the communities where disinformation has the most impact, and in targeted efforts to foster democratic values.

References

Abilov, A., Hua, Y., Matatov, H., Amir, O., & Naaman, M. (2021). *VoterFraud2020: A multi modal dataset of election fraud claims on Twitter* [arXiv:2101.08210]. arXiv. http://arxiv.org/abs/2101.08210

Alba, D. (2020, Nov. 7). No, 20,000 dead people in Pennsylvania did not vote. *The New York Times*. https://www.nytimes.com/2020/11/06/technology/dead-voters-pennsylvania.html

BBC. (2022, June 9). Capitol riots timeline: What happened on 6 January 2021? https://www.bbc.com/news/world-us-canada-56004916

Corley, C. (2021, May 25). Black Lives Matter fights disinformation to keep the movement strong. NPR. https://www.npr.org/2021/05/25/999841030/black-lives-matter-fights-disinformation-to-keep-the-movement-strong

Dempsey, S., Suk, J., Cramer, K., Friedland, L., Wagner, M., & Shah, D. (2020). Understanding Trump supporters' news use: Beyond the Fox News bubble. *The Forum*, *18*, 319–346. https://doi.org/10.1515/for-2020-2012

Ember, S. (2017, May 13). Sinclair requires TV stations to air segments that tilt to the tight. *The New York Times*. https://www.nytimes.com/2017/05/12/business/media/sinclair-broadcast-komo-conservative-media.html

Feuer, A., Schmidt, M. S., & Broadwater, L. (2022, Mar. 29). New focus on how a Trump tweet incited far-right groups ahead of Jan. 6. *The New York Times*. https://www.nytimes.com/2022/03/29/us/politics/trump-tweet-jan-6.html

Friedland, L. A., Shah, D. V., Wagner, M. W., Wells, C., Cramer, K. J., & Pevehouse, J. (2022). *Battleground: Asymmetric communication ecologies and the erosion of civil society in Wisconsin*. Cambridge University Press.

Gabbatt, A. (2021, Nov. 17). The fake news sites pushing Republicans' critical race theory scare. *The Guardian*. https://www.theguardian.com/us-news/2021/nov/17/fake-news-sites-republicans-critical-race-theory-scare

Gottfried, J., & Liedke, J. (2021, Aug. 30). Partisan divides in media trust widen, driven by a decline among Republicans. Pew Research Center. https://www.pewresearch.org/fact-tank/2021/08/30/partisan-divides-in-media-trust-widen-driven-by-a-decline-among-republicans/

Grigoropoulou, N., & Small, M. (2022). The data revolution in social science needs qualitative research. *Nature Human Behaviour*, 1–3. https://doi.org/10.1038/s41562-022-01333-7

Hardee, H., & Chen, K. (2020, Nov. 13). Misplaced Milwaukee flash drive morphs into false reports of election fraud. Madison.com. https://madison.com/news/local/govt-and-politics/misplaced-milwaukee-flash-drive-morphs-into-false-reports-of-election-fraud/article_7298a123-f102-5220-b6f3-cc3ba39e1e2b.html

Hodges, L. (2022, Jan. 2). Trump still says his supporters weren't behind the Jan. 6 attack—But I was there. NPR. https://www.npr.org/2022/01/02/1068891351/january-6-insurrection-capitol-attack-trump-anniversary

Hoft, J. (2020, Nov. 13). Developing: Milwaukee elections chief lost elections flash drive in morning hours of November 4th when Democrats miraculously found 120,000 votes for Joe Biden. *The Gateway Pundit*. https://www.thegatewaypundit.com/2020/11/developing-milwaukee-elections-chief-lost-elections-flash-drive-morning-hours-november-4th-democrats-miraculously-found-120000-votes-joe-biden/

Hopkins, D. J. (2018). *The increasingly United States: How and why American political behavior nationalized*. University of Chicago Press. https://press.uchicago.edu/ucp/books/book/chicago/I/bo27596045.html

Johnson, R. B., & Onwuegbuzie, A. J. (2004). Mixed methods research: A research paradigm whose time has come. *Educational Researcher, 33*(7), 14–26. https://doi.org/10.3102/0013189X033007014

Kim, N. Y. (2021, Sept. 29). Fact-check: Did the Maricopa County audit find "over 17,000 duplicates of votes"? *Austin American-Statesman*. https://www.statesman.com/story/news/politics/2021/09/29/did-maricopa-county-arizona-audit-find-17-000-duplicate-votes/5902985001/

Legum, J., Zkeria, T., & Rebecca, C. (2021, Nov. 8). Right-wing operatives deploy massive network of fake local news sites to weaponize CRT. Popular Information. https://popular.info/p/right-wing-operatives-deploy-massive

Litke, E. (2020, Nov. 17). Fact check: Milwaukee flash drive incident unrelated to Biden votes. *USA Today*. https://www.usatoday.com/story/news/factcheck/2020/11/17/fact-check-milwaukee-flash-drive-incident-unrelated-biden-votes/6325022002/

Perrone, A., & Loucaides, D. (2021, Aug. 17). "Spreading like a virus": Inside the EU's struggle to debunk Covid lies. *The Guardian*. https://www.theguardian.com/world/2021/aug/17/spreading-like-a-virus-inside-the-eus-struggle-to-debunk-covid-lies

Piwowarczyk, J. (2020, Nov. 6). Milwaukee election flash drive was briefly lost, sources say. Wisconsin Right Now. https://www.wisconsinrightnow.com/2020/11/06/milwaukee-election-flash-drive/

Putterman, S. (2020, Nov. 18). Inaccurate early vote count in one Michigan county was a human error, not a failure of the software. PolitiFact. https://www.politifact.com/factchecks/2020/nov/18/ted-nugent/inaccurate-early-vote-count-onmichigan-county-was-/

Rubin, O., Bruggeman, L., & Steakin, W. (2021, Jan. 19). QAnon emerges as recurring theme of criminal cases tied to US Capitol siege. ABC News. https://abcnews.go.com/US/qanon-emerges-recurring-theme-criminal-cases-tied-us/story?id=75347445

Small, M. L. (2011). How to conduct a mixed methods study: Recent trends in a rapidly growing literature. *Annual Review of Sociology, 37*(1), 57–86. https://doi.org/10.1146/annurev.soc.012809.102657

Wells, C., Cramer, K. J., Wagner, M. W., Alvarez, G., Friedland, L. A., Shah, D. V., Bode, L., Edgerly, S., Gabay, I., & Franklin, C. (2017). When we stop talking politics: The maintenance and closing of conversation in contentious times. *Journal of Communication, 67*(1), 131–157. https://doi.org/10.1111/jcom.12280

Wilson, J. (2018, Feb. 21). Crisis actors, deep state, false flag: The rise of conspiracy theory code words. *The Guardian*. https://www.theguardian.com/us-news/2018/feb/21/crisis-actors-deep-state-false-flag-the-rise-of-conspiracy-theory-code-words

20

Afflicting the Comfortable

Dave Karpf

There have to be consequences.

If we are to stave off the next insurrection, it is essential that the people who planned the last one face social sanctions. If January 6, 2021, becomes a badge of honor or a pathway to profit and power, then we seal the collective fate of the nation. (This has been the task of the January 6th commission. At the time of this writing, it is too early to gauge their ultimate success.)

We can approach the problem of preventing the next insurrection from three main angles. We can focus on the mass public—the Republican Party-in-Electorate, a majority of whom now tells pollsters that they believe Trump won the 2020 election despite all evidence to the contrary. We can focus on the communication channels—the social media and partisan media that, through a mix of algorithmic and analytics-based optimization, disseminate and amplify these lies because they prove to be good for business even if they are bad for democracy. Or we can focus on the media and political elites—the small set of powerful actors who crafted the Big Lie, sought advantage through it, and are setting plans in motion for next time.

All three angles deserve attention. But it appears to me that they are often prioritized in the wrong order.

It is easiest to bemoan public misinformation and the loss of social trust and cohesion at the mass scale—to ask searching questions about why the Republican electorate has lost faith in our political institutions and to earnestly pursue efforts to rebuild that wellspring of bygone institutional trust. There has never been a social problem that "civic education" could not be rendered a solution to.

It is nearly as easy, in recent years, to blame the social media platforms. Facebook and Google spent the previous decade displacing mainstream media organizations as the gatekeeper of newsworthiness and public information/disinformation. They did so while absorbing mainstream media's advertising revenues, hastening the decline in local journalism. The

Dave Karpf, *Afflicting the Comfortable* In: *Media and January 6th*. Edited by: Khadijah Costley White, Daniel Kreiss, Shannon C. McGregor, and Rebekah Tromble, Oxford University Press. © Oxford University Press 2024.
DOI: 10.1093/oso/9780197758526.003.0020

social platforms have been lousy gatekeepers, far more likely to issue belated apologies than timely corrections. And yet, precisely because of the well-earned animosity between legacy journalism and the digital platforms, there has been a rush to place the lion's share of the blame at the new gatekeepers' feet. (Could Facebook have done a better job of tamping down on the Big Lie in the months leading up to the insurrection? Yes. Was Facebook *responsible* for the insurrection? No. It was a valuable tool that ought to have rendered itself less valuable.)

The partisan elites, meanwhile, behave with an audacity that suggests they have evaluated their situation and determined they have nothing to fear and everything to gain from their association with the insurrection. The Trump-supporting masses who sacked the Capitol face jail time. The Trump lieutenants who incited the attack are invited on *The Masked Singer*. The members of Congress who participated in the plot to overturn the election faced a brief reprisal from corporate donors announcing they would no longer donate to insurrectionists' reelection efforts. Those announcements lasted less than six months before the donations quietly rolled back in. At the time of this writing, it seems likely that Republican elites who supported, funded, or even participated in the insurrection will win contested primaries and go on to serve as secretaries of state, members of the House of Representatives, and governors.

The January 6th commission has done an impressive job of telling a clear story about these Republican elites. These elites lied to the public. They did so loudly and repeatedly. Their lies are well-documented. They made statements of fact that were demonstrably false, and then brazened forth, pretending those statements were true or insisting they had never made such statements in the first place (or sometimes, somehow, both at the same time!). Partisan elites—the Republic Party-in-Government and Party-in-Media—are responsible for spreading, validating, and rewarding the Big Lie. The commission has created a necessary yet insufficient spectacle, using all of the tools at their disposal. It is still unclear, at the time of this writing, whether and against whom the Justice Department will bring charges. It is eighteen months after January 6th, and it is still too early to draw conclusions about efforts at elite accountability. Unless there are legal repercussions, the work of elite accountability is going to require constant normative vigilance. There is still a real risk that the January 6 insurrection will be converted into a Trumpist Woodstock. If that occurs, then future insurrection attempts become a near-certainty.

Of Norms, Laws, and Democratic Myths

We are governed both by formal laws and informal norms.

The law is enforced by the state—law-breaking carries the risk of onerous lawsuits, fines (for misdemeanors), and jail time (for felonies). It is enforced unequally, by design—there are those the law protects but does not bind (elites) and those the law binds but does not protect (subaltern publics). It is also limited by both the will and the imagination of a constrained legislature and judiciary.

The January 6th commission has made clear that the insurrection was part of a coordinated, broader strategy to overturn the results of the election. It is not yet clear whether the Justice Department will pursue any charges against Trump and his accomplices. And felony convictions, even in the face of overwhelming evidence, would still hinge on drawing a jury that lacks a single enthusiastic Trump supporter. It appears unlikely at the time of this writing that the 117th Congress will pass any new laws to protect against future attempts to undermine electoral democracy in the United States. Existing laws did not prevent the last insurrection, and it does not appear as though any new laws will be added to prevent the next one.

Norms are enforced by social pressure. They are rarely explicitly stated. They represent, instead, a shared collective understanding of how one is *supposed to* behave in a given situation. Norms are a powerful force governing social behavior. Violate a norm, and you risk being ostracized. It is not the state that will sanction you—it is your peers. And while laws change through formal channels and are interpreted, slowly and unequally, by the judicial system, norms change in informal and haphazard fashion. When someone violates a long-standing norm and faces no social consequence, that norm ceases to have force.

I have written previously about the importance of the "myth of the attentive public" for maintaining an even barely functional version of American democracy:

> The myth of the attentive public is a normative belief among media and political elites that there is a public trust between politicians and their constituents, that those constituents are aware (or might at any time become aware) of politicians that stray from their public promises or violate the public trust, and that those who are found to violate the public trust or break their public promises will incur a cost. (Karpf, 2019)

Here I deploy the term "myth" in the same sense as Vincent Mosco in his 2004 book, *The Digital Sublime*. "Myths," Mosco writes, "are neither true nor false, but living or dead" (p. 3). Our system of representative democracy operates on the normative assumption that its elite participants adhere, at least loosely, to the myth of the attentive public. As the relevant norms are repeatedly violated without consequence—as the myth of the attentive public withers and dies—democratic failure becomes increasingly likely. You cannot operate a representative democracy if the elected representatives do not believe in democratic norms or think that they will not be held accountable for betraying the will of the voters.

It would certainly be better if the partisan elites who plotted to overturn the election faced legal repercussions. It would also have been better if the U.S. Senate had made voting rights/electoral integrity legislation filibuster-proof and passed some new laws. But staring at the likelihood that our laws will not be enforced or amended in this case, let me suggest that it is especially important that we create a normative social penalty for egregious actions. To stave off the next insurrection, we must vociferously *afflict the comfortable*.

A Guiding Example: Socially Sanctioning John Eastman

On January 6, 2021, John Eastman stood on the rally stage before Donald Trump's outraged supporters and told the assembled masses that they were the only thing standing in the way of an election that he had *proof* was stolen: "We know there was fraud . . . we know that dead people voted . . . [and] we now know . . . how the machines contributed to that fraud." He went on to describe a system of "secret folders" maliciously installed in voting machine software that awarded fake votes to Biden on November 3rd and also to Senators-elect Warnock and Ossoff in the January 5th Georgia runoff election.

Eastman was, at that time, the dean of Chapman University's Law School and a Visiting Professor of Conservative Thought and Policy at the University of Colorado, as well as the founding director of the Claremont Institute's Center for Constitutional Jurisprudence. He was a former Supreme Court clerk and a member in good standing of the Federalist Society. He was also a member of President Trump's legal team. He was, in other words, exactly the person that you would be predisposed to trust on these matters if you were a supporter of the outgoing president.

It's worth pausing to consider the alternate universe where the speeches John Eastman, Rudy Giuliani, and their co-conspirators delivered on the stage that day were actually true. *What if* we lived in a world where the opposition party had, in fact, seized control of the voting machines, installed software that fixed the vote so they could never lose, and were just hours away from installing a permanent government? Under such circumstances, the insurrectionists would be courageously breaking formal laws in support of a higher moral principle. Just as Facebook made an exception in its "no calls for violence" rules for Ukrainians calling for violence against invading Russian soldiers (Dwoskin, 2022), the insurrectionists' attempt to overturn the results of the 2020 election would be justified if the election had, in fact, been revealed as a massive fraud.

Likewise, in the alternate universe where the Democrats had in fact hacked the ballot machines to steal the election, it would be important for social media platforms *not to crack down* on posts questioning the integrity of our election system or groups planning mass protests of an *actually* stolen election.

The central fact we must grapple with is that *Eastman was making it all up.* There were no "secret folders" in the voting machines. Trump's legal team had filed over 60 lawsuits asserting claims of systematic voter fraud. All of them had been laughed out of court. In Georgia, Democrats were not even the party in control of election administration! Eastman, Giuliani, and the rest of Trump's team invented a fiction, spread that fiction through social media and partisan media, and deployed that fiction to Trump's assembled angry supporters. Chapman University and the University of Colorado both severed ties with Eastman in the aftermath of the insurrection. But the Claremont Institute—which had played an active role disseminating the "Stop the Steal" narrative (Field, 2021)—vocally supported him.

What next for partisan elites like John Eastman, who chose to abandon the norms that undergird American electoral democracy? What next for the Claremont Institute?

The answer, I believe, is *social shaming.* Eastman ought to be ostracized—disinvited from conferences, barred from professional associations, stripped of all of the status markers that he used to perpetrate dangerous lies that contributed to the January 6th attack. If he is rewarded with sinecures and speaking engagements, invited on cable news to share his unique perspective on things, then it is a signal that his actions were just politics-as-usual. If, instead, he is denied access to the status privileges to which he has grown

188 RESEARCH AFTER JANUARY 6, 2021

accustomed, then it signals there are, in fact, lines that cannot be crossed without social consequence. Eastman ought to become a cautionary tale; partisan elites ought to worry about becoming the "next John Eastman."

And that social shaming ought to extend to those civic associations that refuse to condemn Eastman. The Claremont Institute spent the Trump years positioning itself as the think tank providing ideological heft to Trumpism. Its leadership could have treated the January 6th insurrection as a breaking point, a bridge too far. Instead, the Claremont Institute has forged ahead, supporting Eastman and insisting that he has been unfairly maligned, another instance of "cancel culture" run amok. Their continued association with Eastman is a strong, clear signal about their stance on the January 6th insurrection. If that stance does not carry normative consequences, then the norms cease to function.

One benefit of focusing on normative consequences for political elites like Eastman is that it can create leverage points where we can be more than just passive spectators, doomscrolling and tweeting comments into the void. The Department of Justice can bring charges against Eastman if they determine they have sufficient evidence that he has broken the law. The January 6th committee can subpoena him. These entities have formal authority that you and I lack. But in September 2021, as news broke about Eastman's involvement in the attempt to subvert the formal counting of electoral votes, a few political scientists pointed out that he was scheduled to speak on two Claremont-sponsored panels at the American Political Science Association (APSA) annual meeting.

John Eastman appearing on an APSA panel is not a major event. APSA hosts thousands of concurrent panels. They are sparsely attended by people with overlapping research interests. Claremont Institute–sponsored panels are attended by Claremont Institute members and their fellow travelers (traditionally a group of political theorists from the "West Coast Straussian" tradition). One could certainly adopt the logic of the proverbial tree-falling-in-the-forest here. If an insurrectionist appears on a panel and no one is there to hear it except his long-standing allies, does it make a sound?

But in the days after January 6th, the APSA Council issued a statement formally condemning "President Trump, Republican legislators, and all those who have continuously endorsed and disseminated falsehoods and misinformation, and who have worked to overturn the results of a free and fair Presidential Election." Eastman appearing on an APSA panel alongside his Claremont Institute colleagues would signal that the APSA statement was just cheap talk. Disinviting Eastman and ending Claremont's status as an APSA "related group" would signal that APSA has an actual normative commitment to electoral democracy that it is willing to defend.

As a professor of political science, I have far more agency to make meaningful demands of my professional association than of the Department of Justice. I took it upon myself to draft an open letter to the APSA Council, requesting that APSA rescind the Claremont Institute's status as a related group (meaning Claremont would no longer host panels at the convention) and Eastman be stripped of his status as an APSA member (Karpf, 2021). I circulated a link to the letter on Twitter, and it was signed by over 280 political scientists. Similar to the activist campaigns described by Jackson et al. (2020), it developed into an organizing tool that attracted media attention, further ratcheting up the social media pressure.

APSA responded by moving all of the Claremont Institute's panels to "online-only" status in order to prevent potential in-person confrontations at a convention that was occurring amid COVID-related public health concerns. (Shouting matches, circa 2021, can also be super-spreader events.) Claremont then canceled all 10 of their scheduled panels, declaring the woke mob had taken over APSA. As of the time of this writing, Eastman is no longer a member of APSA and the Claremont Institute is no longer listed as an APSA related group. It is a small victory, but a victory nonetheless.

Notice here that what I am calling for is, in fact, a selective *increase* in polarization. The Federalist Society is also an APSA related group, and Eastman is a longtime member of that organization. But the Federalist Society quietly distanced itself from Eastman in the aftermath of January 6th, so it would be a strategic overreach to demand they be held responsible for their previous association with him. The point is to create meaningful normative distance between individuals who provided material support for the insurrection and those who did not.

"Legitimate Political Discourse" and the Future of the Republican Party

Let us be clear about limitations, though: If we manage to prevent the next January 6th, it will not be because of the courageous actions of the professoriate. We all have a contribution to make, but some have a much greater mix of power and responsibility than others.

190   RESEARCH AFTER JANUARY 6, 2021

A standard refrain in my post–January 6th writing has been *Only the Republican Party can fix the Republican Party*. The U.S. government is structured such that it can function only when both parties are at least nominally committed to the work of governance. And, particularly between the geographic biases of the Senate and the electoral comforts provided by gerrymandered House districts, there is little direct pressure that Democrats, mainstream media figures, policy experts, or public intellectuals can put on Republican politicians. If conservative media and political elites abandon all pretense of belief in the myth of the attentive public, and if furthermore they decide that they simply do not have any attachment to electoral democracy, then the only hope in the short or medium term is that they be *replaced by other Republicans*.

It was a particularly foreboding sign when, on February 4, 2022, the Republican National Committee formally declared that the January 6th attack was "legitimate political discourse" and passed a motion of censure against Liz Cheney and Adam Kinzinger for the sin of agreeing to serve on the House Select Committee on the January 6th Attack. It is the official position of the Republican Party that a Republican can attempt to sack the Capitol building in support of Donald J. Trump, but participating in an investigation of a plot to overthrow the government is grounds for expulsion.

As I write this chapter, some of the most extreme members of the Republican Party's Trumpist faction are running credible campaigns to become secretaries of state or governors in key swing states. They are running explicitly on the platform that the 2020 election was stolen, that incumbent Republican election officials did not do enough to "stop the steal," and that, if elected, they will ensure Trump's victory in 2024 regardless of the vote totals.

Even if Democrats win every close race against these authoritarian extremists, American democracy simply cannot last if it hinges on Democrats winning every close race, every time. The normative pressure must come from institutional Republicans as well. It must be significant and sustained and ultimately successful.

Creating sustained normative penalties for those associated with the insurrection is one way to help these efforts. It signals that there are still lines that cannot be crossed (and that those lines are not merely "Republican-versus-Democrat").

Pressuring, shaming, and shunning the political and media elites behind the "Stop the Steal" message is not the sole lever for preventing the next January 6th. Other contributors to this volume will surely make the case for focusing on the mass public and/or the partisan media and digital media platform. Those efforts will be important too.

But I believe it is essential that scrutiny, criticism, and pressure also be brought to bear on the elites. We must *afflict the comfortable*, so to speak.

Otherwise, predicting the next insurrection will be a matter of when, not if.

References

Dwoskin, E. (2022, Mar. 10). Facebook breaks its own rules to allow for some calls to violence against Russian invaders. *Washington Post*. https://www.washingtonpost.com/technology/2022/03/10/facebook-violence-russians/

Field, L. K. (2021, July 13). What the hell happened to the Claremont Institute? The Bulwark. https://www.thebulwark.com/what-the-hell-happened-to-the-claremont-institute/

Jackson, S. J., Bailey, M., & Welles, B. F. (2020). *#HashtagActivism: Networks of race and gender justice*. MIT Press.

Karpf, D. (2019, Dec. 10). On digital disinformation and Democratic myths [Expert Reflection]. Social Science Research Council. https://mediawell.ssrc.org/expert-reflections/on-digital-disinformation-and-democratic-myths/

Karpf, D. (2021, Sept. 23). An open letter to the American Political Science Association regarding John Eastman and the Claremont Institute. Medium. https://medium.com/@davekarpf/an-open-letter-to-the-american-political-science-association-regarding-john-eastman-and-the-5c450b0ffa14

Mosco, V. (2004). *The digital sublime: Myth, power, and cyberspace*. MIT Press.

21

Taking It to the States

Lewis Friedland

I write this chapter having retired from academia (formally) in January 2022, which paradoxically has freed me to speak my mind. While I am still involved in scholarship in social theory and political communication, I am also more directly involved in politics in my home state of Wisconsin. As I will argue here, we are in a state of democratic emergency leading up to the 2024 elections with very immediate, practical, and dangerous consequences. The 2022 midterm elections saw Democratic gubernatorial victories in the swing states of Wisconsin, Pennsylvania, and Michigan, attenuating the immediate threat of these states illegally handing the election to a Republican presidential candidate in 2024 with the likely aid of the U.S. Supreme Court (SCOTUS).[1] But this is not the end.

Here, I will move quickly through some observations about the current state of American politics probably obvious to anyone reading this book. I will then analyze the current balance of power in these swing states, focusing on my home state of Wisconsin. Finally, I will point to some steps that all citizens can take, but particularly those with political communication skills.

Likely Shared Assumptions

The United States is precariously balanced between a weakening democracy and potential authoritarian rule by a radicalized, minority Republican Party split among different factions working in coalition and overlapping

---

[1] As I write, SCOTUS has just taken up a North Carolina case concerning the so-called independent state legislature doctrine promulgated by insurrectionist lawyer John Eastman and others which will allow state legislatures to override electorates and state supreme court decisions. It is a road map for Republican authoritarianism, and only a fool would bet against a favorable decision from the current radical right-wing Court (Liptak & Corasaniti, 2022).

Lewis Friedland, *Taking It to the States* In: *Media and January 6th*. Edited by: Khadijah Costley White, Daniel Kreiss, Shannon C. McGregor, and Rebekah Tromble, Oxford University Press. © Oxford University Press 2024.
DOI: 10.1093/oso/9780197758526.003.0021

in multiple ways: a ruthless, authoritarian faction, currently led by Donald Trump but which could equally (and more effectively) be led by Florida governor Ron DeSantis or others; a right-wing libertarian faction, backed by the Koch group and others, organized around opportunistic careerists exemplified by Senator Mitch McConnell (R-KY), congressional Republicans, and the effective seizure of the SCOTUS, whose primary goal is the dismantling of the New Deal state; a Christian authoritarian faction whose goal is a reversion to a form of patriarchy, exemplified by the *Dobbs* decision and potential rolling back of contraception, LGBTQ rights, and same-sex marriage; a white nationalist faction whose goal is to promote the racist "great replacement" theory and roll back both civil rights and immigration. This coalition has its own media ecosystem, consisting of Fox News and One America News Network, conservative talk radio, and a range of internet and social media actors (from Breitbart to Infowars) which promotes and amplifies their messages. This adds discipline and cohesion as well as amplifies and exaggerates the right wing's strength to non-right-wing media and political actors.

It is easy to forget, however, that while these groups form a majority of the Republican *Party*, the party represents about 30% of the country (Gallup, 2022). And, as the August 2022 Kansas abortion amendment vote importantly demonstrated, not even a majority of Republicans and independent leaners support all of the party's signature extreme views. A significant minority of Republicans (~33%) are opposed to Trump; these are traditional conservatives who believe in the rule of law or moderates who are simply concerned with taxes and pocketbook issues (Pew Research, 2021). Crucially, rolling back authoritarian one-party rule in the northern swing states absolutely requires winning *some* percentage of this electorate.

The Republican coalition operates in a system which gives it structural advantages in the electoral college and U.S. Senate, even while losing majority support in national and some statewide elections. These structural advantages are mirrored at the state level, where rural and exurban districts have outsized political power, which is greatly magnified by gerrymandering that has now been effectively blessed by SCOTUS and is therefore simply not going to change quickly (Daley, 2017). Further, as Jane Mayer (2022) has shown using the case of Ohio, gerrymandering not only guarantees one-party rule, but it amplifies the most extreme right-wing voices within the party. Despite real and legitimate arguments that U.S. politics has been nationalized, my colleagues and I (Friedland et al., 2022) have shown in our in-depth analysis of Wisconsin that, at best, nationalization is incomplete. Political themes are often set nationally, but they play out in local and state geographies differently. States and even counties are fractal, meaning that cities are more "blue" than suburbs, suburbs than exurbs, towns than rural surrounds (Wells et al., 2021).

In response to the exurban-rural skew of the nation and states, progressive political strategies have emerged in varying forms that build on what was once called the "emerging Democratic majority" (Judis & Texeira, 2002): The educated, young, people of color, LGBTQ people, and others are growing in number, and (for reasons often unclear) they are likely to vote increasingly for the left. Many progressives and academics infer from this that the continuing majorities of white working-class people in the swing states and moderate suburbanites who have skewed Republican can be ignored.

States Are Different

But this is wrong for several reasons. First and foremost, the demographics of states vary tremendously. The emerging coalition strategy has had some success in Georgia, where 47% of people are African American, Latino, or Asian (although here as well, suburban moderates were essential in 2020 and 2022 Senate victories). However, the demography of the northern swing states is different. Numbers vary, but in Wisconsin, the census category of "white alone" is 86.6% of the state (in Michigan and Pennsylvania ~75%) (U.S. Census, n.d.). The majority of African Americans in Wisconsin are concentrated in five Democratic counties. This means that winning the statewide races (governor, attorney general, secretary of state) that can serve as a partial break on authoritarian rule requires a plurality of white voters. Second, because Wisconsin's gerrymander is the worst in the nation, in the wave year of 2018 Democrats won 53% of votes statewide but only 36.4% of state assembly seats. Republicans are only a few seats away from supermajorities in both houses, which would give control to (an even more) extreme right wing, similar to Ohio, which would almost certainly attempt to illegally hand the 2024 election to the Republican candidate. Any possibility of holding these controlling swing seats depends on winning white voters outside of Madison and Milwaukee. Third, polling and voting trends show that the issues that working-class African American and Latino voters care most about mostly overlap with those of their white counterparts: inflation and the economy, but also healthcare costs and crime.

How to navigate these cross-class, cross-racial issues goes well beyond this short chapter. Any just and equitable politics must be inclusive and oppose racism, sexism, and other deeply rooted inequalities. As Heather McGee (2021) has argued, the zero-sum paradigm that uses racism to separate Blacks and whites with common interests is at the heart of American politics. But any hope of progress on these questions also requires holding the line in the swing states and winning nationally. Any political strategy that does not take the need to win *now*, in 2024, should not be taken seriously as a defense of democracy.

Simply, winning executive offices in the upper swing states is essential to keep Trump or another authoritarian out of the White House in 2024. Wisconsin is already rife with phony (expensive taxpayer-financed) "investigations" of the 2020 election, and the Republican gubernatorial candidate in 2022 pledged to "overturn" the results if elected. Wisconsin's senior senator sought to give Vice President Pence an alternative slate of electors for the state. In short, this threat is neither hypothetical nor only long term. Anyone who doubts this should study the U.S. right's fascination with Victor Orban, Hungary's neofascist leader. When the Conservative Political Action Committee hosted him at its 2022 conference, the plan was explicit: Bring Orbanism (e.g., the end of "race mixing") to the United States. (Marantz, 2022). The battles in the swing states are pivotal to American democracy. If we lose them, it is all but certain that an authoritarian Republican will be elected president in 2024, with fewer and weaker checks, and a range of Orbanist programs will likely be put into place.

What, Then, Can Be Done?

What's happening in the states should become a more central focus of U.S. political communication research.

In the short run, I would ask my communication colleagues to focus on usable, practical questions. Scholars of political communication should begin to move away from the obsession with Twitter (X) simply because the data is there. In addition to our longer-term research programs, ask what the field can teach about persuasion and messaging in local and state-level communication ecologies. Actively translate your work wherever possible into clear, practical, nonacademic language that can be read and implemented by political activists and citizens. I work with a group of leaders of grassroots field efforts in 10 states. They lead local canvassing, postcarding, and other forms of field persuasion and have a working group to glean best practices from the political communication and political science literature. Even for someone who has been inside the academic tent for about 40 years, I can report that this is not easy. A few simple acts of translation would go a long way. Simply asking "How is my current research helping those who are on the front lines in the democracy fight, and what lessons can be learned?" would be very helpful, as would writing those lessons in clear, short prose.

Another step is to recognize explicitly that we will live in a very imperfect two-party system for the foreseeable future, and that altering it (with ranked choice voting, etc.) will require that Democrats win political power. There is no way around the fact that the Democratic Party is the party of democracy; the Republican Party is now an authoritarian party. Both-sides-ism in research obscures this truth, and therefore actually distorts our understanding of the political field. Scholars should build this recognition into research agendas and results.

Further, the hostility to the Democratic Party among much of the left academic community leads to a bias in favor of "grassroots" "tax-exempt" C3 and C4 groups (themselves often funded by big donors and foundations), which leads to a greater focus on social media–based communication, where left activism dominates. As some have recently argued, the power of large donors and foundations leads to a distortion of the field of center-left politics. But regardless of whether one accepts this premise, on the ground in Wisconsin, Michigan, and Pennsylvania, but also Arizona, Texas, Georgia, North Carolina, and Nevada, the institutional force working for equity and democracy is the Democratic Party.

State Democratic Parties range from good to imperfect to inept to bad. But in a two-party system, they are the only organizations that effectively can build year-round organizational infrastructure to defend democracy. Rather than lob criticisms, scholars would do well to actually look at these parties and examine how they work with grassroots groups or do not and what can be done to improve their organization (for examples, see Skocpol & Tervo, 2021; Putnam & Skocpol, 2018).

As communication scholars at this moment in history, we should be ruthlessly practical. What are the actual barriers to getting a political message across in the state and local ecologies where people actually live? What are the plausible pathways of persuasion? How do they vary for different groups? What kinds of messages have the potential to build coalitions for the defense of democracy that are broad enough to win majorities over some periods of years?

But we are also scholar-citizens. Here in Wisconsin, I have been working with the Democratic Party to understand how messaging can be improved at the state assembly and senate level, leveraging my knowledge of local networks and community communication ecologies. There is not a swing state party in the country that can't use similar assistance, and a pool of scholar-citizens working on this problem could leverage knowledge more quickly and practically and across a wider domain.

I have also been advising a new talk radio network that is covering the state. This is an institutional problem (how to build a network) but also a set of communication problems: What kind of programming is most likely to differentially affect the broadest swath of voters in the different subecologies of the state? What kind of local news can be built that will have local appeal to different audiences? How do we cost-effectively monitor messages and their effects for maximum impact? What is the effect on local voting, civic engagement, and civil society?

Of course, we all make our own decisions. It may be that you have a long-term research project that you are reluctant to take your focus away from or have other reasons to not shift your agenda. In that case, consider taking your skills in messaging and social media and helping your county Democratic Party, or if not the party, your favored independent grassroots group. County parties are closer to the grassroots (more democratic), but because of this, they are more like voluntary associations than big organizations. They are usually neglected by state parties (although this is slowly changing) and lack professional skills. Our own research has found that county Republican parties have actively spread the Big Lie about 2022 on Facebook (and are preparing the ground for 2024). This is an asymmetric fight because county Democratic parties are less skilled and active on Facebook (probably the most important medium outside of deep-blue areas, neglected in both research and practice). If you can't spare any of your research focus, volunteer your communication skills locally.

Being smart and critical is not nearly enough in these times. Provocations are not enough. People in the United States and around the world are taking to the front lines in the fight for democracy. We should do no less in our own backyards.

References

Daley, D. (2017). *Ratf**ked: The true story behind the secret plan to steal America's democracy*. W. W. Norton.

Friedland, L. A., Shah; D. V., Wagner, M. W., Wells, C., Cramer, K. J., & Pevehouse, J. C. W. (2022). *Battleground: Asymmetric communication ecologies and the erosion of civil society in Wisconsin*. Cambridge University Press.

Gallup. (2022, July). U.S. party affiliation. https://news.gallup.com/poll/15370/party-affiliation.aspx

Judis, J. B., & Texeira, R. (2002). *The emerging Democratic majority*. Scribner.

Liptak, A., & Corasaniti, N. (2022, June 30). Supreme Court to hear case on state legislatures' power over elections." *The New York Times*. https://www.nytimes.com/2022/06/30/us/politics/state-legislatures-elections-supreme-court.html

Marantz, A. (2022, June 27). Does Hungary offer a glimpse of our authoritarian future? *The New Yorker*.

Mayer, J. (2022, Aug. 6). State legislatures are torching democracy. *The New Yorker*.

McGhee, H. C. (2022). *The sum of us: What racism costs everyone and how we can prosper together*. One World.

Pew Research. (2021, Oct. 6). Two-thirds of Republicans want Trump to retain major political role; 44% want him to run again in 2024. https://www.pewresearch.org/fact-tank/2021/10/06/two-thirds-of-republicans-want-trump-to-retain-major-political-role-44-want-him-to-run-again-in-2024/

Putnam, L., & Skocpol, T. (2018, Aug. 21). Women are rebuilding the Democratic Party from the ground up. *The New Republic*. https://newrepublic.com/article/150462/women-rebuilding-democratic-party-ground

Skocpol, T., & Tervo, C. (2021, Feb. 4). Resistance disconnect: How Indivisible's national advocates and grassroots volunteers have pulled apart—and what could happen instead. *The American Prospect*. https://prospect.org/politics/resistance-disconnect-indivisible-national-local-activists/

U.S. Census. (n.d.). Quick Facts, Wisconsin. Retrieved August 11, 2022, from https://www.census.gov/quickfacts/fact/table/WI/PST045221

Wells, C., Friedland, L. A., Hughes, C., Shah, D. V., Suk, J., & Wagner, M. W. (2021). News media use, talk networks, and anti-elitism across geographic location: Evidence from Wisconsin. *The International Journal of Press/Politics*, *26*(2), 438–463.

22

Reparation through Reporting

Meredith D. Clark

When I consider the purpose of this volume, I am instantly reminded of similar questions that framed the 1968 Kerner Commission Report, an 11-month inquiry into race riots that rocked the country in the latter years of the civil rights movement:

What happened?
Why did it happen?
What can be done to prevent it from happening again?

One section of the report called out newsrooms across the country for their failure to hire, retain, and promote Black journalists who could intimately cover the other side of the color line—disrupting the fictions of social stability that surprised the privileged classes as race riots broke out in the late 1960s. In the decades since, programs to diversify news media have been launched, halfheartedly supported, and jettisoned. More recently, news media's so-called racial reckoning compelled the industry to examine its shortcomings on covering racialized inequality in the United States, and scores of outlets pledged to improve.

So Why Are We Here Again?

Because for all of the lessons from the past half-century, we have failed to consider discernment as a critical value in journalism. Informed by an ethic of care, discernment—the ability to judge well—goes beyond basic news savvy. As a central tenet of reparative journalism, its application on issues of sources and subjects is an essential tool for critiquing the coverage that ushered in the January 6th insurrection. Through its practice, journalists

Meredith D. Clark, *Reparation through Reporting* In: *Media and January 6th*. Edited by: Khadijah Costley White, Daniel Kreiss, Shannon C. McGregor, and Rebekah Tromble, Oxford University Press. © Oxford University Press 2024.
DOI: 10.1093/oso/9780197758526.003.0022

can resume their active role in parsing information while avoiding the media manipulation that furthers the goals of bad faith actors on the far right.

Three resolutions of reparative journalism are applicable to the selection and use of sources and subjects:

- Report with discernment by envisioning the possibilities of amplifying harmful speech and imagery.
- Be critically intentional about source and story selection, as both components of reporting are instrumental in normalizing bigoted and antisocial behavior.
- Center the perspectives of the vulnerable in news reporting, recognizing that the history and fate of the ignored offer prophetic wisdom for understanding the impact of allowing hegemonic narratives to be published unchecked.

Months after the Capitol insurrection, the online landing page of the *New York Times* offered a clear reminder of how subversive the idea of discernment as a defense mechanism will be for news workers. Below a bold, screaming headline, "Trump Takes Fifth Amendment in New York Deposition," a photographer got *the shot:* an image that sends an undeniable message to all who see it. Question is, what message? Depends on who sees the image.

In the picture, the former president walks toward a black vehicle, surrounded by his security detail. Behind them, a maroon awning emblazoned with a circular "45" icon frames their heads, just left of the main subject, almost as if the composition itself doesn't want to seem *too* obvious. Trump, facing the camera, salutes with his right fist in the air, a gesture that signals power, strength, resolution.

Admittedly, it *is* a great shot.

But alongside brooding portraits of "election deniers" like Kari Lake, a candidate for governor in Arizona, and profiles of white nationalist figures who are presented as everyday people, these stylings are subtle reminders of how news media's impulses are being exploited for political gain. At its core, the idea of "newsworthiness" functions on conflict—a struggle between two forces. In the years leading up to January 6, news media routinely failed to interrogate the racially motivated conflicts it covered, especially those in which the former president was involved. Repeating falsehoods without question (the nativist narrative), echoing white male machismo without criticism ("I could shoot someone on Fifth Avenue"), and adopting/creating euphemisms to politely discuss white nationalism—such as the inclusion of "alt-right" as a term in the *AP Stylebook*, while staying silent on "racism" for decades—are all indicators of how news media serves the interests of whiteness. Those who seek to uphold such interests have learned to speak in new languages. Recognizing that news media seeks out conflict, unusualness, and prominence as part of its calculus, they use inferences, images, and "gaffes" as indirect statements about their ideologies, making themselves photogenic and quote-worthy. Even "misspeaking" is story-worthy if the slip of the tongue can lash audiences into a frenzy.

This crafty approach is layered onto media routines that have historically privileged the same groups who are now working to maintain their power through racial and social hierarchies. In a 1988 replication of newspaper research studies undertaken two decades before, Brown et al. (1987) analyzed news coverage for source diversity, emphasizing the who, how, and where of sources to construct a picture of which voices actually shape our news. In retrospect, their findings are chilling: Newspaper stories about conflict were shaped by the voices of the state and elite agents of commerce. Where those sources were identified, they were overwhelmingly white and more than 85% were male. Too often, the authors wrote, the sources were "veiled," individuals quoted on deep background. Overreliance on these sources redirect power away from journalists as gatekeepers and allow elites to control news narratives without warranting critique, as they operate within the confines of normal reporting routines.

The authors, confirming findings from foundational research about who influences the news (Gandy, 1989; Gans, 2004; Sigal, 1973), concluded that "newspapers have relinquished control to their sources," a finding that highlights a target of opportunity for agents of misinformation and chaos (Brown et al., 1987, p. 52). Twenty years later, Daniels (2009, p. xx) warned of an era in which an overbroad application of the First Amendment gave individuals "the right to be racist online." Ultimately, there are more than 50 years of news research that indicate sourcing—from who gets to speak to what they get to say—is a central lever in the social construction of news as reality. Thus, a reparative journalism approach would first require news media to consider who it quotes—and why.

Reconsidering Sources, Subjects, and Soundbites

What would past and present coverage of far-right extremism, white nationalism, and the former president look like through a reparative journalism lens? It would have provided context for understanding how Trump used his celebrity status to seize upon the news value of prominence, making even his most asinine comments newsworthy. It would have called "birtherism" by its rightful name: a nativist lie. It would have rightly ignored nonsensical utterings from the president ("covfefe," anyone?) and his ilk, focusing instead on issues that impact vulnerable populations. For instance, practicing discernment would have questioned the mechanisms that enabled his social media presence to drive fluctuating interest rates—illustrating the direct impact on entrepreneurs and homeowners. Reporting with discernment would lead news professionals to ask how the American electorate came to prefer celebrities with no experience to public servants as candidates for office, and detail the impact of their tenure in politics.

Extending this commitment to intentionality to outlets such as the *New York Times*, which routinely profiles white supremacists and white nationalist idealogues alongside dating-app founders and Instagram personalities, discernment in choosing sources and stories would prompt media workers to examine how their "view from nowhere" coverage that selects its objects of inquiry based on this misapplication of oversimplified values, including prominence, conflict, and unusualness, allows bad actors to make a mockery of their work by amplifying hateful messages, ultimately sowing civic mistrust.

A Call for a New Creed

News media must find ways to present information with historical and factual context; practice discernment in deciding when, whether, and how to quote someone directly; and present information in ways that require readers to consider multiple perspectives at once. For instance, as one far-right provocateur continues to post his strategy for weaponizing language to silence divergent political thought, news outlets should consider how repetition of his strategy and claims contributes to social polarization—even when such reporting is taken to draw attention to these strategies in their public ideation phase. How can news media report on Christopher Rufo's public intentions to make people associate? In keeping with the purview of reporters who challenged the scope of the Federal Communications Commission on the Fairness Doctrine, editorial leaders, alongside individuals and groups that represent those who are and have been harmed by ethnonativist speech and activity, might work to propose and adopt (even informally) a responsive fairness creed that recognizes the harms caused by treating all subjects equally: *We recognize that no story, no source, no soundbite is neutral, and pledge to present information that considers the relationships between the powerful people/entities we quote, and the publics who live out their consequences. We recognize that there are more than two sides to every story, and prioritize coverage that considers historical perspective as part of each report's central narrative.*

It is difficult to imagine glossy features on facists being produced through journalistic routines that demand a presentation of evidence of how extremism harms in light of adopting such a creed.

Beginning with the recognition of past harms, local news outlets might commit to reporting on the history of voting rights access in their coverage area, and how those legacies shape contemporary turnout. From the development of invisible boundaries used to create minority-driven districts to the placement and staffing of polling stations, journalists would examine the process for unanticipated obstacles that keep each area's eligible but nonparticipatory voting public from turning out, as well as elevating the stories of disenfranchised voters. Instead of asking political parties to comment about their base in areas where government and private-sector interventions created jobs via the prison-industrial complex, journalists might report on those nearing the end of their sentence about how each candidate's proposed policies could impact their ability to avoid recidivism.

Finally, reparative journalism's most significant task in the lead-up to the 2024 election may well be the promotion of social solidarity. For this reason, I acknowledge that its implementation is "the work of generations." Despite my commitment to reparative journalism as an application of radical imagination, it is difficult to visualize the transformation of the treasonous mob into a redeemable group whose worldview can be reconciled with a shared social commitment to equity and justice.

An intersectional reading of January 6, 2021, indicates that the problem of the color line is still to blame for ongoing social stratification. White, property-owning Christian men have for centuries been assured of their position in the racial hierarchy that is American society. To many in this group, the civil rights movement, affirmative action, the election of President Barack Hussein Obama, and the relative speed at which the Black Lives Matter movement solidified a normative understanding of racial justice struggle in the 21st century presented a series of threats that stretched beyond the existential and into the tangible. Headlines that proclaim the "browning" of the country seem to warn of white demise rather than reflect the evolution of a nation with sufficient raw human capital to actively address its broken and uneven foundation, laid in the blood of indigenous peoples and built through the exploitation of kidnapped Africans forced into chattel slavery. And thus I argue that we must pressure and pursue likewise the evolution of the business of news media, building on what we have learned from its early existence and tools—particularly adherence to narrowly defined, market-oriented news values—to reporting practices that engage our highest and best cognitive abilities.

Our ability to recognize that, as recorded in the pages of the Kerner Commission's findings, and reflected in decades of data and reporting on the pervasiveness of white culture and ideology in news media, the norms and values of U.S. journalism must evolve to center a racial justice mission in its work in order to address the full measure of its function of social responsibility to its people. If we are to develop news media that is useful in creating a more cohesive social order—absent race, gender, or other identity-based subjugation—the most powerful people in the field must concede and redistribute their power to those striving to escape its permanent underclass.

The publishers, executive and managing editors, and other editorial decision-makers must elevate those who have been pushed out or are systematically underrepresented, and be willing to step out of the way for leadership from the margins to recenter our priorities. The empty rallying cry of the years prior to Trump's election, "Listen to Black women!," has merit here. But those Black women, and their compatriots, must not come from the ruling classes, nor must they be compelled to emulate the examples of those whose works have narrated our collective experience thus far. A final example to illustrate this is drawn from my observations of how political communication experts have handled this crisis, emerging only in its aftermath to recognize the dangers that vulnerable people warned the public about all along.

What if decision-makers in news had strategically elevated the voices of so many journalists from marginalized backgrounds who warned about the waves of anti-Black sentiment embedded in the rhetoric of the so-called Tea Party movement and its progeny? What if they had heeded the cautions from disabled people, Hispanic/Latinx journalists, and media students from poor backgrounds, and recognize warnings, like the ones repeated by Dr. Melissa Harris-Perry, who told a Texas university crowd about the chilling realization that fell upon her as she recorded the final days of her cable news show in 2016:

> Anything you point a camera at takes on value—normative value. So if you point a camera at something, a broadcast camera at something . . . He's going to be president, period. It's not neutral. Anything you put the camera on will grow, guaranteed. You can't watch it and not make it.

The former president's words and images, amplified by mainstream news media in the months before and after Trump's election, were delivered so readily because of adherence to a set of journalistic practices and values that met their full utility in the time before the third age of political communication, when the cash flow unleashed by *Citizens United* converged with the rise of Political Twitter and abused the embrace of the culture of celebrity. Trump, a legendary figure in the business and entertainment world, was able to game news values of conflict, prominence, unusualness, and timeliness, among others, to keep himself and his narratives in the headlines. Over time, as news outlets relented to economic pressures of always-on production, every utterance he made (particularly as president) became newsworthy and, thus, a form of truth.

The generative power of media is to train the public's eye to hold precedent and possibility on the same plane, and to reinforce our collective belief that potential can eventually become a reality. That is the challenge of committing to reparative journalism work: to review the mistakes of the past, to read them in comparison with the events of the present, and to help multiple publics recognize what is possible, without promoting favor for one in exchange for exploitation of the Other.

References

Brown, J. D., Bybee, C. R., Wearden, S. T., & Straughan, D. M. (1987). Invisible power: Newspaper news sources and the limits of diversity. *Journalism Quarterly, 64*(1), 45–54. https://doi.org/10.1177/107769908706400106

Daniels, J. (2009). *Cyber racism: White supremacy online and the new attack on civil rights.* Rowman & Littlefield Publishers.

206 RESEARCH AFTER JANUARY 6, 2021

Gandy, O. H., Jr. (1989). The surveillance society: Information technology and bureaucratic social control. *Journal of Communication, 39*(3), 61–76.

Gans, H. J. (2004). *Deciding what's news: A study of CBS Evening News, NBC Nightly News, Newsweek, and* Time. Northwestern University Press.

Sigal, L. V. (1973). *Reporters and officials: The organization and politics of newsmaking* (Vol. 10). Jossey-Bass.

23

Epilogue

Daniel Kreiss, Shannon C. McGregor, Rebekah Tromble,
and Khadijah Costley White

Across 104 pages of text, the summary of the Select Committee to Investigate the January 6th Attack on the United States Capitol's core findings mentions media just two times and social media a mere six times. The Committee does call attention to the ways in which Trump and his allies relied on the media to spread election denial claims. It also highlights how Trump used social media to summon his supporters to the Capitol and to foment rage, particularly against Mike Pence, while the attack was underway. And the summary text does note that far-right extremists and militia groups used social media to coordinate ahead of January 6th, including devising plans to bring weapons to the Capitol.

Yet both the summary material and the full 845-page report reflect the Select Committee's primary focus on Trump's own actions leading up to and on January 6, 2021. While this focus is understandable—especially as the Committee sought to investigate potential criminal activity—we believe this was a missed opportunity. The Committee's important, but ultimately narrow, focus largely obscures the role of the media—and its relationship to politics—in fomenting the attempted coup on January 6th. As the 22 chapters in this volume make clear, an understanding of media, history, the relationship between communication and social identity, and reinforcing dynamics between media and politics are necessary to fully grasp the attempted coup at the U.S. Capitol and its implications for democracy.

While the 845-page public report spends little time on social media, a 122-page special section on social media—initially kept private—was ultimately leaked to the press (Zakrzewski et al., 2023). This special section was completed by a team tasked with considering "how the spread of misinformation and violent extremism contributed to the violent attack on our democracy, and what steps—if any—social media companies took to prevent their platforms from being breeding grounds for radicalizing people to

---

Daniel Kreiss, Shannon C. McGregor, Rebekah Tromble, and Khadijah Costley White, *Epilogue* In: *Media and January 6th*.
Edited by: Khadijah Costley White, Daniel Kreiss, Shannon C. McGregor, and Rebekah Tromble, Oxford University Press.
© Oxford University Press 2024. DOI: 10.1093/oso/9780197758526.003.0023

208 EPILOGUE

violence" and built in part on information gathered by subpoena from 15 tech companies (Technology and Democracy, 2022). The special section notes that social media played a role in spreading the disinformation that fomented the attempted coup (spiking after Trump tweeted on December 19th that the January 6th rally would "be wild") and provided a platform for organizing and planning violence. It suggests that inconsistent content-moderation policies, faulty detection algorithms, and outright inaction from top social media company executives all contributed to the spread of messages that helped fuel the attempted coup. At the same time, this leaked special section argues that social media is just one factor at play. In particular, the special section highlights how mainstream news outlets helped generate a political environment conducive to political anger and violence. This included spreading and repeating election denial claims from political leaders and partisan news outlets, as well as stoking election conspiracy theories and disinformation.

The Committee's findings reveal the blatant lies that undergirded the extrajudicial, and ultimately deadly, attempt to overturn a free and fairly run election. And yet crucial historical, social, and political context is still lacking, even from this more detailed investigation of social media. Though the Committee emphasizes the central role both mass and social media actors played in laying the groundwork for January 6th, the special section pays little attention to the powerful identity-driven rhetoric within which the attempted coup was situated or to the perceived threats to dominant white, religious, political, social, and economic power that motivated the attack. None of the Committee's findings sheds light on the long-simmering political and racial animus at the heart of January 6th.

Reflecting our shared commitment to a true multiracial democracy in the United States, the chapters collected in this volume center our focus on historical and contemporary racial, ethnic, and power dynamics within the context of media and communication. Absent this focus, we fail to see how our country can withstand ongoing and future threats to democracy. The contributions in this volume lay out promising research agendas at the intersection of democracy and media, which we urge scholars in the fields of communication, political science, and sociology—and their related subfields of political communication, political psychology and behavior, media studies, and journalism studies—to pursue. Researchers whose work builds on normative ideals of democracy must, as the contributors to this volume do, center historical and contemporary dynamics of identity—including race and ethnicity, and how these feed into and inform political and partisan identities—as they map onto political power and other social structures. Descriptive accounts that lack this important contextual grounding risk promoting overly simplistic, even potentially harmful, narratives in media coverage, as well as naïve and ineffective policies and interventions by social media platforms and policymakers.

The events of January 6, 2021, cast this in very stark relief. Relying on a simplistic and politically convenient interpretation of the threats afoot, social media companies focused on risks to the voting process but did little to prepare for or prevent postelection violence. For their part, mainstream media outlets largely covered the postelection period as spectacle. The sitting president, his supporters, and their outlandish claims were given endless coverage. The audience was often reminded that the president's claims were false, but they were repeated with little or none of the vital context that might help Americans understand just how dangerous these claims could and would prove to be.

What should technology companies, social media platforms, and mainstream media outlets do going forward? First and foremost, they must recognize that they have a responsibility to support and protect democracy. Inaction in the face of threats to democratic norms, values, and institutions is irresponsible. When tech and social media executives—driven by their desire to appear nonpartisan—looked the other way or delayed their responses to the rise of far-right extremism, they ultimately helped facilitate the attacks on January 6th. When journalists and editors focused on the spectacle of the Big Lie and portrayed efforts to overturn the election as one more example— extreme though it might be—of expected political gamesmanship, they helped to undermine confidence in democracy itself.

We do not suggest that tech and social media executives, journalists, or news leaders should embrace political partisanship, nor even that they should stand up in defense of the U.S. government per se. Democracy is not equivalent to the government. Rather, democracy is represented in the norms and institutions (read: rules of practice) that undergird checks and balances on power, full franchise, freedom of expression, equality under the law, and the peaceful transfer of power through elections. While in the wake of the 2020 election the threat to these rights, norms, and values was indeed posed by a sitting president, and while he and his supporters had captured the governing apparatus of one political party, taking these threats seriously— and acting on them—need not and should not be seen as an embrace of

210 EPILOGUE

partisanship. Instead, the defense of democracy should be seen as a commitment to the very norms and practices that permit technology, social media, and news organizations to exist in the first place. After all, authoritarian impulses threaten social media companies' ability to host lawful content and develop content rules in ways protected by freedom of expression. And they clearly undermine the very foundations of a free press. In this environment, purported "balance," "objectivity," and "neutrality" are in fact position-taking. Dangerous position-taking that leaves democracy vulnerable.

As we look ahead to the presidential election in 2024, we are profoundly concerned that American democracy remains under threat. Drawing on the research-based guidance offered by the Election Coverage and Democracy Network[1]—a group of more than 60 journalism, media studies, and political communication scholars—we share a series of recommendations tailored specifically for news organizations covering the 2024 elections, but with broader principles that can apply to social media companies as well:

- **Employ a "democracy-worthy" frame in election and postelection coverage.**
  Editorial decisions about how to cover the elections must be motivated by the peaceful transfer of political power, protection of democratic institutions, and rejection of political falsehoods and violence. It is important to elevate public-interest sources of expertise. Consider lessons from science reporting: highlighting expert, not partisan, sources best serves the public. As Heesoo Jang, Daniel Kreiss, Shannon McGregor, and Erik Peterson conceptualize "democracy-framed coverage," it is news that

    > foregrounds democracy both as an established norm and as a polit-
    > ical ideal. This frame of coverage goes beyond just pointing out that
    > claims of widespread voter fraud are false and not substantiated with
    > evidence—it also positions election denial as a violation of democratic
    > norms with deleterious implications for democracy itself; for example,
    > the norm of losing candidates accepting the results of free and fair
    > elections. This coverage treats election denial—or ex ante assertions
    > that a candidate will not accept the result of an upcoming election—
    > as fundamentally different from other campaign issues. Journalists
    > may analyze these actions as a political tactic designed to gain power

[1] See its website, https://mediafordemocracy.org/.

outside of the electoral process. Journalists may bring in sources other than politicians (such as an election administrator or academic) to rebut claims of voter fraud or to discuss the norms of democracy.

- **Highlight democratic institutions and norms.**
If the 2024 election proves as contentious as expected, it will be imperative to emphasize the role that the peaceful transfer of power plays in democracy. Party leaders historically have publicly addressed their supporters about the importance of a peaceful transfer of power and recognized the legitimacy of the next president. Journalists can remind people that the peaceful transfer of power continues to be a hallmark of democratic governance, even as modes of communication change over time (Mirer & Bode, 2015).

- **Help the public understand what to expect from an election.**
This includes informing the news audience about the work of local and state election officials, the time it takes to count votes, and the process experts use to forecast winners on election night. Even in the most challenging of times, to date, the U.S. election system has proven reliable and secure (Burden & Stewart, 2014; Jacobs & Choate, 2022). This conclusion was confirmed in 2020, just as it has been during previous elections, according to extensive research (Brennen Center, 2020). Reporting can clearly and consistently remind the public of this fact.

- **Minimize the influence of false claims that contest the election results.**
Unless there is clear evidence, backed by public-interest experts, that fraud has occurred, wherever possible afford such claims little or no attention. If it is necessary to cover these claims, sandwiching false claims (Clark, 2020) between reminders that they are unsupported and that the elections were free, fair, and secure helps diminish undue influence.

- **Use clear definitions in the context of antidemocratic behavior and political violence.**
As this volume has highlighted, it is important that we deploy clear terminology with respect to partisan political violence, distinguishing between legitimate, constitutionally protected protest and violence aimed at political intimidation or seizing political power. The U.S. Constitution is clear about the rights of citizens to speak, write, and assemble

212 EPILOGUE

peaceably when they object to government behavior. However, the Constitution does not permit violent activity, or even the stoking of violence. Journalists can continue to help their audiences understand the difference between peaceful political protests and politically motivated violence (Kreiss & McGregor, 2023).

Each of these recommendations has an analogue for social media platforms. Policies about whether and how to moderate election-related content should be guided by these very same principles and commitments. Platforms should develop content moderation policies that seek to protect elections and deny political leaders and their supporters the ability to undermine accountability at the ballot box. They should also develop content policies in race-conscious ways that acknowledge differences in power and vulnerability to expression that silences and undermines political power (Kreiss et al., 2021). Voter and civic information centers, which most of the major platforms have deployed ahead of recent elections, can highlight democratic institutions and norms and help the public understand the nuances and complexities of democratic elections, all while carefully deploying clear definitions of antidemocratic behavior.

For those who value and support multiracial democracy in the United States, this is an all-hands-on-deck moment. Policymakers, tech and social media executives, journalists, news media organizations, and scholars alike must undertake our work with a commitment to the normative ideals of democracy. This means acknowledging and centering analysis of political, partisan, racial, and ethnic identities and their place in political and social structures of power. It means resisting the temptation to do nothing or fall silent lest we risk accusations of partisanship. (Those accusations will come, even when we choose inaction or silence.) But most of all, it means grappling with the fragility of American democracy—contextualizing it and helping others to better understand both the threats at hand and the difficult, but essential, measures that may bolster it going forward.

References

Brennen Center. (2020). It's official: The election was secure. https://www.brennancenter.org/our-work/research-reports/its-official-election-was-secure

Burden, B. C., & Stewart III, C. (Eds.). (2014). *The measure of American elections.* Cambridge University Press.

Clark, R. P. (2020). How to serve up a tasty "truth sandwich?" The secret sauce is emphatic word order. *Poynter*. https://www.poynter.org/reporting-editing/2020/how-to-serve-up-a-tasty-truth-sandwich/.

Jacobs, L. R., & Choate, J. (2022). Democratic capacity: Election administration as bulwark and target. *Annals of the American Academy of Political and Social Science, 699*(1), 22–35.

Kreiss, D., Barrett, B., & Reddi, M. (2021). The need for race-conscious platform policies to protect civic life. Tech Policy Press. https://techpolicy.press/the-need-for-race-conscious-platform-policies-to-protect-civic-life/

Kreiss, D., & McGregor, S. C. (2023). A review and provocation: On polarization and platforms. *New Media & Society*. https://doi.org/10.1177/14614448231161880

Mirer, M. L., & Bode, L. (2015). Tweeting in defeat: How candidates concede and claim victory in 140 characters. *New Media & Society, 17*(3), 453–469.

Technology and Democracy. (2022, Jan. 14). January 6 Committee issues subpoenas to social media platforms. https://techpolicy.press/january-6-committee-issues-subpoenas-to-social-media-platforms/

Zakrzewski, C., Lima, C., & Harwell, D. (2023, Jan. 17). What the Jan. 6 probe found out about social media, but didn't report. *The Washington Post*. https://www.washingtonpost.com/technology/2023/01/17/jan6-committee-report-social-media/

Index

For the benefit of digital users, indexed terms that span two pages (e.g., 52–53) may, on occasion, appear on only one of those pages.

Tables and figures are indicated by *t* and *f* following the page number

American democracy, 54–55, 190, 210
  democratic backsliding, 63, 65, 128–29, 130, 137, 142–43
  existential racial threat and, 63–64, 65–67
  January 6th and, 1, 2–4, 7, 8–10, 12, 91–92, 136, 147, 153–54
  myth of the attentive public for, 185–86
  right-wing media as threat to, 104–5, 164, 170
American Enterprise Institute, 99
American Political Science Association (APSA), 136, 188–89
antidemocratic agribusiness, 7–8, 147–51
antidemocratic behavior, political violence and, 211–12
antidemocratic counterpublics, 90–91
antidemocratic movements, 7–8, 9–10, 12, 13, 14, 86, 116–17
antidemocratic views, 148
  racial demographic change and, 63, 64–65, 66*f*
  right-wing media and, 111–12, 142, 164, 169, 170
Antifa, 80–81, 83, 84, 98–99, 105
application programming interfaces (APIs), 122–23, 126–27
APSA. *See* American Political Science Association
Arbery, Ahmaud, 79–80
Associated Press, 35
attempted coups, 17, 18, 19, 20–21, 30, 41, 79, 164
attempted dissident coup, 17, 20–21
authoritarianism, 64–65, 128–29, 132, 133, 192–93, 195, 196

Bannon, Steve, 167–68
Barr, William, 147
Bauer, A. J., 157
Benkler, Yochai, 166–67
Bennett, W. L., 150–51
Berger, P. L., 59
Biden, Joe, 46, 54, 55, 58–59, 108–9
Big Lie, the, 51, 73–74, 75–76, 146, 147–50, 170, 183–84, 197
Black Americans, 47–50, 51, 204
Black Lives Matter, 12–13, 27, 80–81, 83–84, 88, 203–4
  false equivalences with January 6th Capitol stormers, 104, 105–8, 112, 141
Bland, Sandra, 24–25
Borysenko, Karlyn, 105
Breitbart, 110*f*, 116–17, 157, 163–64, 165–66, 167–68, 192–93
Brexit, 88–89
Brill, Kenneth, 95
Brown, Danielle K., 6, 13–14
Brown, J. D., 201
Brown, Megan A., 7, 115–16
Brown, Michael, 24–25, 79–80, 82–83
Buckley, William F., Jr., 168–69
Buck v. Bell (1927), 48–49
Burack, Cynthia, 7, 9, 117–18
Burden-Stelly, Charisse, 80–81

Cambridge Analytica scandal, 122–23
Carlson, Tucker, 34–35, 109–11
Carusone, Angelo, 37
Castile, Philando, 24–25
Cawthorn, Madison, 163
CBS This Morning, 32–34

216 INDEX

Center for Communication and Civic Renewal, 173
Cernovich, Mike, 109
Chamberlain, Will, 109
Cheney, Liz, 133–34, 190
Christian conservative movement, 128, 132
citizen-activist function, of news media, 31–32, 36–38, 41
Citizens United v. FEC (2010), 205
civil rights movements, 24–25, 199
Claremont Institute, 187, 188–89
Clark, Meredith, 8, 9, 118–19
Clark, Stephon, 24–25
Cline Center for Advanced Social Research, 6, 11–12, 17–19, 17n.2, 20–21
Clinton, Hillary, 45–46
CNBC, 39–40
CNN, 35–36
connective action, 12–13, 87–90, 91, 92
conservatism and conservative tradition, 79–80, 81, 84–85, 157
conservative media, 35, 50–51, 75–76, 153, 156
　conservative news cultures, 7–8, 117, 142, 154–55, 157, 158–59, 160–61
　normative claims and, 159–61
　racial and cultural resentments and, 157–58
　in transformations on the right, 157
conservative populism, 12, 79, 82–83
Constitution, U.S., 1, 27, 50–51, 211–12
cooperative journalistic standards, 39–41
Costley White, Khadijah, 6, 11–12, 31, 169
counterpublics, 90–91
Coup d'État Project, of Cline Center for Advanced Social Research, 17–19, 20–21
coups and attempted coups, 17–19, 20–21
COVID-19 pandemic, 55, 73–74, 121–22, 178, 189
critical media scholarship, 156, 159–60
critical race theory (CRT), 137, 179–80
Cruz, Ted, 34–35, 163
Cudd, Jenny, 71

Daily Caller, the, 116–17, 163, 164, 165–66, 167
Daily Wire, The, 108–9, 163, 164
Daniels, J., 201
Davis, Damon, 82–83
democracy, 209–10. *See also* American democracy
　Democratic Party on, 196
　digital participation and, 87–88
　Election Coverage and Democracy Network recommendations on, 210–12
　multiracial, 3, 4, 31–32, 41, 118–19, 208–9, 212
　norms and normativity, 185–86, 208–10, 211, 212
Democratic Party and Democrats, 64–65, 73, 118, 157–58, 190, 194, 196, 197
Dempsey, Sadie, 8, 9, 116
DeSantis, Ron, 45, 46, 192–93
digital fascism, 7, 12–13, 89–92
digital media, 7, 12–13, 88–90, 148, 190–91
digital mobilization, 87, 91
digital organizing, 87, 89, 91, 92, 129
digital platforms, 86–87, 88, 92, 183–84
disinformation, 6–7, 27, 39–40, 41, 98, 101
　in antidemocratic agribusiness, 148–51
　election, 6, 44–45, 47–49, 51, 140
　on Fox News, 39–40, 165
　January 6th and, 139, 140, 153–55, 176
　local sources of, 177, 179–80
　power and interest in studies of, 139–41
　in right-wing media, 165–66
　of Stop the Steal phrase and movement, 44–45, 47
disinformation studies, 139–41, 154–55
Dobbs v. Jackson Women's Health Organization (2022), 192–93
domestic terrorism, 30, 34–35, 40–41, 80–81
Dominion Voting Systems Corporation, 98–99
Dominion Voting Systems Corp v. Fox News Network LLC, 2023, 5

INDEX 217

Dorstewitz, Michael, 107
Drudge Report, The, 157
Du Bois, W. E. B., 48, 49

Eastman, John, 118, 186–89, 192n.1
Edison, Michael, 95
Edwards, Carolyn, 30
Election Coverage and Democracy
    Network, 41, 210–12
election disinformation, 6, 44–45, 47–49,
    51, 140
election fraud claims, 116, 124, 147
    the Big Lie, 51, 73–74, 75–76, 146,
        147–50, 170, 183–84, 197
    by Eastman, 186, 187
    election denial, 51, 200–1
    on Facebook, 173, 174–75, 176, 177,
        183–84, 197
    local-national feedback loop of, 174,
        177, 178, 180
    local political institutions and actors in
        spreading, 173, 174–76, 178–79
    minimizing influence of, 211
    by Trump, 1, 5, 44, 45, 54–58, 97–98,
        129, 146, 147, 178–79, 183, 187
eugenics, 48–49
Evangelical Christians, 99–100

Facebook, 40, 54, 55–59, 92, 109, 122–23,
    123n.4, 124–25, 126
    election fraud claims on, 173, 174–75,
        176, 177, 183–84, 197
Faris, Robert, 166–67
Federal Communications Commission,
    202–3
Federalist Society, 189
Figliuzi, Frank, 95
First Amendment, 27, 37, 201, 211–12
Floyd, George, 27, 79–81, 121–22
Folayan, Sabaah, 82–83
Fox News, 11–12, 34–35, 95, 109–11,
    130–31, 140, 163–64, 192–93
    in citizen-activist role for January 6th,
        36–38
    commercialism of, 167, 168
    disinformation on, 39–40, 165

*Dominion Voting Systems Corp v. Fox
    News Network LLC,* 2023, 5
    misinformation on, 37, 39–40
    in Tea Party Movement, 169
Freiss, Foster, 167
Friedland, Lewis, 8, 118

Gab, 90, 122–23, 126
Gaetz, Matt, 163
Garner, Eric, 24–25
Gateway Pundit, The, 177
gerrymandering, 190, 193–95
Gettr, 122–23, 123n.3
Gillum, Andrew, 45
Gitlin, Todd, 131–32
Giuliani, Rudy, 98–99, 187
Gohmert, Louie, 163
Google, 183–84
Google Trends, 46
Gray, Freddie, 24–25
Great Awakening concept, 96–97,
    99–101
Great Replacement conspiracy theory, 63,
    84, 96, 170, 192–93

Haidt, Jonathan, 130
Hannity, Sean, 5, 37, 38, 109–11
Harris, Kamala, 108–9
Harris-Perry, Melissa, 204–5
Hawley, Josh, 109, 163
Hayes, Chris, 38
Hemmer, Nicole, 157, 167
Hendershot, Heather, 157
Heritage Foundation, 50
Hinck, R. S., 24
Hooker, Juliet, 137
House Select Committee to Investigate
    the January 6th Attack on the United
    States Capitol
    congressional report, 1–2, 5, 9, 58, 183,
        184, 185, 207–8
    hearings, 95, 106, 107, 109–11, 133, 147,
        149–50, 188
    Republican National Committee on,
        190
hyperpartisan media, 163–64

218 INDEX

identity, power and, 9, 208–9
identity-driven wrongness, 71–76
illiberalism, 118, 128–29, 132
InfoWars, 45, 192–93
Ingraham, Laura, 37, 109–11

Jackson, S. J., 189
January 6th Capitol attack
  accusations of bias in mainstream
    media reporting on, 106–8
  American democracy and, 1, 2–4, 7,
    8–10, 12, 91–92, 136, 147, 153–54
  in antidemocratic agribusiness, 148,
    149–50
  antidemocratic counterpublics in,
    90–91
  antidemocratic feedback loop on right-
    wing media about, 111–12
  as attempted coup d'état, 17, 18–19,
    20–21, 30, 41, 79, 164
  Breitbart coverage of, 110*f*
  conservative news cultures and, 154–55
  as digital fascism, 89–92
  disinformation and, 139, 140, 153–55,
    176
  Eastman in, 186, 187–89
  event descriptors in coverage of, 25–26,
    26*f*, 26*t*
  false equivalences between Black Lives
    Matter and, 104, 105–8, 112, 141
  Fox News in citizen-activist role for,
    36–38
  identity-driven wrongness and, 71, 75
  local political institutions and actors in,
    173, 176, 180–81
  misinformation in, 73–74, 121–22
  news narratives on anniversary
    commemoration of, 30–35
  OANN on, 163
  platform data access and, 115–16,
    124–25
  political and social scientists on, 136
  as political violence, 118, 143, 160–61
  preventing future attacks, 129, 183, 186,
    189
  protests *versus,* 24–26, 27–28

  QAnon and, 100, 140–41
  race, racism and, 81, 83–84, 203–4
  racial demographic changes and, 62–63,
    65–67
  radicalization and, 95–96
  reparative journalism and, 199–200
  Republicans and, 95–96, 184, 189–91
  right-wing victimhood claims and,
    108–12, 117
  rioters on "Black Lives Matter" and
    "Antifa," 80–81, 83–84
  rioters on home and "the house," 81–83
  riots *versus,* 27–28
  Shapiro on, 153–54, 156
  status threats and, 117–18, 138,
    140–41
  Tea Party movement and, 6, 11–12,
    31–32, 35–36, 38–39, 41, 173
  Trump and, 1–2, 5, 6, 9–10, 19, 20, 30,
    31–32, 37, 41, 44, 54–55, 58, 70–71,
    73–74, 79, 90, 91–92, 95, 128–29, 173,
    184, 185, 207–8, 209
  violence of, 30, 86, 87, 118, 143, 154–55,
    209
  white Christian nationalists at, 141
Johnson, Paul Elliott, 6–7, 12
Johnson, Theodore R., 133
Jones, Alex, 45, 141
journalism, 199–201, 204
  reparative, 8, 9, 118–19, 199–200,
    201–5

Karpf, Dave, 8, 9, 118
Kelly, Ryan, 149
Kerner Commission Report, 199, 204
Khoury, Christy, 6, 11–12
Kim, Pyeonghwa, 6, 11–12
Kinzinger, Adam, 133–34, 190
Klein, Ezra, 73
Koch, Charles, 167
Kreiss, Daniel, 7–8, 41, 117–18
Kydd, Andrew, 95

Lake, Kari, 51, 200–1
Lawrence, Regina, 7–8, 9, 116–17
Lear, Norman, 132–33

INDEX 219

Lewis, Becca, 7, 13, 45
Li, Jianing, 8, 9, 116
Loeffler, Kelly, 163
Luckmann, T., 59

Maddow, Rachel, 40
mail-in balloting, 55–56, 57–59, 75
mainstreaming, 96–97, 101
Mamdani, Mahmood, 143
Manion, Clarence, 168–69
Maraj, Louis, 79–80
Marlow, Alex, 165
Martin, Trayvon, 24–25
Marwick, Alice, 7, 13, 45
Mason, Lillianna, 158–59
Mayer, Jane, 193–94
McCarthy, Kevin, 51
McConnell, Mitch, 192–93
McGee, Heather, 195
McKernan, Brian, 6, 11–12
McMaster, H. R., 167–68
McVeigh, Timothy, 84–85
Media Metric, 179–80
Mercer, Rebekah, 167–68
Mercer family, 167
Mercieca, J., 45
metadata, 125–26
#MeToo movement, 88
Miller, Stephen, 167–68
Miller-Idriss, Cynthia, 39, 40–41
misinformation, 27, 40, 41, 183
   about COVID-19, 73–74
   on Fox News, 37, 39–40
   in identity-driven wrongness, 72,
      73–74
   in January 6th Capitol attack, 73–74,
      121–22
   racial demographic change and, 67
   during Reconstruction, 48
mixed-methods, 174–75
   multilevel perspective and, 173–74,
      178–80
Mogelson, Luke, 82
Mosco, Vincent, 186
Mouffe, C., 169
MSNBC, 39–40, 163–64

multilevel perspective, 175–76
   mixed-methods and, 173–74, 178–80
   quantitative analysis for studying
      content flows in hybrid information
      environments, 177–78
multiracial democracy, 3, 4, 31–32, 41,
   118–19, 208–9, 212

Nadler, Anthony, 7–8, 9, 117
National Republican Congressional
   Committee, 163
nativism, 200–1, 202–3
Newsmax, 106, 107–8, 165–66
NewsWhip, 25–26
New York Times, 39, 107, 200–1, 202
Nichols, Terry, 84–85
Nixon, Richard, 79–80, 84–85
norms and normativity, 8, 9, 159–61,
   185–86, 190, 208–10, 211, 212

OANN. See One America News Network
Oath Keepers, 1–2, 86–87, 141, 147
Obama, Barack, 6, 11–13, 30–31, 63, 203–4
Oklahoma City bombing, 84–85
One America News Network (OANN),
   116–17, 163, 164, 192–93
online data
   ephemerality of, 115–16, 121–22,
      122n.1, 124–25
   platform data access, 115–16, 121–25,
      126–27
Orban, Victor, 195

Palin, Sarah, 32, 79
Panahi, Rita, 107
Pape, Robert, 95–96
Parler, 81, 90, 109, 122–23, 126, 177
partisan media, 163–66
patriotism, for the left, 131–33
Pence, Mike, 1–2, 44, 86, 146, 195, 207
Perlstein, Rick, 157
Pew Research, 61
Pfetsch, B., 150–51
Phillips, Whitney, 7–8, 9, 116–17
platform data access, 115–16, 121–25,
   126–27

220 INDEX

polarization, 130–31, 137–39, 142, 202–3
police violence and police killings, 24–25,
27, 79–80, 82–83, 121–22
political communication research and
scholars, 8, 118, 150–51, 195–97, 204
political identity salience, 74–75
political violence, 7–8, 11, 12, 62, 84–85,
86, 90, 118
antidemocratic behavior and, 211
Cline Center for Advanced Social
Research on, 17n.2
disinformation and, 101
January 6th Capitol attack as, 118, 143,
160–61
Politico, 35
Pool, Tim, 107–8
Popular Information, 179–80
popular right, 7–8, 156
Powell, Sidney, 98–99
propaganda and, 166–68
ProPublica, 81
protests, 24–26, 27–28
Proud Boys, 1–2, 86–87, 90, 141, 147

QAnon, 13, 96–97, 98–101, 124–25,
140–41

race, 6–7, 12, 14, 31–32, 38–39, 83–84,
137, 203–4, 212
racial demographic changes, in U.S.,
61–67, 66f
racial threat, 63–67
racism, 35–36, 38–39, 45–46, 47–49, 81,
83–84, 137, 157–58, 200–1, 203–5
radicalization, 95–97, 111
Reagan, Ronald, 79–80, 84
Reconstruction period, 47–48, 51
Regnery, Henry, 168–69
reparative journalism, 8, 9, 118–19, 199–
200, 201–5
Republican National Committee, 50, 190
Republican Party and Republicans, 6–7,
14–15, 50–51, 62, 128–29, 149, 193
authoritarianism, 192–93, 196
disinformation and, 140
distrust of electoral process, 62–63, 75
election fraud claims by, 146, 183
gerrymandering by, 193–95

identities in, 72–74, 75–76
on January 6th as "legitimate political
discourse," 189–91
January 6th insurrection and, 95–96,
184
local and county level, 173–74, 175–76
mainstreaming of extremism
in, 96–97
National Republican Congressional
Committee, 163
Never Trump Republicans, 133–34
on racial demographic changes, 63–64,
67
on racial threat and authoritarianism,
64–65
victimhood claims of, 108–11
Rice, Tamir, 24–25
Rich, Seth, 165
right-wing media, 8, 104–12, 116–17
activist model for, 168–70
American democracy threatened by,
164, 170
antidemocratic views and, 111–12, 142,
164, 169, 170
commercialism, propaganda and,
166–68
disinformation in, 165–66
partisan media paradigm on, 163–66
right-wing mobilizations, 154–55, 157–58
right-wing populism, 87, 89–90, 92
right-wing victimhood claims, 108–11
riots, 27–28, 83–84
Roberts, Hal, 166–67
Roe v. Wade (1973), 49
Rubin, Dave, 105
Rubio, Marco, 149–50, 167–68
Rudkowski, Luke, 107, 108f
Rufo, Christopher, 202–3
Rumble, 122–23

Sanders, Bernie, 33–34
Santelli, Rick, 36
Save America March and Save America
Rally, 19, 23, 44, 146
Scalise, Steven, 51
Schiff, Adam, 38
Schmitt, Rob, 106
Scott, Rick, 46

Searles, Kathleen, 41
Sedassee, Alicia, 33–34
Shapiro, Ben, 108–9, 153–54, 156,
    159–60
Shirkey, Mike, 2
Sicknick, Brian, 70
Singh, N., 24
slavery, 35–36, 48, 138, 203–4
Snyder, Timothy, 132
social media, 121–22, 140, 183. *See also*
    Facebook; Twitter; YouTube
  content moderation policies, 124–27,
    212
  democracy and, 209–10
  platform data access, 115–16, 121–25,
    126–27
social sanctions, 183, 185, 186–89
Social Science One URL Shares Dataset,
    122–23
social solidarity, 138, 203
Soros, George, 45–46, 98–99
sources, subjects, and soundbites, 202
Starbird, Kate, 97–98
status threats, 117–18, 137–39, 140–42
Sterling, Alton, 24–25
Stone, Roger, 45, 97–98
Stop the Steal movement and phrase, 6,
    9–10, 11–12, 23, 31–32, 45–47, 51, 57,
    58, 70, 72, 97–99
  in antidemocratic agribusiness, 148,
    149
  Claremont Institute and, 187
  disinformation of, 44–45, 47
  on Facebook, 124–25
  local political institutions and actors in,
    173, 174, 178–79
  Republican election officials on, 190
  Stone and, 45, 97–98
  Trump on, 11–12, 44, 47, 49, 57, 58,
    96–99
Stop the Steal rally, 70, 86–87
Storey, Sharon, 32–34
Stromer-Galley, Jennifer, 6, 11–12
swing states, demographics of, 194–95

Tarrio, Enrique, 90
Taylor, Breonna, 79–80
Taylor, C., 54–55

Taylor Greene, Marjorie, 163
Tea Party movement, 6, 11–12, 30–32,
    35–37, 38–40, 41, 169, 173, 204–5
Teixeira, Ruy, 130–31
Thompson, Andrew, 6–7, 14, 117–18
Tripodi, Francesca, 6, 11–12, 50–51,
    97–98, 118–19
Trump, Donald, 51, 88–89, 138, 157,
    167–68, 200–1
  authoritarianism of, 192–93, 195
  Biden and, 46, 54, 55, 59
  The Big Lie, 73–74, 75–76
  on Black Lives Matter and Antifa,
    80–81
  celebrity and news value of, 202, 205
  in democratic backsliding, 128–29
  deplatforming, 40
  Eastman and, 186, 187
  election fraud claims, 1, 5, 44, 45, 54–58,
    97–98, 129, 146, 147, 178–79, 183,
    187
  on Facebook and Twitter, 54, 55–58, 90,
    109, 148
  January 6th and, 1–2, 5, 6, 9–10, 19, 20,
    30, 31–32, 37, 41, 44, 54–55, 58, 70–
    71, 73–74, 79, 90, 91–92, 95, 128–29,
    173, 184, 185, 207–8, 209
  Pence and, 1–2, 44, 207
  presidential campaigns, 2016 and 2020,
    45, 46, 55, 57
  QAnon and, 13, 98–99, 100–1
  on Stop the Steal movement and phrase,
    11–12, 44, 47, 49, 57, 58, 96–99
Trumpism, 31, 133, 188, 190
Truth Social, 123n.3
Twitter, 40, 45–46, 92, 107, 122–23, 126
  Biden on Facebook and, 58–59
  election fraud claims on, 177
  QAnon on, 98–99, 100, 124–25
  Trump on Facebook and, 54, 55–58, 90,
    109, 148

voter suppression, redistricting efforts
    and, 49–51

Wagner, Michael, 41
Waisbord, Silvio, 7, 12–13
Washington Post, 36, 40, 86, 95–96

222 INDEX

Watkins, Ron, 98–99, 100
Welch, Edgar Maddison, 100–1
white nationalism and white nationalists,
96, 107, 148, 192–93, 200–1, 202
   Christian Nationalists, 96–97, 117–18,
   138, 141
white supremacy and white supremacists,
30–31, 40, 45–46, 47, 48, 86, 95–96,
101, 173, 202
   mainstreaming of, 31–36, 41

Williams, Mark, 35–36
Wilson, Darren, 79–80, 82–83
Wisconsin, 192, 193–95, 197

Yang, Yunkang, 8, 9, 116–17
Yiannopoulos, Milo, 45
Young, Dannagal, 6–7, 14, 117–18
Young, Iris, 169
YouTube, 104, 105, 107, 108–9, 122–23,
124–25, 126